Wrestling the Angel

Wrestling the Angel

Charles Wesley Struggles with Vital Questions of Faith

Response and Commentary by
S T KIMBROUGH, JR.

Foreword by
Richard P. Heitzenrater

RESOURCE *Publications* · Eugene, Oregon

WRESTLING THE ANGEL
Charles Wesley Struggles with Vital Questions of Faith

Copyright © 2022 S T Kimbrough, Jr. All rights reserved. Except for brief quotations in critical publications or reviews, no part of this book may be reproduced in any manner without prior written permission from the publisher. Write: Permissions, Wipf and Stock Publishers, 199 W. 8th Ave., Suite 3, Eugene, OR 97401.

Resource Publications
An Imprint of Wipf and Stock Publishers
199 W. 8th Ave., Suite 3
Eugene, OR 97401

www.wipfandstock.com

PAPERBACK ISBN: 978-1-6667-0571-3
HARDCOVER ISBN: 978-1-6667-0572-0
EBOOK ISBN: 978-1-6667-0573-7

04/11/22

Contents

Abbreviations | ix
Foreword by Richard P. Heitzenrater | xi
Preface | xiii
Introduction | xvii

SECTION 1: GOD THE FATHER
1. Who is God? | 3
2. What is God's will? | 8
3. Is God dead? | 10
4. What is in a name? | 13
5. How do we experience God? | 16
6. What is life, patterned after the Holy Trinity? | 18

SECTION 2: GOD THE SON
7. Who Is Jesus? | 25
8. Why was Jesus Born? | 27
9. Can we believe the mystery? | 30
10. Can we live the mystery? | 32
11. Was Jesus born to set all people free? | 36
12. What shall we proclaim and why? | 38
13. What does it mean to be consumed by love? | 42
14. Why did Jesus die? | 45
15. What shall we remember? | 48
16. What holds a family together? | 51

SECTION 3: GOD THE HOLY SPIRIT

17. Can there be an end to bloodshed? | 57
18. What is true freedom? | 61
19. Are we filled with the Spirit? | 63
20. How do we read the Bible? | 65
21. How do we prepare to read the Bible? | 68
22. What shall I desire above all else? | 71

SECTION 4: FAITH

23. What shall I do with my life? | 77
24. How are we to respond to God's call? | 81
25. How can I know how to live each day? | 84
26. Can we prove faith? | 87
27. How do we relate believing and doing? | 89
28. What is eternal life? | 91
29. What do we really want? | 95
30. Where do we start? | 99
31. For what shall we pray? | 102
32. Why will you die for nothing? | 105
33. How can I overcome the power of sin? | 110
34. How shall I approach my work? | 114
35. What are the marks of faith? | 117

SECTION 5: OTHERS AND THE WORLD

36. Do we care about others? | 123
37. Do we care about God's creation? | 125
38. Can there be peace on earth? | 128
39. How does love for others grow? | 131
40. Do we give unbelievers a chance? | 134
41. Is the church really for everyone? | 136
42. Can people be united? | 139
43. What shall be our covenant with God? | 141
44. Can there be unity among God's people? | 144
45. Can all be one? | 148

46. Who will sound the alarm of freedom? | 151
47. What does a faith community do when it gathers? | 155
48. Are these really united as one: slaves, free, males, females, parties, sects? | 159
49. Why celebrate yet another feast? | 163
50. How shall I cope with the death of a faithful friend? | 167
51. What is the true nature of the church? | 170
52. What is the path to peace, not war? | 173

SECTION 6: OURSELVES
53. How do we overcome trials and persecution? | 179
54. What are we really like? | 182
55. What is our outlook on life? | 185
56. How do we deal with sickness? | 188
57. Are we bigots? | 191
58. Are we saints? | 193
59. Are we ablaze with love? | 195
60. Are we forgiving? | 197
61. Are we hard-hearted? | 200
62. Are we all alone? | 203
63. Are we ministers? | 205
64. How do we do God's will? | 207
65. Why is music important in our lives? | 209
66. How do our hearts become pure? | 213
67. What will keep me from sin? | 217

SECTION 7: DAILY LIVING
68. What makes the impossible possible for us? | 223
69. What can we learn? | 225
70. How can we grow? | 227
71. What is most important? | 229
72. How do we prepare for the evening and rest? | 232
73. How do we prepare for the day? | 234
74. How shall we spend our time? | 236

75. Do we eat for the right reasons? | 239
76. Why pray before eating? | 241
77. How do we wait on God? | 244
78. How shall we live our lives? | 247
79. Which is the most important meal? | 251
80. What does one experience at Holy Communion? | 254
81. Why do we observe Holy Communion? | 257
82. What does Holy Communion really mean? | 261
83. How can we know and feel that God and love are one? | 265
84. Whom will we invite to supper? | 268
    Conclusion | 273

APPENDIX A: CHARLES WESLEY TIME LINE | 275

Selected Bibliography | 279

Index of First Lines | 281

Index of Scripture Passages | 283

Index of Subjects | 287

Abbreviations

HGEL 1742 = *Hymns on God's Everlasting Love*, 2nd series. London: Strahan, [1742].

HIM 1758 = *Hymns of Intercession for All Mankind*. Bristol: Farley, 1758.

HLR 1746 = *Hymns for Our Lord's Resurrection*. London: Strahan, 1746.

HLS 1745 = *Hymns on the Lord's Supper*. Bristol: Farley, 1745.

HNL 1745 = *Hymns for the Nativity of Our Lord*. London: [Strahan], 1745.

HNYD 1749 = *Hymns for New Year's Day*. Bristol: Farley, [1749].

HSP 1739 = *Hymns and Sacred Poems*. London: Strahan, 1739.

HSP 1740 = *Hymns and Sacred Poems*. London: Strahan, 1740.

HSP 1742 = *Hymns and Sacred Poems*. Bristol: Farley, 1742.

HSP 1749 = *Hymns and Sacred Poems*. 2 vols. Bristol: Farley, 1749.

HTTP 1744 = *Hymns for Times of Trouble and Persecution*. [London: Strahan, 1744].

HUF 1767 = *Hymns for the Use of Families*. Bristol: Pine, 1767.

MSJ = *The Manuscript Journal of the Reverend Charles Wesley, M.A.* 2 vols. Edited by S T Kimbrough, Jr., and Kenneth G. C. Newport. Nashville: Abingdon, 2007.

PW = *The Poetical Works of John and Charles Wesley*. 13 vols. Edited by George Osborn. London: Wesleyan-Methodist Conference Office, 1868–1872.

RH 1747 = *Hymns for those that seek, and those that have Redemption in the Blood of Christ*. London: Strahan, 1747.

ABBREVIATIONS

SH 1762 = *Short Hymns on Select Passages of the Holy Scriptures.* 2 vols. Bristol: Farley, 1762.

UP = *The Unpublished Poetry of Charles Wesley.* 3 vols. Nashville: Kingswood, 1988, 1990, 1992.

WH 1746 = *Whitsunday Hymns* (subtitle); original title is *Hymns of Petition and Thanksgiving for the Promise of the Father.* Bristol: Farley, 1746.

1780 Collection = *A Collection of Hymns for the Use of the People Called Methodists.* [Edited by John Wesley]. London: John Mason, 1780.

Bible translations are usually quoted from the *New Revised Standard Version of the Bible.* New York: National Council of Churches of Christ in the U.S.A., 1989. However, since Charles Wesley often used the language of the Authorized Version or King James Version (KJV) of the Bible, where it is important for his use of such language, biblical quotations are cited from the KJV.

Where Charles Wesley gave titles to his hymns and poems, these are included immediately following the initial question.

Foreword

Charles Wesley, one of the world's most beloved hymn writers, never composed a piece of music, so far as we know. Although the mention of "O for a thousand tongues to sing" or "Hark! the herald angels sing" or "A charge to keep I have" elicits the memory of familiar tunes, it is the words, not the music, that give these hymns their power. With all due respect to the many composers (from Carl von Weber to Felix Mendelssohn-Bartholdy to Lowell Mason) who gave melodies to Charles's poetry, we recognize that the lasting grasp on our hearts and minds comes from what Shakespeare called "the force of a heaven-bred poesy."

Poetry is perhaps the most appropriate form for a theology of the heart; the words often communicate to the soul even before they are understood by the mind. The power of Wesley's poetry is its evocative nature—the words call forth images that are immediately sensible and personally relevant. Wesley's poetry is conceived within a vibrant sense of the divine-human relationship, and from the experience of his reality emerge words and images that convey the depth and breadth of Christian experience. The vigor and intensity of his own experience is transmitted in images that speak with clarity and power in a form that transcends the pedantic tendencies of prose theology. Charles has mastered the art of poetic expression by marshaling verbal symbols that give perceptive form to the palpitations of the heart.

His brother John felt that Charles's poetry unfolded "the purity, the strength, and the elegance of the English language" as well as "the true spirit of poetry." But the practical impact of his work was even more easily definable. Charles's hymns came to represent the popular form of Wesleyan theology; the eighteenth-century revival was to a great extent borne on the wings of Charles's poetry. Charles's hymns not only helped form the texture of the Methodist mind but also, perhaps more importantly, set the temper of the Methodist spirit.

The language of Wesley's poetry is biblical and personal; the images have vigor and intensity. While some of the hymns have been sung in public worship for generations, others of the poems were written intentionally for private use. Both are works of devotional art and can appropriately be incorporated into private devotion and meditation.

From the vast depository of Wesleyan poetry, not all of it equally masterful, S T Kimbrough, Jr., has here chosen some of the best examples of Charles's hymns and poems that continue to speak to our own conditions and situations. His selection further illustrates John Telford's comment on Charles that "every side of life stirred his muse." These poems and the commentary upon them are more than meditations upon personal experience; they exhibit and examine many of the basic questions of human existence. With prayerful use, the reader cannot only expect to wrestle with the "Traveler unknown," but can also hope to share the joy of a life "lost in wonder, love, and praise."

Richard P. Heitzenrater
Emeritus Professor
Duke Divinity School
Durham, NC

Preface

This book begins with "Come, O thou Traveler unknown," of which Isaac Watts is reported to have said "That single poem, 'Wrestling Jacob,' is worth all the verses I myself have written." It is Charles Wesley's spiritual autobiography and summarizes his life, work, and ministry. It raises the question he is ever asking:

> Wilt thou not yet to me reveal
> Thy new, unutterable name?

In his hymns and poems, Charles Wesley takes all who sing and read on an inward journey, asking soul-searching questions which are as up-to-date now as they were in the eighteenth century. They reflect his quest for identity as a human being, clergyman, and follower of Jesus Christ. His questions about God, Jesus, faith, others, self, the world, and daily living are still today's questions. This book is not an exhaustive study of such questions in the context of Wesleyan history, theology, or hymnody. It is simply an attempt to look afresh at questions we are asking with which Charles Wesley often wrestled in familiar and unfamiliar hymns and poems, just as Jacob wrestled with the angel in Genesis 32, asking "What is your name?"

In some instances, more stanzas are included than will be found in most hymnbooks, especially where they enhance understanding. However, no attempt has been made to print every poem in its entirety because of the length of some poems. For those texts that have appeared in hymnbooks, the most common selection of stanzas appears here. The stanzas as printed here often are designated in the discussions by number, such as stanza one or two. This is for clarity in reference to the order in which they appear on the printed pages of this book and does not necessarily indicate Wesley's own sequence of the stanzas. Nevertheless, the original number of stanzas is usually noted in the footnotes where relevant.

PREFACE

Widely accepted revised forms of some hymns as they appear in many hymnbooks are often used. Occasionally, however, an original wording has been restored where the revised form has greatly changed Wesley's original intention. While Wesley lived in a time which did not express the kind of concern for inclusive language voiced today, he used much language which is quite compatible with that concern, such as, "Parent of Good" as a form of divine address and occasionally "human kind" instead of "mankind"[1].

Very little has been done to adjust the language of his hymns which have become a part of the "memory bank" of English-speaking Christianity. In some instances, inclusive language changes which do not affect rhyme, assonance, and alliteration have been made, as well as a few for clarity and contemporary relevance. On the whole, the attempt has been made to be faithful to Wesley's texts as written. They possess an integrity on their own as theology, literature, and art. Where revisions occur, they have been made from the viewpoint of hymns as living worship or liturgy and not as dead, verbal relics of the past, and by utilizing Wesley's own vocabulary. Significant changes are noted in the footnotes. In using the traditional language in Wesley's hymns and poems today, it is paramount to remember the overarching pluralistic, inclusive, and universalistic spirit of his theology.

The Charles Wesley poetry is the largest lyrical commentary on the Christian faith, life, and the Scriptures to be found in the English language. About 9,000 hymns and poems may be attributed to him. While hundreds of them, if not thousands, were written as hymns, many were never intended to be sung. His primary biblical sources were the King James Version of the Bible or Authorized Version, the Hebrew Bible or Old Testament, the Greek New Testament, the Book of Common Prayer, the early fathers of the church, numerous poets of his day, and the people whom he served.

Over the past thirty years the renewal of interest in Charles Wesley studies has made all of his works of prose and poetry available. It is increasingly important to evaluate the works of the other poets in the Wesley family: father Samuel, brothers John and Samuel, sister Mehetabel, as well as the prose works of mother Susanna. It is also of vital importance to study Charles's poetry in relation to other poets of his time and those who preceded him.[2]

1. See *HUF* 1767.
2. See the following examples in *Proceedings of The Charles Wesley Society*. J. Richard Watson, "Hymns on the Lord's Supper, 1745, and Some Literary and Liturgical Sources," 2 (1995): 17–33; James Dale, "Holy Larceny? Elizabeth Rowe's Poetry in Charles Wesley's Hymns," 3 (1996): 5–19; James Dale, "Charles Wesley and the Line of Piety: Antecedents

PREFACE

The hymns and poems included here take one on an inner spiritual journey of growth in faith, encountering questions which are as up-to-date now as they were in the eighteenth century. Who is God? What is God's will? Is God dead? Who is Jesus? Can we believe mystery? Can we prove faith? What is eternal life? Charles's response to such questions helps us to make our own response to these questions today!

S T Kimbrough, Jr.,
Research Fellow
Center for Studies in the Wesleyan Tradition
Duke Divinity School

---

of the Hymns in English Devotional Verse," 8 (2002): 55–64; J. Richard Watson, "Charles Wesley and the Thirty-Nine Articles of the Church of England," 9 (2003–2004): 27–38. Additional sources: Percy E. Burtt, "Comparison of Charles Wesley and Isaac Watts," *Pittsburgh Christian Advocate* 77, 17, p. 21, 1910. A. C. Capey, "Charles Wesley and his literary relations," Retford: Brynmill Press, 1983, off-printed from the *Gadfly*, 6:1, 17–26. James Dale, "Charles Wesley, the Odyssey, and Clement of Alexandria," *Methodist History* 30 (1992): 100–102. Thomas H. Gill, "Watts and Charles Wesley Compared," *Congregationalist* 7 (1878): 129–44. E. M. Hodgson, "Poetry in the Hymns of John and Charles Wesley," *Proceedings of the Wesley Historical Society*, 38 (1972): 131–5, 161–5. E. E. Kellett, "The Poetic Character of Charles Wesley's Hymns," *Methodist Recorder*, 18 (August 1910), 10–11. John R. Tyson, "Charles Wesley and Edward Young: Eighteenth-Century poetical apologists," *Methodist History*, 27:2 (1989): 110–19. Dissertations: James Dale, "The Theological and Literary Qualities of the Poetry of Charles Wesley in Relation to the Standards of his Age," University of Cambridge, 1960. Herbert John Roth, "A Literary Study of the Calvinistic and Deistic Implications in the Hymns of Isaac Watts, Charles Wesley and William Cowper," Texas Christian University, 1978.

Introduction

Charles Wesley is unquestionably one of English-language Christianity's greatest poets. Many of the approximately 9,000 poems written during his lifetime have been set to music for use as hymns by many distinguished composers, including George F. Händel (1685–1759), John F. Lampe (1703–1751), Jonathan Battishill (1738–1801), and others. They may be found in almost every English-language Christian hymnal regardless of denomination. Wesley was a master of words and was steeped in a strong classical educational tradition which gave him facility in Latin and biblical languages, and a firm foundation in history, theology, and literature. Charles's father, Samuel, a village Anglican clergyman and astute classical scholar, and his mother, Susanna, a master of children's education, provided solid classical training in the home during their children's early years.

Charles was surrounded by strong poetical influences in his family: his father; two brothers, Samuel and John; and his sister Mehetabel all of whom published poetry. Interestingly, some of Mehetabel's poems appeared in the eighteenth-century *Gentleman's Magazine*. The three brothers also shared with their father ordination as priests of the Church of England.

At eight years of age Charles left home to attend Westminster School in London and later entered Christ Church College at Oxford where he received the B.A. and M.A. degrees. It was there that his poetical prowess began to develop as he transcribed, translated, and paraphrased some of the great classical poets, such as Virgil, Juvenal, and Ovid in metrical English verse. Thus it was that Charles's poetical and spiritual interests were destined to be wedded throughout his life.

During Charles's third or fourth year at Oxford, Charles and John became part of a small group of students later called "Methodists" because of their methodical concern for the daily routine of living a holy life. They were committed to study, prayer, social service, and weekly attendance at

INTRODUCTION

Holy Communion. A lifelong partnership in the journey of faith and ministry began for Charles and John.

In 1735, they traveled to America as missionaries of the Church of England to the Colony of Georgia, and after their return to England both had life-changing spiritual experiences in 1738, which greatly influenced the course of their lives. They traveled and preached side by side; sang, prayed, and worshiped together. Both co-edited hymn books, were often persecuted by mobs, and shared many of their deepest thoughts with each other.

Unfortunately, because of John's and Charles's close identity, the uniqueness of Charles's individual creativity, thought, and contributions were often overlooked. Charles was often overshadowed by his older brother, the superb organizer of the Methodist movement within the Church of England. John was seen as the organizer, leader, systematic thinker, writer, and publisher, while Charles was the troubadour, bard, and poet. However, Charles was no less a systematic thinker or effective preacher and theologian than John, but he tended to couch his thought in the mystery and eloquence of poetical language which for many could not always be easily subjected to the closely-reasoned theological apologetic often characteristic of John's writing.

Nevertheless, Charles proceeded systematically through the Bible, writing poems on passages from all of its books. His two volumes, *SH* 1762, remain one of the richest lyrical commentaries on the Bible in the English language.

Indeed, Charles and John were much alike in many aspects of doctrine and faith perspectives. Both were evangelical and sacramental Christians who sought a fervent inner encounter with God through Christ and a strong practice of living worship centered in regular attendance at Holy Communion, preaching, daily prayers, and whatever good they might do for the bodies and souls of all whom they encountered.

Nevertheless, Charles was very different from John. He was a modest man and consumed with passion to communicate the Christian faith and to capture its wonder and mystery in the language of poetry. From 1738 onward, rarely a day passed without Charles writing poetry. John was also an excellent poet, as his translations of over thirty German hymns reflect. But he was more involved in the organization and distribution of Charles's poetry than in writing his own. We can find many clues to differences in their thinking in the stanzas of hymns and poems John often omitted and/

or changed when he edited Charles's works for publication. Though occasionally he may have found some of Charles's lyrics too sentimental, mystical, and occasionally misleading theologically, it is incorrect to maintain, as some sources have done, that John omitted "Jesu, Lover of my soul" from his distinguished 1780 *Collection* because he thought its language was too sentimental. In fact, in the musical companion to the 1780 *Collection*, which is titled *Sacred Harmony: or a Choice Collection of Psalms and Hymns, Set to Music in Two and Three Parts for the Voice, Harpsichord & Organ*, which was edited by John Wesley, he includes "Jesu, lover of my soul."

Charles ardently opposed John on the separation of the Methodist societies from the Church of England and on the "ordination" of "Methodist bishops" for America. In the 1762 volumes mentioned above he also articulated his views on gradual sanctification. His views on sanctification were by no means in every point synonymous with John's. John often expressed his opposition to Charles's views in marginal notes he entered in his personal copy of *SH* 1762.

John has often been designated the preacher-organizer-theologian and Charles the poet-artist-theologian. More simply put, some would say John was the preacher and Charles was the singer. Charles, however, was also a forceful preacher and invested much time and energy in the improvement of preaching, a role very important to him. One of the most widely distributed Methodist pamphlets during the lifetime of the Wesleys was Charles's sermon, "Awake, Thou That Sleepest!" first delivered in 1742 at Oxford.

John was certainly a more prolific writer of prose than Charles, and his contributions to Christian theology and religious awakening are extremely significant. By comparison, however, many more people around the world today sing Charles's hymns than read John's theology. This has more to do with the nature of the hymns than with John's closely reasoned sermons. Charles's poetry generally transcends the idiosyncrasies of denominations and points directly to the inward witness of God's Spirit in human lives.

Many of Charles's poems were born out of conflict, crisis, violence, oppression, and opposition, and are still timely today. They have spread around the world where people suffer, rejoice, and worship, for their message of self-giving love, as Wesley experienced it in Christ, redeems the time and those who sing them. The questions he was asking throughout his life are still questions people are asking today. Therefore, we can see our lives mirrored in his words. The questions may take other forms, be they

INTRODUCTION

expanded or altered, but the basic questions are in many ways the same, because they have to do with what life ultimately means.

The goal here is to take a fresh look at the unique way in which Charles Wesley asked questions in the eighteenth century which are still relevant today, and how he responded to them. This is something he did through his poetry, which was distinctively different from John.

At the time of Charles's conversion in May 1738, he wrote a hymn which begins with the question: "Where shall my wondering soul begin?"[3] His boldness to ask himself and others this question in the face of commitment to Christ and the church is a valuable guide for Christian discipleship and life's pilgrimage as a follower of Jesus. We must always be bold to inquire and question. Charles helps us to do that. Above all, he helps us to ask ourselves questions that matter most.

Before we begin, however, remember that it is much easier to *read* a question mark than to sing one. How does one *sing* a question mark? This is why the time spent here with questions, which often appear in Charles's hymns is so important. Even though at times he does entertain specific questions within a text, very often there are underlying questions he is addressing in the text itself. Perhaps if we contemplate them properly, we will not pass over them so easily when we sing.

One often thinks of Charles Wesley's theology as a lyrical theology of declamation because of his popular declamatory hymns: "O for a thousand tongues to sing," "Hark! the herald angels sing," "Christ the Lord is risen today." It is better, however, to think of his theology as a lyrical theology of questions. His hymns and poems are filled with questions of faith and a living response to faith, questions of how we relate to one another and to God, questions of personal and societal behavior, questions of the daily order of one's life. The danger is that as one sings Wesley's hymns or reads his poems one may be so captivated by his elegance of expression or the strength of his affirmations that one does not see the questions he is addressing.

This volume is divided into seven sections. The first three address a variety of questions related to the Holy Trinity. Charles devoted an entire volume, *Hymns on the Trinity* (1767), to the identity of the Father, Son, and Holy Spirit and how the persons of the Trinity shape our lives, so that we become "transcripts of the Trinity." What is the primary question with

---

3. This hymn is thought by many scholars to be the hymn written at the time of his conversion in 1738.

INTRODUCTION

which these texts are concerned? — How do we become transcripts of the Trinity? This question is a subject of almost every text in the volume.

In section four we move to questions of faith. What are the marks of faith? How are we to understand sin in relationship to faith? What difference can faith make in one's life? Is it possible to prove faith? Often Charles's responses to such questions are not direct, but rather subtle, for faith is often not direct. It involves continual, lifelong growth. Faith matures as we mature, and Wesley wants us to ask ourselves to what extent we can follow a path whereby this transpires.

Section five brings together some texts of Wesley that raise questions about our relationship to others and the world. Do we care about others? Do we love others? Can there be unity among human beings? Can there be peace among peoples? Is the church really intended for everyone? What are our attitudes toward war? How will we deal with the death of others, especially family and friends? Charles Wesley was not an only child, but rather he had two brothers and many sisters. Therefore, many of his questions about life with others came from real life experience. Furthermore, as a young man in his twenties he made a voyage to America and lived under adverse conditions on St. Simon's Island, Georgia, which included false accusations of misconduct by two angry women. Moreover, he encountered the horrors of slavery in Charleston before departing on his return voyage to England. Charles knew that we cannot stop asking ourselves questions about how we relate to others and the world around as Christians.

Section six is concerned with personal matters. What are the ongoing questions we must continue to ask ourselves? If we go through trials and persecutions, how will we respond to them? How will persistent illness, which Charles endured, affect our faith and attitudes toward life? What about those who are bigots? Do we see bigotry only in others? Do we have the ability to forgive? If not, how do we learn to forgive? What is the measure by which we know God's will for our lives? How do we discern the principles by which we shall live? One of the interesting things about Wesley's lyrical theology of questions is that what he asks of others, he is committed to ask of himself.

Section seven concerns daily living. Charles spends a lifetime asking himself how he can grow in faith and learn the meaning of life. This concerns not only the expansion of the mind and heart, but he also asks how shall one rest in order to meet the challenges of the next day? How shall one properly nourish the body, which is the temple of the Spirit.

INTRODUCTION

This question of nourishment brings him to the lifelong question—What is the most important meal for human existence? For Charles it is unquestionably Holy Communion, to which he and his brother John devoted an entire volume, *HLS* 1745. Herein lies one of the most important questions of hospitality. Who is welcome at the Lord's table? Charles's response is: "ye need not one be left behind."

While throughout this volume we will search for the questions Charles is ever asking, we shall also comb his texts for his responses. Why do we not say "his answers"? We do not say "his answers," because Charles often asks the questions, and we, like Charles, as servants of Christ, must seek the answers for ourselves.

SECTION 1

God the Father

Father, in whom we live,
    In whom we are and move,
The glory, power, and praise receive
    For thy creating love.

CHARLES WESLEY

1.

Who is God?
Come, O thou Traveler unknown[1]

WRESTLING JACOB

Come, O thou Traveler unknown,
    Whom still I hold, but cannot see!
My company before is gone,
    And I am left alone with thee.
With thee all night I mean to stay,
And wrestle till the break of day.

I need not tell thee who I am,
    My misery or sin declare;
Thyself hast called me by my name;
    Look on thy hands and read it there:
But who, I ask thee, who art thou?
Tell me thy name and tell me now.

In vain thou strugglest to get free;
    I never will unloose my hold!
Art thou the Man that died for me?
    The secret of thy love unfold;
Wrestling, I will not let thee go,
Till I thy name, thy nature know.

---

1. *HSP* 1742, 115–18; based on the story of Jacob wrestling the angel in Genesis 32.

SECTION 1: GOD THE FATHER

Wilt thou not yet to me reveal
    Thy new, unutterable name?
Tell me, I still beseech thee, tell;
    To know it now resolved I am;
Wrestling, I will not let thee go,
Till I thy name, thy nature know.

'Tis all in vain to hold thy tongue,
    Or touch the hollow of my thigh:
Though every sinew be unstrung,
    Out of my arms thou shalt not fly;
Wrestling, I will not let thee go,
Till I thy name, thy nature know.

What tho' my shrinking flesh complain,
    And murmur to contend so long?
I rise superior to my pain,
    When I am weak, then I am strong;
And when my all of strength shall fail,
I shall with the God-Man prevail.

My strength is gone, my nature dies,
    I sink beneath thy weighty hand,
Faint to revive, and fall to rise,
    I fall, and yet by faith I stand,
I stand, and will not let thee go,
Till I thy name, thy nature know.

Yield to me now—for I am weak,
    But confident in self-despair;
Speak to my heart, in blessings speak,
    Be conquered by my instant prayer;
Speak, or thou never hence shalt move,
And tell me if thy name is love.

'Tis love! 'Tis love! Thou diedst for me!
    I hear thy whisper in my heart.
The morning breaks, the shadows flee,
    Pure universal Love thou art;
To me, to all thy mercies move,
Thy nature and thy name is love.

My prayer has power with God; the grace
    Unspeakable I now receive;
Thro' faith I see thee face to face,
    I see thee face to face, and live!
In vain I have not wept, and strove:
Thy nature and thy name is Love.

I know thee, Savior, who thou art,
    Jesus, the feeble sinner's friend;
Nor wilt thou with the night depart,
    But stay, and love me to the end;
Thy mercies never shall remove:
Thy nature and thy name is love.

The Sun of Righteousness on me
    Hath risen with healing in his wings;
Withered my nature's strength, from Thee
    My soul its life and succor brings;
My help is all laid up above:
Thy nature and thy name is love.

Contented now upon my thigh
    I halt, till life's short journey end;
All helplessness, all weakness, I
    On thee alone for strength depend;
Nor have I power from thee to move;
Thy nature and thy name is love.

Lame as I am, I take the prey,
    Hell, earth, and sin with ease o'ercome;
I leap for joy, pursue my way,
    And as a bounding hart fly home,
Thro' all eternity to prove
Thy nature and thy name is Love.

With these lines Charles Wesley has written his spiritual autobiography. He sees the struggles of his own life mirrored in Jacob's wrestling with the angel. Wesley's life was a struggle to know the Unknown Traveler. Even after the revelation of May 21, 1738, when he grasped for the first time the reality of God's love for him in Jesus Christ, the struggle to know the heights and depths of such love and the God who gave and gives of self in that love continued until his death at age eighty-one.

SECTION 1: GOD THE FATHER

This poem is not only his spiritual autobiography; it is ours as well. The questions he was asking are those we are asking:

> Who is God? Who, I ask thee, who art thou? (stanza 2)
> Who is Jesus? Art thou the Man that died for me? (stanza 3)
> Can I know God? Wilt thou not yet to me reveal / Thy new, unutterable name? (stanza 4)

Wesley's search is our search, and it is the experience of faith which goes back for centuries. We struggle to know the name and nature of God. We grasp for the Unknown, and we hold fast to that which we cannot see. Charles's brother John eloquently expressed the search for the unseen God in his translation of a German hymn by Gerhard Tersteegen:

> Thou hidden love of God, whose height,
>   Whose depth unfathomed, no one knows,
> I see from far thy beauteous light,
>   And inly sigh for thy repose;
> My heart is pained, nor can it be
> At rest, till it finds rest in thee.[2]

The struggle is an identity crisis: Who is God and who am I? If I want divine vitality in my life, how can I receive it? In the Bible story of Genesis 32, Jacob must first be asked who he is before he can receive the blessing. Wesley says, however:

> I need not tell thee who I am,
>   My misery or sin declare;
> Thyself hast called me by my name;
>   Look on thy hands, and read it there.

God knows the generations of humankind by name—"sinner"—and that name is written in the pierced hands of Jesus upon the cross. God knows who we are.

The struggle requires endurance.

> Wrestling, I will not let thee go,
> Till I thy name, thy nature know.

It is easy to give up in the midst of the struggle to know God. When we despair, lack confidence, and doubt, we must hold fast to the Unknown

---

2. From an eight-stanza hymn *Verborgne Gottesliebe du* from the Herrnhut *Gesangbuch*, 1735. Wesley's English translation first appeared in *A Collection of Psalms and Hymns*, 1738.

Traveler whom we cannot see, namely, God. We must "wrestle till the break of day," which is a lifelong struggle. This was Jacob's experience. It is ours also. If we endure and do not let go, we will emerge from the struggle knowing that God's name and nature are one and the same—Love.

Stanzas 1–6 tell of the agony of the struggle, the mental and physical pain, and the soul-searching questions which often drive many away from God. Stanzas seven through twelve, however, describe the discovery of faith which resounds in the refrain: "Thy nature and thy name is Love."

Love with a capital "L" is who God is, what God is like, and the way in which God's self-disclosure is revealed to us. It is God's love made known in Jesus which makes the shadows of doubt flee as dawn breaks and we confess with Wesley: "Pure, universal Love thou art!"

Who is God? Love! Who is Jesus? The One who shows us how God's love acts in the world. Can we know God? Yes! If we endure in the struggle to grasp God whom we cannot see, we will experience that love, God's love, acted out in life—which is what matters most.

2.

What is God's Will?
Thy will, O Lord, whate'er I do

> Thy will, O Lord, whate'er I do,
>   my principle of action be.
> Thy will I would through life pursue,
>   impelled, restrained, and ruled by thee;
> and only think, and speak, and move,
>   as taught and guided by thy love.[1]

How often we have heard that we are to do God's will, and yet we are not always certain we know what it is. Some would excise the freedom God has given human beings from the divine creative process and say that whatever happens is God's will. Hence, knowing God's will is simple. When you know what happens, you know God's will, because whatever happens is God's will. This, however, imposes evil, hatred, war, destruction, even murder upon God's will in a way contrary to the Scriptures and removes responsibility from human beings for their own actions and the evil which issues from human will.

Whatever happens is not always God's will. To be sure, daily occurrences do not take place outside the context of God's will for love and wholeness for all people and the world at large. We can, however, oppose God's will and stand in its way.

---

1. *PW*, 10:205.

This short poem stresses some important aspects of the role God's will is to play in our lives. First, it is to be the principle on which we are to act. Second, it is to be the goal of our lives. God's will is something we seek all our lives long. It gives momentum to all we do. It restrains us and gives structure, form, and shape to our lives. And third, God's will is to guide our thoughts, words, and actions by love.

Those seem to be fine principles regarding God's will, but what is God's will? How can we *know* it in any given situation? What is God's will for my life vocationally? What is God's will for me when I am at school, at work, single, married, divorced, male, female, disabled, wronged, angry, poor, rich, unemployed? How do I know what the will of God is? Charles Wesley suggests a way:

> And only think, and speak, and move,
> as taught and guided by thy love.

God's love should be the principle which shapes our understanding of God's will. How does that help us in knowing God's will? We know how God's love expressed itself. It was personified in Jesus, who willingly gave of himself in pursuit of others and their needs at all costs, even death upon a cross. In any situation in life we are to use the measure of God's love as expressed in Jesus as the means of determining our own actions.

What is God's will? It is the willingness to live out the principle of sacrificial love which goes in search of others at all costs, even to death. When we submit to that love, we will know God's will. To do God's will one must live by sacrificial love. When we love enough, we will know it.

3.

Is God Dead?

O Love divine, what hast thou done![1]

DESIRING TO LOVE

O Love divine, what hast thou done!
    The immortal God hath died for me!
The Father's co-eternal Son
    Bore all my sins upon the tree:
The immortal God for me hath died!
My Lord, my Love is crucified!

Behold him, all ye that pass by,
    The bleeding Prince of life and peace!
Come, sinners, see your Maker die,
    And say, was ever grief like his?
Come, feel with me his blood applied:
My Lord, my Love is crucified!

Is crucified for me and you,
    To bring us rebels near to God;
Believe, believe the record true,
    We all are bought with Jesus' blood,

---

1. *HSP* 1742, 26–27.

Pardon for all flows from his side:
My Lord, my Love is crucified!

Then let us sit beneath his cross
    And gladly catch the healing stream,
All things for him account but loss,
    And give up all our hearts to him;
Of nothing think or speak beside,
My Lord, my Love is crucified!

Some years ago there was much discussion about the so-called "death-of-God theology," which hailed the inevitability of God's death. Although the popularity of this school of thought tended to wane, there was much deliberation over the significance of a dying God and/or the death of the idea of God. It did bring Christians to a new realization that there is a death-of-God theology inherent in the Scriptures. It has been eloquently summarized by Charles Wesley in the above hymn. Unfortunately, some hymn editors changed the word "immortal" to "incarnate." Wesley is expressing the mystery and wonder of the immortal Being who has created life, and whose co-eternal Son dies on behalf of all humankind. In stanza two he phrases this another way: "Come, sinners, see your Maker die." The Creator dies for the created. The editorial change of "Maker" to "Savior" in some hymnbooks radically changes Wesley's intention.

    The death of God has personal and universal implications, for the Son "bore all *my* sins upon the tree" but is "crucified for *me* and *you*." As particular and personal as his death may be for me, its effect is universal. It is a death for friends and enemies, peace lovers and war mongers, the loved and the hated, the moral and the immoral. God's death is for *all* in order "to bring us rebels back to God."

    When we see God's death in the context of creation, our own understanding of life and its complexities is more clearly focused. We view grief differently. All our pain and agony are seen against the backdrop of the excruciating death at Calvary and the groaning of the Creator for the whole creation. Charles asks, "Was ever grief like his?" Our complaints, sufferings, and sorrows are placed in proper perspective. Therefore, we will not break under them for they are minuscule when seen in the light of our own Creator's suffering for us.

    A woman arrived at her pastor's home one morning to begin her ritual complaint about how people in the church and community were saying unkind and unjust things about her. When met at the door by the pastor's wife, she began her liturgy and hastily posed the question: "It is just not right for anyone to be treated the way I am, is it?" The pastor's wife perceptively replied, "I don't know. They nailed Jesus to a cross." The woman was speechless. She paused, stutteringly offered a "good day," and departed. The death of God at Calvary places all our grief and complaints in proper perspective.

From beneath the cross we "catch the healing stream" and are made whole. We are cured of the illness of greed, malice, and lust as we grasp that "all things for him account but loss." Our hearts are no longer sick with false allegiances. The healing stream of God's love which flows from the cross restores us to health and singleness of purpose. With Charles we learn to let "all things for him account but loss." As we focus on this reality: "My Lord, my Love is crucified," the life of self-giving love, experienced in the crucifixion of Jesus, becomes the goal, purpose, and style of our lives.

4.

What is in a name?
Thou hidden Source of calm repose[1]

HYMNS FOR BELIEVERS

Thou hidden Source of calm repose,
    Thou all-sufficient Love Divine,
My help and refuge from my foes,
    Secure I am, if thou art mine:
And lo, from sin and grief and shame,
I hide me, Jesus, in thy name.

Thy mighty name Salvation is,
    And keeps my happy soul above;
Comfort it brings and power and peace,
    And joy and everlasting love:
To me, with thy great name, are given
Pardon, and holiness, and heaven.

Jesus, my All in All thou art:
    My rest in toil, my ease in pain,
The med'cine of my broken heart,
    In war my peace, in loss my gain,

---

1. *HSP* 1749, 1:245–46.

SECTION 1: GOD THE FATHER

> My smile beneath the tyrant's frown,
> In shame my glory and my crown.
>
> In want my plentiful supply,
>   In weakness my almighty power,
> In bonds my perfect liberty,
>   My light in Satan's darkest hour,
> In grief my joy unspeakable,
> My life in death, my heaven in hell.

Charles Wesley claimed to have learned the love of knowledge from his mother and the virtue of sound study and the disciplines of hardship and denial from his father. From both he learned the love of God. Even in moments of emptiness and despair it was this love which upheld him. Knowledge and experience taught him that God is the "all-sufficient Love Divine," who sustains us through all of life's daunting polarities and paradoxes.

Although the paradoxes of life often become stumbling blocks to faith, Wesley experienced God as the God of paradoxes: God comes to us in the tensions and complexities of life with strength and wisdom that enable us to endure. When we feel there is no strength or reason to go on, we discover a hidden Source of power. Wesley tells us in stanza one that such power is all-sufficient Love Divine. It is our—

> help in weakness,
> refuge in desperation,
> security in insecurity,
> joy in grief;

and it imparts—

> sinlessness for sin,
> shamelessness for shame.

God is known by many names. We learn in stanza two that one of the most powerful is "Salvation," which is the meaning of Jesus' name, *y^{e}shu`a*, in Hebrew. We can experience the power of that name.

When someone who has been rescued from a disaster says to the rescuer, "You are my salvation!" that person knows that the power and life-giving strength of the rescuer will always be known to the rescued as "salvation."

Wesley affirms that God is Salvation, having rescued us from destruction and given us a new life. God, our Salvation, brings—

> comfort when we are comfortless,
> power when we are powerless,
> peace when we suffer strife,
> joy when we are sad,
> love when we hate;

and imparts—

> holiness for impurity,
> heaven for hell.

Stanza three declares the discovery that Jesus is our All in All, for he personifies the all-sufficient Love Divine who seeks every human being at all costs. Those who follow this Jesus will find—

> rest in toil,
> ease in pain,
> healing in broken hearts,
> peace in war,
> gain in loss,
> smiles amid frowns,
> glory amid shame.

Finally, in stanza four, we learn that faith in God's love as disclosed in Jesus brings—

> abundance in want,
> power in weakness,
> liberty in bondage,
> light in darkness,
> life in death.

Wesley eloquently summarizes God's promises to all in this hymn, and his experience can be ours. He bids us trust the "hidden Source of calm repose" and follow the embodiment of all-sufficient divine love: Jesus.

5.

How do we experience God?
O thou who camest from above[1]

Leviticus 6:13: "The fire shall ever be burning upon the altar; it shall never go out." (KJV)

> O thou who camest from above,
>   The pure, celestial fire to impart,
> Kindle a flame of sacred love
>   On the mean altar of my heart;
> There let it for thy glory burn,
>   With inextinguishable blaze,
> And trembling to its Source return,
>   In humble prayer, and fervent praise.
>
> Jesus, confirm my heart's desire
>   To work, and speak, and think for thee,
> Still let me guard the holy fire,
>   And still stir up thy gift in me.
> Ready for all thy perfect will
>   My acts of faith and love repeat,
> 'Till death thy endless mercies seal,
>   And make my sacrifice complete.

---

1. *SH* 1762, 1:57.

HOW DO WE EXPERIENCE GOD?

It is reported that in John Wesley's later years some preachers came to him to inquire about his experience of God, reminding him that often he had asked them to share their own experiences. His reply is said to have been the quotation of the last stanza of "O thou who camest from above." In the first four lines of stanza 2 above one finds vital insight into the Christian's experience of God.

> Jesus, confirm my heart's desire
> To work, and speak, and think for thee,
> Still let me guard the holy fire,
> And still stir up thy gift in me.

The holy fire which Wesley would guard is the "flame of sacred love" of which he speaks in stanza one. Love is the source of activity, speech, and thought. What a transforming power it is when all we do, say, and think issues from love! The world has yet to experience such total transformation of all people. Yet those who have the courage and vision to follow Jesus know and experience the possibility and reality of this love.

We also experience God by constantly being alert to God's will. This we do by repeating acts of faith and love throughout our lives. Our best experience of God's will and the way we understand it most sensitively is by acting out faith by love. It is a lifelong activity.

> 'Till death thy endless mercies seal
> And make my sacrifice complete.

Both John and Charles Wesley understood life as a sacrifice. Like Paul, they experienced dying daily with Christ. Calvary's cross became for them and becomes for us a pattern of life: give all we have, all our lives, in love for God and others. That is what Jesus did. His sacrifice shapes our own. Thus, the following lines, sometimes attributed to John Wesley, emerged which helped shape the spirit of the Wesleyan movement.

> Do all the good you can,
> By all the means you can,
> In all the ways you can,
> In all the places you can,
> At all the times you can,
> To all the people you can,
> As long as ever you can.

If we act out faith by love as followers of Jesus, we will know God's will.

6.

What is life, patterned after the Holy Trinity?

Father, in whom we live[1]

HYMN TO THE TRINITY

>Father, in whom we live,
>   In whom we are and move,
>The glory, power, and praise receive
>   For thy creating love.
>Let all the angel throng
>   Give thanks to God on high,
>While earth repeats the joyful song
>   And echoes to the sky.
>
>Incarnate Deity,
>   Let all the ransomed race
>Render in thanks their lives to thee
>   For thy redeeming grace.
>The grace to sinners showed
>   Ye heavenly choirs proclaim,
>And cry, "Salvation to our God,
>   Salvation to the Lamb."

---

1. *RH* 1747, No. 34, 44–45. In some contemporary versions of this hymn the first line reads, "Maker, in whom we live."

> Spirit of Holiness,
>   Let all thy saints adore
> Thy sacred energy, and bless
>   Thine heart-renewing power.
> Not angel tongues can tell
>   Thy love's ecstatic height,
> The glorious joy unspeakable,
>   The beatific sight.
>
> Eternal, Triune God,
>   Let all the hosts above,
> Let all on earth below record
>   And dwell upon thy love.
> When heaven and earth are fled,
>   Before thy glorious face,
> Sing all the saints thy love hath made
>   Thine everlasting praise.

Charles Wesley wrote many hymns on the theme of the Holy Trinity. In fact, he published two collections (1746 and 1767) devoted solely to that subject. This hymn entitled "Hymn to the Trinity," however, appeared in a different volume, *RH* 1747. It is a doxology of praise to God the Creator, Incarnate Redeemer, and Holy Spirit. It resounds with the language of Scripture from beginning to end.

Stanza 1 reminds us that God is the One in whom we "live, and move, and have our being" (Acts 17:28). It opens with the spirit and metaphors of many of the Psalms (19, 47, 98, 150). Earth and heaven, including the angel throng, are praising God for "creating love." This is a constant theme of Wesley's—love creates, reclaims, and sustains life. The picture is not, however, one of the inhabitants of creation alone lifting their voices in praise of their Father, but rather the angels ring out God's praise and the "*earth* repeats the joyful song. All creation "echoes to the sky." As the psalmist acclaims:

> Let the floods clap their hands;
>   let the hills sing together for joy
> at the presence of the Lord. (Psalm 98:8–9a)

Stanza 2 extends the doxology to God as the Incarnate Deity, God become flesh, the Redeemer of all humankind. Once again, the way Wesley formulates the doxology is of vital importance for what it means. He declares that the "ransomed race / renders in thanks their lives to thee." Such praise is not merely for the lifting of our voices in thanksgiving to God but our lives, our entire existence. Sinners cry "Salvation to our God / salvation to the Lamb" not merely with melody and word but with their being—who they are and how they live. Wesley draws his imagery and language here from the Scriptures, namely the Revelation of John 7:9–10, where the multitude from every nation breaks forth in the hymn:

> Salvation to our God
> who sits upon the throne,
> and to the Lamb! (7:10, KJV)

Stanza 3 exalts the third person of the Trinity, the Holy Spirit, whom Wesley here addresses as the "Spirit of Holiness." Once again, his unique, eloquent, and poignant language help us to grasp what a true doxology of praise to God's Spirit means. It is to acknowledge and experience the Spirit of Holiness as "the sacred energy" which embodies God's "heart renewing power." We can experience this energy of holiness in our lives, but we shall find our words futile in describing the height of God's love which is "joy unspeakable."

The final stanza returns to the image of all creation in stanza 1: "hosts above" and "all on earth" recall and dwell upon God's love. Imagine a world that actually would "dwell upon [God's] love!" O what a world that would be! O what a church, the church would be, if it would but constantly "dwell upon [God's] love!" What examples we would be of the Savior formed within our souls, if we would "dwell upon [God's] love!"

Wesley concludes with the scriptural affirmation that though earth and heaven pass away, God's creating love remains. That itself seems a thought incomprehensible, but it is one sustained from the beginning of the Scriptures to their end.

What a marvelous pattern for living Wesley provides in this "Hymn to the Trinity." (1) *Put worship at the center of life.* Let your life resound with praise of the Creator, who gives and sustains life. Join with all creation in the joyous praise-song to God. Remember, however, that if God wants the floods and hills to rejoice, the inhabitants of God's earth must see that their lives are not turned toward death by human destruction and misuse of the environment. (2) *Make your life a doxology.* In every facet of existence let it be praise and thanks to God. This means that all we are must render God thanks. (3) *Trust God's "sacred energy,"* the "Spirit of Holiness," for strength. Here is the power that sustains in the needs of every moment. (4)

WHAT IS LIFE, PATTERNED AFTER THE HOLY TRINITY?

Remember to dwell upon God's self-giving love until you become such love! Such is the trinitarian life!—a life patterned after the Trinity!

SECTION 2

God the Son

> One look of Jesus Christ
> can break your heart this moment,
> and bind it up by faith.
>
> CHARLES WESLEY

7.

Who Is Jesus?

Savior of all, what hast thou done?[1]

THE TRIAL OF FAITH

Savior of all, what hast thou done?
    What hast thou suffered on the tree?
Why didst thou groan thy mortal groan,
    Obedient unto death for me?
The myst'ry of thy passion show,—
The end of all thy griefs below.

Pardon, and grace, and heaven to buy,
    My bleeding sacrifice expired:
But didst thou not my pattern die,
    That, by thy glorious Spirit fired,
Faithful to death I might endure,
And make the crown by suffering sure?

Thou didst the meek example leave,
    That I might in thy footsteps tread;
Might like the Man of Sorrows grieve,
    And groan, and bow with thee my Head:

---

1. *HSP* 1749, 2:10–11; stanzas 1, 3, 4 of a six-stanza poem.

> Thy dying in my body bear,
> And all thy state of suffering share.

Sometimes we are asked, "Who has been the greatest influence in your life?" Usually we respond with the name of someone we know or have known during our lifetime: father, mother, teacher, coach, friend. It is often someone who has inspired and encouraged us, fostered our talents and abilities, given us a set of values by which to live, or been a model of character and purpose after which to pattern our lives. How often do we answer that Christ is the most influential person in our lives?

Charles Wesley asks, "But didst thou not *my pattern* die?" It is common to think of Christ as an example of goodness and virtue, as someone who went about doing good. Wesley suggests, however, that Christ's pattern for our lives has a much deeper meaning than that. The overarching pattern he gives us for living is one of suffering and dying. It is the cruciform life in that it draws its form, meaning, and energy from the crucifixion. This is the key to the example of life Christ sets before us.

The apostle Paul understood the cruciform life when he said, "I die daily" (1 Corinthians 15:31). Wesley comprehended this when he wrote, "Thy dying in my body bear." Christians bear the death of Christ in themselves. Like Christ, they are to be faithful through suffering even unto and until death. That is at the heart of Christ's pattern of life. Suffering does not bring faith into question; it affirms it! Christ demonstrates its importance in redeeming and reclaiming life. Suffering crowns existence. "And make the crown by suffering sure."

The shallow quest for "happiness" often involves the attempt to avoid suffering, but suffering is an integral part of living. That is indeed a mystery, just as the redemptive power of Christ's passion, death, and resurrection is a mystery. Yet, suffering is a reality. And when we open ourselves to the mystery of Christ's redemption, the anguish of earthly life is relieved. We are able to endure faithfully to the end.

To pattern our lives after Calvary does not mean we are to have martyr complexes. Rather, it means that suffering and death do not defeat us. They renew, redeem, and reclaim us as do the suffering and death of Christ.

8.

Why Was Jesus Born?
Lo, he comes with clouds descending[1]

Revelation 1:7: "Look! He is coming with the clouds;
every eye will see him,
even those who pierced him;
and on his account all the tribes
of the earth will wail.
So it is to be. Amen"

THY KINGDOM COME

Lo, he comes with clouds descending,
Once for favored sinners slain;
Thousand, thousand saints attending
Swell the triumph of his train:
Hallelujah,
God appears, on earth to reign!

Every eye shall now behold him
Robed in dreadful majesty;
Those who set at nought and sold him,
Pierced and nailed him to the tree,
Deeply wailing,
Shall the true Messiah see.

1. *HIM* 1758, 32–33.

> The dear tokens of his passion
>   Still his dazzling body bears;
> Cause of endless exultation
>   To his ransomed worshippers;
>   With what rapture
>   Gaze we on those glorious scars!
>
> Yea, amen! Let all adore thee
>   High on thine eternal throne;
> Savior, take the power and glory,
>   Claim the kingdom for thine own:
>   Hallelujah,
>   Everlasting God, come down.

This hymn, which anticipates Christ's coming in glory as described in Revelation 1:7, is often sung during the Advent season, but it expresses the Christian's hope at every time of the year. Every day is filled with the expectation of Christ's coming. Wesley tells us why.

Sinners are transformed into saints (stanza one).

> Thousand, thousand saints attending,
>   Swell the triumph of his train.

To the One who will be slain for sinners they cry out: "Hallelujah!" This is quite a different picture from the small band of adoring shepherds at Bethlehem and the Wise Men who followed the star. Even if the angels resounded, "Glory to God in the highest," thousands of saints did not hail Christ's birth. As Christians continue to pray with the early Church, "Come, Lord Jesus," they do so with the confidence that God transforms a small band of worshipers at Bethlehem into thousands upon thousands worldwide resounding, "Hallelujah!" at Christ's coming in glory. History and people are changed! Sinners have now become saints through the redemptive life, ministry, death, and resurrection of Jesus Christ.

Narrow human vision is transformed into God's universal vision (stanza two). Human exclusivity becomes God's inclusivity. *All* "shall the true Messiah see." It is not a select few who will have this vision. "*Every eye* shall now behold him;" even Judas who sold him for thirty pieces of silver and the soldiers who pierced his side with a spear and drove the nails through his hands and feet at Calvary shall see Christ for who he truly is: the Messiah. God's most illuminating view of life will be seen by those with the narrowest vision.

Suffering is transformed into exultation (stanza three). Calvary, the symbol of pain, agony, and death gives cause for jubilation to all who worship Christ, for they have experienced redemption and release from their sins. As they "gaze . . . on those glorious scars," which become symbolic of life, not death, they begin to experience that God transforms life's suffering into joy.

The world's weakness is transformed into God's strength (stanza four). Throughout history, nations, leaders, and peoples have sought to claim the kingdoms of the earth as their own. The results have been appalling: greed, war, destruction, wealth, poverty, the powerful and powerless, masters and servants, etc. The Christian's hope is that in the coming of Christ, God lays claim to the kingdom of the earth, establishing love as the reigning power throughout the world. That day has not yet arrived, and we continue to pray, "Come, Lord Jesus!" With Wesley we plead

> Everlasting God, come down.
> Come and transform—
> sinners into saints,
> narrow vision into universal vision,
> suffering into joy,
> weakness into strength.

It is not surprising that Wesley titled this hymn "Thy Kingdom Come," for it is the coming of God's reign that brings these things to pass.

9.

Can we believe the mystery?
When he did our flesh assume[1]

Jeremiah 31:22: "A woman shall compass a man."

> When he did our flesh assume,
>   That everlasting Man,
> Mary held him in her womb
>   Whom heaven could not contain!
> Who the mystery can believe!
>   Incomprehensible thou art;
> Yet we still by faith conceive,
>   And bear thee in our heart.

"The word was made flesh and dwelt among us" (John 1:14, KJV). Who can explain God's assumption of human flesh in the form of Jesus? Who can explain Mary's conception of the Holy Child? These mysteries are unfathomable to the human mind.

> Who the mystery can believe!
>   Incomprehensible thou art.

We cannot subject the mystery to scientific analysis for verification. There are realities which transcend logic and science. We may say that we love someone and vow that such love is real, but we cannot prove it except by

---

1. *SH* 1762, 2:32.

how we live. Love transcends factual proof. We may produce what we view as tangible evidence of love, but the evidence is not the love itself. Love's reality resides within us. We can communicate that reality in our thoughts, words, actions, and emotions—in who we are. We can personify love's reality.

The Scriptures tell us that "God is love" (1 John 4:8). In other words, God is best defined or described as Love, and Jesus personifies the reality of Love, Supreme Love, which seeks all human beings whatever the cost, even death. Jesus is the evidence that love is real. Through the indwelling Spirit of Jesus, love's reality resides within us. And though we do not fully comprehend it,

> Yet we still by faith conceive
> And bear thee in our heart.

10.

Can we live the mystery?
And can it be that I should gain[1]

FREE GRACE

And can it be that I should gain
    An interest in the Savior's blood?
Died he for me?—who caused his pain!
    For me?—who him to death pursued.
Amazing love! How can it be
That thou, my God, shouldst die for me?

'Tis mystery all! the Immortal dies!
    Who can explore his strange design?
In vain the first-born seraph tries
    To sound the depths of love divine.
'Tis mercy all! Let earth adore,
Let angel minds inquire no more.

He left his Father's throne above—
    So free, so infinite his grace—
Emptied himself of all but love,
    And bled for Adam's helpless race.

---

1. *HSP* 1739, 117–19.

'Tis mercy all, immense and free;
For, O my God, it found out me!

Long my imprisoned spirit lay
   Fast bound in sin and nature's night;
Thine eye diffused a quickening ray—
   I woke, the dungeon flamed with light,
My chains fell off, my heart was free,
I rose, went forth, and followed thee.

No condemnation now I dread;
   Jesus, and all in him, is mine!
Alive in him, my living Head,
   And clothed in righteousness divine,
Bold I approach the eternal throne,
And claim the crown, through Christ, my own.

The soul-searching questions of stanza one above characterize Wesley's lifelong quest for God from his earliest search to his constant realization that this "interest" was indeed the consuming passion of his life. They reflect his spiritual journey and personalize his Christian experience. Therefore, if we consider these questions carefully, our relationship to God may grow and Wesley's questions may become ours.

      And can it be that I should gain
      An interest in the Savior's blood?

Wesley is astounded that he should be concerned with Christ's sacrifice. The events of Calvary had occurred centuries ago. What should draw his attention to them now? He had reluctantly become an Anglican clergyman in 1735 at the insistence of his brother John, whom he accompanied with great reservation to the American colony of Georgia as a member of Oglethorpe's staff and as a missionary. He had thought of spending all his days at Oxford. It was there he had taken his degrees and established himself as a lecturer at Christ Church College. Life at Oxford had won his interest. Yet something was lacking. On board the ship *Simmonds* just off Tibey Island in Georgia he wrote:

> In vain have I fled from myself to America; I still groan under the intolerable weight of inherent misery! If I have never yet repented of my undertaking, it is because I could hope for nothing better in

England—or in Paradise. Go where I will, I carry my Hell about me.[2]

In 1736 Charles Wesley returned to England despondent over his ineffectiveness in Georgia. There was tremendous inner turmoil in his life. It was not until May 21, 1738, that the answer "Yes!" came to the question:

> Died he for me, who caused his pain?
> For me, who him to death pursued?

As he read Martin Luther's commentary on the Book of Galatians, especially the conclusion to chapter two, Wesley knew that his sin was a part of the sin of all humankind for which Christ had given his life on the cross. Therefore, he confessed, "Amazing love!" Wesley had experienced the social evils of his day in England with its outcast, destitute, hungering masses and those of America with its dastardly enslavement of Africans. Now he realized that the sacrifice of Christ at Calvary had been made for those sins; but not for social sins only, for they have their origin in personal sin.

Wesley would spend the rest of his life in wonder over God's amazing love, knowing that he could never fully comprehend it. It would be a constant struggle. Over a year after his conversion he wrote in his *Journal*:

> Never knew till now the strength of temptation, and energy of sin. Who that conferred with flesh and blood would cover great success? I live in a continual storm. My soul is always in my hand. The enemy thrusts sore at me, that I may fall. And a worse enemy than the devil is my own heart. . . . Received, I humbly hope, a fresh pardon in the Sacrament at St Paul's.[3]

> 'Tis mystery all! the Immortal dies!
> Who can explore his strange design?

Wesley learned to live the mystery: that questions and confession go together; that to be emptied of everything but love is what it means to serve a God who in Christ "emptied himself of all but love."

If Charles Wesley's questions become our questions, let his realizations and his confession become ours as well. Let us learn to live the mystery of God's love. In moments when we feel the emptiest, let us boldly "approach the eternal throne" knowing:

---

2. Baker, *Charles Wesley as Revealed by His Letters*, 22.
3. *MSJ*, 1:182.

CAN WE LIVE THE MYSTERY?

'Tis mercy all, immense and free,
For, O my God, it found out me.

11.

Was Jesus born to set all people free?
Come, thou long-expected Jesus[1]

> Come, thou long-expected Jesus,
>   Born to set thy people free;
> From our fears and sins release us;
>   Let us find our rest in thee.
> Israel's strength and consolation,
>   Hope of all the earth thou art;
> Dear desire of every nation,
>   Joy of every longing heart.
>
> Born thy people to deliver,
>   Born a child and yet a King,
> Born to reign in us forever,
>   Now thy gracious kingdom bring.
> By thine own eternal Spirit
>   Rule in all our hearts alone;
> By thine all-sufficient merit,
>   Raise us to thy glorious throne.

This great hymn of freedom and deliverance takes on added dimensions of meaning when we consider one particular occurrence in Charles Wesley's life. Spent and dejected after only five months in the colony of Georgia, he decided to return to England. Charles made his way overland

---

1. *HNL* 1745, 14.

to Charleston where the boat he was to board for England would set sail. But if his spirits were at a low ebb, they were utterly shattered by his first-hand encounter with slavery while in Charleston. Here is a shocking passage from his *Journal* regarding slavery.

> I had observed much, and heard more, of the cruelty of masters towards their negroes. But now I received an authentic account of some horrid instances thereof [at Charleston before I set out on my return voyage to England]. . . . The giving a child a slave of its own to tyrannize over, to beat and abuse out of sport, was, I myself saw, a common practice. Nor is it strange that being thus trained up in cruelty, they should afterwards arrive at so great perfection in it; that Mr Star, a gentleman I often met at Mr Lasserre's, should, as he himself informed Lasserre, first nail up a negro by the ears, then order him to be whipped in the severest manner, and then to have scalding water thrown all over him, so that the poor creature could not stir for four months after. Another much applauded punishment is drawing their slaves' teeth. One Colonel Lynch is universally known to have cut off a poor negro's legs, and to kill several of them every year by his barbarities.
>
> . . .
>
> These horrid cruelties are the less to be wondered at, because the government itself in effect countenances and allows them to kill their slaves by the ridiculous penalty appointed for it, of about 7 pounds sterling (half of which is usually saved by the criminal's informing against himself). This I can look upon as no other than a public act to indemnify murder.[2]

As this hymn declares, Charles Wesley knew that Jesus was born to set *all* people free; yes, the slaves too! Mortified by the terror of slavery, he could only hope that slaves, their masters, and all touched by this savage villainy could be set free from fears and sins and find their rest in Jesus. "This is the only hope of all the earth," Wesley cries out. He understood and had experienced that Jesus was truly born to deliver people from bondage and that when he ruled their hearts, they could no longer subject others to the tyranny of servitude.

In a world teeming with injustice, we need to sing this hymn with great expectancy and live its message until those who are enslaved to sin and all human bondage are set free!

Come, thou long-expected Jesus!

---

2. *MSJ*, 1:46–47.

12.

What shall we proclaim and why?
Jesus! the name high over all[1]

Philippians 2:9–11: "Wherefore God also hath highly exalted him, and given him a name which is above every name: That at the name of Jesus every knee should bow, of things in heaven, and things in earth, and things under the earth; And that every tongue should confess that Jesus Christ is Lord, to the glory of God the Father." (KJV)

AFTER PREACHING

Jesus! the name high over all,
In hell or earth or sky;
Angels and mortals prostrate fall,
And devils fear and fly.

Jesus! the name to sinners dear,
The name to sinners given;
It scatters all their guilty fear,
It turns their hell to heaven.

---

1. *HSP* 1749, 1:305–8.

> O that the world might taste and see
>   The riches of his grace!
> The arms of love that compass me
>   Would all mankind embrace.
>
> Thee I shall constantly proclaim,
>   Though earth and hell oppose;
> Bold to confess thy glorious name
>   Before a world of foes.
>
> His only righteousness I show,
>   His saving grace proclaim;
> 'Tis all my business here below
>   To cry, "Behold the Lamb!"
>
> Happy, if with my latest breath
>   I might but gasp his name,
> Preach him to all and cry in death,
>   "Behold, behold the Lamb!"

When Charles Wesley published this hymn in 1749, he had been a clergyman for fourteen years. In 1735 he had been ordained deacon and priest in the Church of England and immediately thereafter departed with his brother John for the colony of Georgia as a missionary, as Secretary of Indian Affairs, and as Colonel Oglethorpe's personal secretary. It was in Georgia, where he remained only a little more than five months, that he began preaching. His perspectives regarding preaching, however, changed significantly after his conversion in 1738.

After his return to England, Charles was searching for an inner peace he knew he did not have. When he recorded in his *Journal* on May 17, 1738, "I read the scriptures and slept peacefully," it was because he was on the verge of discovering four days later, May 21 (Pentecost Day), that it was by faith in Jesus Christ alone that he stood. After this experience he would never preach in the same manner again. The homiletical cry of his heart became the one couched in this hymn, "Jesus! the name high over all."

Just as his brother John recorded at the conclusion of his sermons that he had offered the hearers Christ, this hymn might be considered Charles Wesley's homiletical signature for the conclusion of every sermon. It would do much to revive the spirit of the Wesleyan revival for clergy today to recite this text inwardly, if not publicly. It can serve as a valuable interpretive evaluation of one's proclamation.

SECTION 2: GOD THE SON

Wesley draws his inspiration and language for this hymn from Paul's canticle of Christ's obedience in Philippians chapter 2, namely, verses 9–11. The first half of this biblical song, verses 5–8, affirms Christ's obedience as a humble, self-emptying, faithful servant, who gave his life for all. The second half, verses 9–11, to which Wesley is responding here, proclaims the efficacy and primacy of Jesus's name in heaven and in earth.

The name comes from the Hebrew *yᵉshu'a* meaning "salvation." It has the same root as the Hebrew name *Joshua*, Moses' successor who led the children of Israel into the promised land.

In stanza 3 Wesley proclaims the scriptural promise that the name of Jesus, the Savior, scatters the fear of guilty sinners and turns hell into heaven. What tremendous power there is in this name––transforming power!

In the assembly of rulers, elders, scribes, the high priest Caiaphas, and members of the high priestly family, the question was raised—By what power or by what name the disciples Peter and John had taught the people in the temple that with Jesus there is resurrection from the dead? Peter responded:

> "This Jesus is 'the stone that was rejected by you, the builders; it has become the cornerstone.' There is salvation in no one else, for there is no other name under heaven given among mortals by which we must be saved." (Acts 4:11–12)

Stanzas 1 and 2 of Wesley's hymn state the centrality of the biblical affirmation that Jesus is "the name high over all" and it removes sinners' fears and transforms the worst into the best, namely, hell into heaven in this life and beyond. After articulating this central message, Wesley turns to the essentials of the preaching office. What gives this office validity and effectiveness?

Stanza 3 expresses the *longing* within the heart and soul of everyone who proclaims the gospel. One yearns that the whole world will "taste and see / the riches of his grace!" Christ's message of love is for all creation. At the heart of preaching is the burning desire for everyone and everything to experience the embrace of God's love. This can be shared authentically, however, only when one can declare with Wesley that "the arms of love . . . compass *me!*"

Stanza 4 contains the averment of every earnest preacher of the gospel.

WHAT SHALL WE PROCLAIM AND WHY?

> Thee I shall constantly proclaim,
> Though earth and hell oppose;
> Bold to confess thy glorious name
> Before a world of foes.

No opposition shall deter the faithful proclaimer of the gospel. Foes may rise time and again, as though all earth and hell had marshaled their forces against the gospel and its proclaimers, but the faithful will boldly confess Jesus' name!

Where can one find a more articulate and succinct expression of the vocation of the preaching office than in stanzas 5 and 6 of this hymn? If I am a preacher of the gospel, my only *business* is "to cry, 'Behold the Lamb!' which taketh away the sin of the world!" (John 1:29. KJV) I *do* this not only by words, however; "I show" God's righteousness and saving truth: in other words, this is also a proclamation of God's saving truth.

Hence one's happiness in life and in death, even with one's last breath, is to repeat the name, the name which itself cries out, "salvation" to all. What is the source of the preacher's happiness?—it is to

> Preach him to all and cry in death,
> "Behold, behold the Lamb!"

What if Wesley's expression of the centrality of the gospel message and his formulation of a preacher's earnest longing, devout vow, and clear understanding of vocation became the posture and lifestyle of every preacher of the gospel today?

13.

What does it mean to be consumed by love?

Jesus, thine all-victorious love[1]

Jesus, thine all-victorious love
    Shed in my heart abroad;
Then shall my feet no longer rove,
    Rooted and fixed in God.

O that in me the sacred fire
    Might now begin to glow;
Burn up the dross of base desire
    And make the mountains flow!

O that it now from heaven might fall
    And all my sins consume!
Come, Holy Ghost, for thee I call,
    Spirit of burning, come!

Refining fire, go through my heart,
    Illuminate my soul;
Scatter thy life through every part
    And sanctify the whole.

---

1. *HSP* 1740, 156–8.

WHAT DOES IT MEAN TO BE CONSUMED BY LOVE?

These four stanzas are part of a longer hymn which originally had twelve stanzas when published in *HSP* 1740. They have appeared often in some hymnbooks in a hymn which opens with Wesley's original first stanza beginning "My God, I know, I feel thee mine." The four stanzas of "Jesus, thine all-victorious love" emphasize important aspects of *knowing* and *feeling* that God is personally active in one's life, namely, the experience of divine love and of the working of the Holy Spirit.

The hymn opens and closes with a prayer and includes Wesley's reflections on the Holy Spirit as a cleansing or refining fire. Stanza 1 is a prayerful plea for the victorious love of Jesus to fill his heart, a constant prayer of Charles throughout his life and ministry. He knew that if his life were rooted and fixed in the kind of love God has revealed to him and the world in Jesus, love that gives and gives of itself again and again for others, he would not stray from the path toward God in all that he did.

Stanzas 2–4 reveal Wesley thinking, as he often did, in biblical imagery. John the Baptist had proclaimed centuries before that One would come after him who "will baptize you with the Holy Spirit and with fire" (Luke 3:16). In stanzas 2 and 3 Wesley yearns for the baptism of sacred fire, that it "might begin to glow" within him. Whatever he desires that is unworthy of the godly life, he is confident will be consumed by the flames of the Spirit.

In stanza 3 his desire intensifies, as he hopes for the descent of the Spirit's fire from heaven to consume "all my sins."

> Come, Holy Ghost, for thee I call,
> Spirit of burning, come!

Such a baptism of the Spirit which cleanses from sin is integral to the path toward holiness. Wesley fervently prays in stanza 4 for the inner illumination of the soul which alone comes through the refining fire of the Holy Spirit. Imagine a world filled with those who have every facet of their inner being illuminated, enlightened, by the refining fire of the Holy Spirit. This divine Spirit is the Spirit that fills every breast with the burning desire of self-giving love. Imagine humankind throughout God's creation so wholly sanctified that this desire literally consumes every individual and society so that everyone lives to give of self in love to God, others, and all creation. This is the constant, passionate prayer of Charles Wesley. Would that we might make his prayer our own so that its possibility might be realized in our lives! When we are consumed by such love, we will *know* it and we will *feel* it!

SECTION 2: GOD THE SON

What does it mean to be consumed by love?—The flame of desire within us to empty ourselves in love never goes out.

14.

Why did Jesus die?
"'Tis finished! The Messiah dies"[1]

John 19:29–30: "A jar full of sour wine was standing there. So they put a sponge full of the wine on a branch of hyssop and held it to his mouth. When Jesus had received the wine, he said, "It is finished. Then he bowed his head, and gave up his spirit."

'Tis finished! The Messiah dies,
    Cut off for sins, but not his own.
Accomplished is the sacrifice,
    The great redeeming work is done.

The veil is rent; in Christ alone
    The living way to heaven is seen;
The middle wall is broken down,
    And all the world may enter in.

'Tis finished! All my guilt and pain,
    I want no sacrifice beside;
For me, for me the Lamb is slain,
    and I am more than justified.

---

1. *SH* 1762, 2:234 (stanzas 1 and 3 of above hymn); and MS Richmond (1749–51), 44 (stanzas 2 and 4 of above hymn).

> The reign of sin and death is o'er,
> And all may live from sin set free;
> Satan hath lost his mortal power;
> 'Tis swallowed up in victory.

This is a hymn text on which Charles Wesley continued to work over a number of years, though all of his forty lines of poetry on this theme in this meter were never recorded in one place, either in published or manuscript form. All of the stanzas appeared for the first time together in *UP* 1990.[2]

Stanza 3 first appeared in *The United Methodist Hymnal* (1989) and is extremely important to the sequence of the hymn and the wholeness of Wesley's theology of Christ's atonement. Stanzas 1, 2, and 4 were written in the third person and are descriptive of the power and effect of Christ's death. Stanza 3 is in the first person and emphasizes the personal aspect of the atonement.

Stanzas 1 and 2 are *Christ's story*. Stanza 1 describes the occurrence of Christ's death, emphasizing that he has been cut off, not for his own sins, but for those of others. It is his sacrifice which accomplishes "the great redeeming work." As Paul affirms in Galatians 1:3-4, "Grace to you, and peace, from God our Father and the Lord Jesus Christ, who gave himself for *our sins* to set us free from the present evil age." And John the Baptist declares, "Here is the Lamb of God who takes away the *sin of the world!*" (John 1:29).

Stanza 2 begins with the mention of the rending of the veil of the temple at Christ's death (Mark 15:38; Luke 23:45). No longer does there need to be a veil in the temple which separates anyone from the holiest of the Holy, namely, God's own self revealed in Jesus Christ. Christ's death removes such separation once and for all. Everyone has access to the holiest of the Holy. The middle wall between "insiders" and "outsiders" has been broken down, and *all the world may enter in.*

Stanza 3 is no longer Christ's story, but rather *Charles Wesley's story* and *our story. My* guilt and pain are finished, Wesley declares. Here once again he stresses the reality of personal justification by faith.

> *For me, for me* the Lamb is slain;
> and I am more than justified.

This personal realization is a recurrent theme in Wesley's hymns and poetry.

---

2. *UP,* 2:277-9.

WHY DID JESUS DIE?

> I felt my Lord's atoning blood
> Close to my soul applied;
> *Me, me* he loved, the Son of God,
> *For me, for me* he died.[3]

The immortal God for me hath died.

> 'Tis thine the blood to apply
> And give us eyes to see,
> Who did for every sinner die,
> Hath surely died for me.[4]

'Tis love! 'tis Love! Thou diedst for me.[5]

From the time of his conversion on Pentecost Day, May 21, 1738, the words of Galatians 2:19–20 resonated throughout Charles Wesley's life and ministry: "I have been crucified with Christ; and it is no longer I who live, but Christ who lives in me. And the life I now live in the flesh I live by faith in the Son of God, who loved *me* and gave himself for *me*."

This personal story is, however, everyone's story; hence Wesley breaks forth in the words of stanza 4:

> The reign of sin and death is o'er,
> And *all* may live from sin set free;
> Satan hath lost his mortal power;
> 'Tis swallowed up in victory.

The triumph of the universal power of Christ's death is celebrated by Wesley recalling the Apostle Paul's declaration: "Death is swallowed up in victory" (1 Corinthians 15:53, KJV). This is the triumph of Good Friday, of Christ's death, and resurrection!

This hymn provides an eloquent summary of Wesley's confidence in the Scripture's promise of personal and universal redemption.

---

3. *HSP* 1740, 120.
4. *HSP* 1742, 26–27.
5. *WH* 1746, 30–31.

15.

What shall we remember?
Hail the day that sees him rise[1]

Hail the day that sees him rise
To his throne above the skies!
Christ, awhile to mortals given,
Re-ascends his native heaven.

There the glorious triumph waits:
Lift your heads, eternal gates!
Christ hath conquered death and sin,
Take the King of glory in.

See! the heaven its Lord receives,
Yet he loves the earth he leaves;
Though returning to his throne,
Still he calls the world his own.

See! he lifts his hands above:
See! he shows the prints of love.
Hark! his gracious lips bestow
Blessings on his church below.

This is the most well-known of Charles Wesley's hymns for Ascension Day, commemorating Jesus' ascent to union with God's presence, transcending

1. *HSP* 1739, 211–13.

earthly existence. It was not a part, however, of his collection of hymns devoted to this theme published in 1746, *Hymns for Ascension-Day*. Wesley viewed the events of Christ's life as worthy of Christian celebration. They are a part of the great recital of God's salvation history or saving action which call to mind what God has done for all humankind and what it cannot do for itself. Though Wesley composed many collections of hymns on themes from landmark occurrences in Christ's life, such as *HNL* 1745, *HLR* 1746, and *WH* 1746, he also wrote and published other hymns which treat these themes that are scattered throughout numerous publications during his lifetime. Such is the case with "Hail the day that sees him rise," published in *HSP* 1739.

What is it about the recital of salvation history which is important to individual believers and the community of faith? The roots of such a tradition go back to the Hebrew Scriptures. An examination of this question turns our attention especially to the Psalms in which Charles Wesley was so deeply steeped, for he read them every day. In the Psalms the recital of God's mighty deeds has a number of functions, some of which we mention here. (1) It shapes the identity of the faithful. When they remember what God has done for them, they know who they are—God's own people. In Psalm 111 recounting God's saving acts is the heart of the consciousness that God's people are indeed God's own to whom the power of divine saving action has been revealed "giving them the heritage of the nations" (111:6). They have been sent redemption forever through God's covenant (111:9). They are the redeemed community. (2) In remembering God's salvation history, the faithful know they are not orphans of history but are a part of a dynamic and meaningful ancestry. They are not an isolated anomaly of history. It is here that the recitation of the great hymn of Deuteronomy 26 is vital for the link to the faith community of the ages, for "you shall make this response before the Lord your God:

> A wandering Aramean was my ancestor; he went down into Egypt and lived there as an alien, few in number, and there he became a great nation, mighty and populous. When the Egyptians treated us harshly and afflicted us, by imposing hard labor on us, we cried to the Lord, the God of our ancestors; the Lord heard our voice and saw our affliction, our toil, and our oppression. The Lord brought us out of Egypt with a mighty hand and an outstretched arm, with a terrifying display of power, and with signs and wonders; and he brought us into this place and gave us this land, a land flowing

with milk and honey. So now I bring the first of the fruit of the ground that you, O Lord, have given me."[2]

(3) Celebrating God's redemptive deeds is the divine mandate of proclamation for all the faithful. The preface to the recital of God's mighty deeds on behalf of the people in Psalm 107 is: "Let the redeemed of the Lord say so" (107:2a). Let them recite to the world what God has done.

Charles Wesley spent his adult life reciting what God has done. In this hymn he calls the community to the recitation of a doxology of praise and thanksgiving that remind the faithful of vital matters for their life perspectives. (1) God's power encompasses and transcends earthly existence. There is a cosmic reality which is not bound by the earth. Christ (the revealed God of the universe), who is given a while to mortals, is not bound by mortality and earthly existence. (2) God's victory over sin and death encompasses the earth with the power of God's love. As the community of faith celebrates Christ's absence in body, it celebrates God the Creator's caring love of the world, the world God has made; it is not a world made by mortals (stanzas 2 and 3). "Still he calls the world his own." The doxology ends affirming that those who recite God's saving act of redemption on the cross, "the prints of love" in Christ's hands, reiterate the divine words of forgiveness from the cross to the church for all time: "forgive them; for they do not know what they are doing." Hence, in the singing of Wesley's hymn the faithful are reminded that they are the forgiven, who become in Christ's place the forgiving, loving community.

What shall we remember? God's eternally ascending song. It is a song to sing, and a song to become.

---

2. Deuteronomy 26:5–10.

16.

What holds a family together?
Jesus, Lord, we look to thee[1]

FOR A FAMILY

Jesus, Lord, we look to thee;
Let us in thy name agree;
Show thyself the Prince of Peace,
Bid our strife forever cease.

By thy reconciling love
Every stumbling block remove;
Each to each unite, endear;
Come, and spread thy banner here.

Make us of one heart and mind,
Gentle, courteous, and kind,
Lowly, meek, in thought and word,
Altogether like our Lord.

Let us for each other care,
Each the other's burdens bear;
To thy church the pattern give,
Show how true believers live.

---

1. *HSP* 1749, 1:248.

SECTION 2: GOD THE SON

> Free from anger and from pride,
> Let us thus in God abide;
> All the depths of love express,
> All the heights of holiness.
>
> Let us then with joy remove
> To the family above;
> On the wings of angels fly,
> Show how true believers die.

While this hymn may clearly be construed as being applicable to the family of God as a whole, when Charles Wesley published it in 1749, he gave it the title "For a Family." The year 1749 was the year he married Sarah Gwynne, and no doubt many thoughts regarding establishing his own family were going through his mind.

Charles wrote particularly about his own family experience, knowing the necessity for unity and forbearance in the home for harmony and understanding to meet the needs of each day. He grew up in a very large family, having seven sisters and two brothers who survived out of nineteen children. They lived on the edge of poverty in the rectory of the parish at Epworth, where father Samuel, the local Anglican priest, was arrested in his own churchyard once for debts. The rectory at Epworth in which the Wesley family lived was razed by fire, perhaps set by adversaries of Samuel. For a time, the family members were scattered among other homes until living quarters could be rebuilt. Many of Charles's sisters had extremely difficult and sad marriages, and one of the sisters had grave physical problems from birth. With his own children Charles was not free from controversy, for many thought that raising his sons, Samuel and Charles, Jr., to be musicians was a worldly endeavor, and this invoked criticism, even from his brother John.

Throughout his life Charles matured in the understanding that a family must be forbearing and must look to Jesus Christ for its sustenance and peace in all strife and joy.

This hymn throughout is a prayer that should be constantly on the lips of every family member. It can do more to hold families together and resolve tension than can be imagined. Here Wesley provides an excellent picture of Christians living as a family, stressing Christ as the mediator of peace, living in love and unity, caring for one another, freedom from strife and anger, holiness, how to live, and how to die.

Stanza 2 articulates the heart of the matter: "reconciling love" alone removes the stumbling blocks we encounter. Only as we unfurl the banner of love in our families can we be united and endeared to one another.

Stanza 3 discloses the change reconciling love makes in our demeanor. As we become one in heart and mind, we are gentle, courteous, kind, lowly, and meek in what we think and say. This was Christ's demeanor and it becomes our own. Wesley perceived that words and thoughts can hurt and heal.

Stanza 4 reveals how reconciling love affects our attitudes toward one another. We become bearers of one another's burdens. We show that we really care about each other. Hence our behavior becomes the example, the pattern, the model of "how true believers live."

Stanza 5 further elaborates how reconciling love affects the overall posture of a family whose members exemplify reconciling love. They are "free from anger and from pride." By abiding in God they learn to express the "depths of love" and the "heights of holiness," for submission to reconciling love is the path to holiness.

Finally, in stanza 6 Wesley emphasizes that a family which lives out reconciling love is a joyful family. In celebrating a life of love together it anticipates the joyful union with God's family of all ages and not only shows "how true believers live," but also "how true believers die."

What Wesley has written for the individual family becomes exemplary for the whole of the family of God. There is more food for thought in Wesley's text for the future of Christian unity throughout the world, there is more here to shape a new vision of an ecumenical movement, than Christians have been willing to realize in their relationships with one another and with others. Would that we might pray this prayer and become its example!

SECTION 3

God the Holy Spirit

I fully resolved to obey the motions
of the Holy Spirit by leading
a new life.

CHARLES WESLEY

17.

Can there be an end to bloodshed?
Spirit of faith, come down [1]

    Spirit of faith, come down
    Reveal the things of God,
And make to us the Godhead known,
    And witness with the blood.
    'Tis thine the blood to apply
    And give us eyes to see,
Who did for every sinner die
    Hath surely died for me.

    No one can truly say
    That Jesus is the Lord,
Unless thou take the veil away
    And breathe the living Word.
    Then, only then, we feel
    Our interest in his blood,
And cry with joy unspeakable,
    "Thou art my Lord, my God!"

    O that the world might know
    My dear atoning Lamb!
Spirit of faith, descend and show
    The virtue of his name;

---

1. *WH* 1746, 30–31.

SECTION 3: GOD THE HOLY SPIRIT

> The grace which all may find,
>   The saving power impart,
> And testify to humankind,
>   And speak in every heart.
>
> Inspire the living faith
>   (Which whosoe'er receive,
> The witness in themselves they have
>   And consciously believe),
> The faith that conquers all,
>   And doth the mountain move,
> And saves whoe'er on Jesus call,
>   And perfects them in love.

In this hymn Wesley lays down four distinct needs of human beings in relation to the gift of the Holy Spirit: revelation, recognition, reclamation, and regeneration.

Stanza 1 is a prayer for revelation, a prayer to have one's inner eyes opened to see the "things of God" more clearly; namely, knowing the Godhead (who God is) and God's activity (what God does). It may seem rather strange that Wesley prays for the Spirit to "witness with the blood." History tells us, however, that this is a human preoccupation. People in every age often witness at some point to some cause, or way of life that spills the blood of others. Life today is haunted by terrorists representing political, national, and religious interests. They seek to further their interests by "applying blood," that is by taking the lives of others, even children and other innocent people. Wesley emphasizes here that God's Spirit reveals to those who will hear the meaning of Christ's death, i.e., how *the witness of his blood was for all people* so that they might understand how much God loves them. Therefore, they seek to live together in the spirit of that love.

Stanza 2 is a prayer of personal recognition: "Thou art my Lord, my God!" The corporate and communal recognition of the lordship of Christ begins with the individual. This transpires when the veil between the human and the divine is taken away and one breathes the living word. This is reminiscent of Wesley's prayer in the hymn, "Love divine, all loves excelling":

> Breathe, O breathe thy loving Spirit
> Into every troubled breast.[2]

---

2. *RH* 1747, 11–12.

It is the loving Spirit, the living Word, which evokes an interest in the blood of Christ. One is filled with the Spirit of love and sees the futility of all human bloodshed. That indeed is worthy of human concern! Christ's sacrifice brings the reign of love on earth, "because God's love has been poured into our hearts through the Holy Spirit that has been given to us" (Romans 5:5).

Stanza 3 is a prayer for the universal reclamation of humankind. As definitive as Wesley is in stanza 2 about personal confession of Christ's lordship, this stanza is wholly inclusive in its language as he pleads for the descent of the Spirit on all humankind.

> O that the world might know
> The *all*-atoning Lamb!
> ...
> The grace which *all* may find,
> ...
> And speak in *every* heart.

Eighteenth-century England was plagued with religious disunity. There were divisions indicated by names the Wesleys and others were called: Papists, Dissenters, Calvinists, Jacobites, non-Jurors, etc. Furthermore, Charles Wesley saw a schism developing between the Methodist Societies and the Church of England. There were political divisions as well—those who were loyal to the crown and others who favored a Pretender to the throne.

Human loyalties are willing to sacrifice others to their causes and breed enmity. Wesley cries out for the reclamation of broken humankind through the descent of God's Spirit of love upon *every* heart—through universal awareness that it is no longer necessary to live by the false notion that others must be sacrificed to a human cause. God's sacrifice of Jesus has shown us the virtue of his name which is "Salvation" and given us a pattern for living in harmony: give of self in love for others and God.

Stanza 4 is a prayer for regeneration. The faith which moves mountains and gives life a new beginning is one which perfects in love those who call on the name of Jesus. The verb *perfects* is at the heart of redemption and social harmony, for it reflects the process of maturing love as followers of Jesus. "O that the world might know" that it can grow in love and peace instead of hatred and war. Such a worldwide regeneration, new birth, or new beginning is the hope of the descent of the Spirit of love which God pours into our hearts. The shedding of Christ's blood is the sign and seal

SECTION 3: GOD THE HOLY SPIRIT

of the Spirit which can fill human hearts with love so that there will be no more bloodshed on earth.

18.

What is true freedom?
Spirit of faith, come down on me[1]

Judges 15:14: "The Philistines shouted against him, and the Spirit of the Lord came mightily upon him." (KJV)

> Spirit of faith, come down on me,
> For where thou art is liberty;
> Thy presence looses all my bands,
> And melts the fetters from my hands,
> Consumes like flax the cords of sin,
> And burns up all my foes within.

Some years ago, at the height of the Cold War, my youngest son, Mark, and I went to a summer camp in the country then known as Czechoslovakia, which was attended by Christians from over twenty countries. During our first gathering we were divided into groups of three and asked to discuss the words: *faith, hope,* and *freedom*. In my group was a young married man from the host country and a soldier in its army. I recall that when we came to the word *freedom*, he was asked what freedom(s) he felt had been taken from him by the Russian military domination of his country. His reply was direct, immediate, and convincing. "None at all," he said, "because when you have the inner freedom of God's Spirit, no one can take away your freedom. They can restrict your mobility, but they cannot take away your

---

1. *SH* 1762, 1:132.

freedom, because it is eternally yours within." He was living the fulfillment of Charles Wesley's prayer:

> Spirit of faith, come down on me,
> For where thou art is liberty.

Although he could not travel to any destination of his choice, the Spirit of faith had descended to dwell within him and he was free indeed! No military presence from any country of the world could take away that freedom.

When the Spirit of God comes to dwell in us by faith in the gift of love expressed in Jesus Christ (God among us in life, ministry, death, and resurrection), we are liberated from the tyranny of others and ourselves. No matter the situation in which we are found, it is God's *presence* in us which shatters all external and internal shackles or chains that bind us. This is why the church lives on in times of persecution and oppression. The tyranny of governments and dictators is no match for the Spirit of faith dynamically alive in the lives of all who make up the church, the body of Christ.

The Spirit of faith also frees us from the tyranny of ourselves. We can be ruled inwardly by many forces: greed, hate, lust, hunger for power, wealth, and success. But when we allow the Spirit of faith to be our indwelling power, these burning desires are consumed by the flame of love which overtakes us as rapidly as flax vanishes in a fire.

Christians will struggle to free all people because of their commitment to the reign of God's justice on earth; nonetheless, they know that if they are not free within—if the Spirit of faith has not come to dwell within them—they shall never be free, even if liberated from some worldly bondage.

19.

Are we filled with the Spirit?
Jesus, plant thy Spirit in me[1]

Galatians 5:22–23: "The fruit of the Spirit is love, joy, peace, long-suffering, gentleness, goodness, faith, meekness, temperance." (KJV)

> Jesus, plant thy Spirit in me;
> Then the fruit shall sow the tree,
> Every grace its Author prove,
> Rising from the root of love.
>
> Joy shall then my heart o'erflow,
> Peace which only saints can know,
> Peace, the seal of canceled sin,
> Joy, the taste of heaven within.
>
> Gentle then to all and kind
> To the wicked and the blind,
> Full of tenderness and care,
> I shall every burden bear;
>
> Glad the general servant be,
> Serve with strict fidelity,
> Life itself for them deny,
> Meekly in their service die.

---

1. *SH* 1762, 2:309.

The New Testament parable of the sower stresses the importance of where the seeds are cast, for the nature of the soil on which they fall determines the growth. Wesley speaks in this prayer of the seed of the Spirit which is *sown within us* by Jesus. Our inner being, heart and soul, is the soil. As in the first psalm, people are likened in this poem to fruit-bearing trees.

When the seed of the Spirit has been planted in us by Jesus, the main root of the tree—which becomes the primary source of growth, strength, and food for all of the branches—is *love*. It gives life and fruit-bearing ability to the Spirit tree. The Christian is the Spirit tree and bears fruit according to the growth of the power of the Spirit within. The line, "Every grace its Author prove," tells us that a tree's fruit-bearing posture is determined by its roots. If they are in shallow ground, the tree may bend over easily or be blown down by the wind. If they are not watered and nourished, and if the surrounding soil is not kept fertile, the tree will wither and die. Every grace which Christians exhibit attests to the Author of their lives, their source of strength and nurture. That is, the demeanor of Christians—how people exhibit their actions and manner of speech—reveals whether or not the grace in their lives stems from the root of *love*.

Often you can determine the type of tree by its bearing or posture. The drooping limbs of a weeping willow may project an image of pathos. A giant redwood reigns as a tower of strength over the smaller trees of the forest. The sprawling stumps and winding limbs of a cypress tree reflect survival at all costs in water or on land. How does one determine whether persons are Spirit trees?—by their bearing or posture, physically, mentally, and spiritually.

Trees are often identified by the fruits they bear. Orange, lemon, apple trees are so named because they bear those fruits. Spirit trees are also known by the fruits they bear: gentleness, tenderness, caring, service, joy, peace, faithfulness, meekness. How can others tell if we are Spirit trees? They will know God's Spirit has been planted within us if our hearts overflow with joy; if we personify peace in all that we are; if we are gentle and kind to everyone; if we are tender, loving, caring, and bear the burdens of others; if we happily and faithfully serve God and others; if we live lives of self-denial for the sake of service; and if we live as meek servants all our days.

20.

How Do We Read the Bible?
Come, Holy Ghost, our hearts inspire[1]

BEFORE READING THE SCRIPTURES

Come, Holy Ghost, our hearts inspire,
    Let us thy influence prove;
Source of the old prophetic fire,
    Fountain of life and love.

Come, Holy Ghost, (for moved by thee
    Thy prophets wrote and spoke:)
Unlock the truth, thyself the key,
    Unseal the sacred book.

Expand thy wings, prolific dove,
    Brood o'er our nature's night;
On our disordered spirits move,
    And let there now be light.

Through God's own self we then shall know
    If thou within us shine,
And sound, with all thy saints below,
    The depths of love divine.

---

1. *HSP* 1740, 42–43.

SECTION 3: GOD THE HOLY SPIRIT

There may be many simple messages in the Bible, but it is by no means a simple book. It spans numerous centuries and is not written in chronological order. To grasp its message and meaning, some knowledge of the world from which it came, the ancient Near East, is essential. It is written in three languages—Hebrew, Aramaic, and Greek—and all who do not read them must read translations. As faithful as translators try to be to the original languages in the form they have been received in the biblical books, it is not always easy to capture the nuances of idioms, expressions, and words for which there may be no direct equivalents in many languages.

Serious students of the Bible use every possible means to study it. For example, the science of archeology has yielded a wealth of information which greatly enhances the understanding of the world, language, history, and message of the Bible. Unquestionably, diverse avenues of investigation and research have developed in biblical studies which illuminate the Bible. For example, the discovery of the Dead Sea Scrolls provided the earliest Hebrew manuscript of the Book of Isaiah yet known to biblical scholars and by which they now may compare previously existing Hebrew manuscripts of Isaiah, but of a much later period.

In spite of the intensive efforts to authenticate the earliest Hebrew and Greek manuscripts of the Old and New Testaments, the Scriptures embody a quality which transcends and complements all methods of their study. While many of them prove useful in interpreting the Bible in order to glean the most authentic meaning possible, the Scriptures have a self-appropriating power: an ability to find people where they are and to speak to them and their needs.

Wesley's hymn, "Come, Holy Ghost, our hearts inspire," affirms an approach to the Bible which allows its self-appropriating quality to empower and enlarge our understanding of God's word. Regardless of the method or tools utilized to study the Bible, there must be an inner openness to allow God's Spirit to speak through the word. There is a divine influence which pours from its pages into our lives: "Let us thy influence prove." Wesley bids us prayerfully seek that influence as we read the Bible, for it is the source of God's past and present inspiration and is the "fountain of life, and love."

The "influence" is God's own Spirit, which moves throughout the Scriptures with a dynamism that imparts truth..

> Unlock the truth, thyself the key,
> Unseal the sacred book.

Those who find their lives shattered and desperate can search the Scriptures and discover the truth about God, themselves, and their needs which heals and makes new beginnings possible.

God's Spirit not only unlocks the truth of the Scriptures, it sheds light upon the darkness of our lives. It brings order to disordered spirits.

> On our disordered spirits move,
> And let there now be light.

Stanza 4 affirms that it is God's own self that is revealed through the Scriptures, and thus it is God whom we come to know as we read them. The light which floods our lives from the pages of the Bible is God's own radiance.

How do we read the Bible? We do so in an attitude of prayer with heart and being open to the Spirit's influence, truth, and light. In so doing we sound the depths of love divine. Ships make soundings to determine the depth of the water through which they go to secure a safe voyage. When we read the Bible, we are sounding the depths of divine love to steer us through the waters of life. Its depths cannot be determined, however, as one measures the depth of water to the ocean floor, for God's love is fathomless. Nevertheless, each time we read the Bible with openness to God's Spirit, we shall discover new depths of that love. The deeper we go into God's word, the deeper we plunge into God's love. In Jesus, divine love ascends a cross, goes down to the grave, and rises to earth and heaven for us.

Each time we read the Bible we search for God's love. Hence the act itself becomes an act of love.

21.

How do we prepare to read the Bible?
Come, divine interpreter[1]

> Revelation 1:3: "Blessed is the one who reads aloud the words of the prophecy, and blessed are those who hear and who keep what is written in it; for the time is near."

> Come, divine Interpreter,
>   Bring me eyes thy book to read,
> Ears the mystic words to hear,
>   Words which did from thee proceed,
> Words that endless bliss impart,
> Kept in an obedient heart.
>
> All who read, or hear, are blessed,
>   If thy plain commands we do;
> Of thy kingdom here possessed,
>   Thee we shall in glory view
> When thou comest on earth to abide,
> Reign triumphant at thy side.

Charles Wesley wrote many hymns and poems to be read or sung in preparation for reading Holy Scripture. This is an endeavor he did not take lightly. His brother John has often been spoken of as a man of one book, namely, the Bible. Both were alike in this matter. Yet that does not mean they read

---

1. *SH* 1762, 2:412.

the Bible at the expense of all other literature. To the contrary, they were voracious readers of secular literature as well. John was also a publisher of non-religious works, especially abridged editions of other authors. He sincerely believed that human beings were not created in a vacuum, and that there is *universal* knowledge of creation which *universal* humankind should absorb in order better to understand the universe in which all God's creatures have been placed. Clearly for Charles and John, however, the Bible formed the central focus of their reading. Their understanding of the universal impact of God's redemptive love was a mandate to comprehend as much knowledge of the whole of creation as possible; hence they shared an insatiable appetite for knowledge. Nevertheless, it was to the Holy Scriptures that they returned time and again to give focus to what they had learned. It was the book of books, for from its pages they gleaned the view of God's real world, which makes life worth living. It was not just another book to them, although they unquestionably brought the full breadth of their literary understanding to its reading and study.

The centrality of Holy Scripture in the lives of the Wesley brothers is perhaps nowhere better expressed than in the following words of Charles, which were precipitated by reflection on Deuteronomy 6:6–7, "These words which I command thee this day shall be upon thine heart. And thou shalt teach them diligently unto thy children, and shalt talk of them when you sit in your house" (KJV).

> When quiet in my house I sit,
>   Thy book be my companion still
> My joy thy sayings to repeat,
>   Talk o'er the records of thy will,
> And search the oracles divine,
> 'Till every heartfelt word is mine.[2]

Today as in Wesley's day, people often read the Bible and find what they want to find there. Charles cautions that the Bible should be read with prayerful preparation. The preface to the opening of the Scriptures, the prelude to all reading of them, should be his words, "Come, divine Interpreter." One puts aside the presumptions of human understanding and seeks a wiser insight than one's own, a divine Interpreter, the Spirit of God.

During the week prior to Charles Wesley's conversion on May 21, 1738, one finds him hungering and thirsting for God and searching the Scriptures for insight, wisdom, and guidance. On May 13th he was comforted by the

---

2. Ibid., 1:92.

promises of Psalm 68 which his friend W. Delamotte read to him, and he recorded, "*At night* received much light and comfort from the Scriptures."[3] On May 15th he wrote, "Found comfort in the 102nd Psalm."[4] The turning point came in reading Martin Luther's commentary on Galatians, especially his conclusion to chapter two: "I labored, waited, and prayed to feel 'who loved *me* and gave himself for *me*'"[5] (Galatians 2:20). On the morning after his conversion, May 22nd, Wesley was renewed once again by words from the Bible: "Under his [Christ's] protection I waked next morning, and rejoiced in the reading the 107th Psalm, so nobly describing what God had done for my soul."[6]

Against the backdrop of such experience it is not surprising that Wesley prayed in this hymn for eyes, ears, and a heart that will respond to God's Word. This trilogy of words (eyes, ears, heart) underscores the ultimate goal—that to the inner depths of our being we will respond with an obedient heart. The reading and hearing may seem to be mere physical responses, but heeding God's Word means "thy plain commands we do" and we are "of thy kingdom here possessed." The Scriptures relate us to God's reign on earth. There is an inner response to the Word which transcends all physical seeing and hearing. Yes, the blind shall see and the deaf shall hear, for the divine Interpreter speaks to the human heart.

---

3. *MSJ*, 103.

4. *MSJ*, 103.

5. *MSJ*, 104. Wesley incorrectly cites the passage as Galatians 1:6–7. However, it is actually Galatians 2:20.

6. *MSJ*, 108.

22.

What shall I desire above all else?
O come and dwell in me[1]

2 Corinthians 3:17: "Now the Lord is that Spirit: and where the Spirit of the Lord is, there is liberty." (KJV)

> O come and dwell in me,
> Spirit of power within,
> And bring the glorious liberty
> From sorrow, fear, and sin.

2 Corinthians 5:17: "Therefore if anyone be in Christ, there is a new creation:[2] old things are passed away; behold, all things are become new."

> Hasten the joyful day
> Which shall my sins consume,
> When old things shall be done away,
> And all things new become.
>
> I want the witness, Lord,
> That all I do is right,
> According to thy mind and word,
> Well-pleasing in thy sight.

1. *SH* 1762, 2:298, 301, 367.
2. KJV = "if any man be in Christ, he is a new creation."

SECTION 3: GOD THE HOLY SPIRIT

Hebrews 11:5: "By faith Enoch was translated that he should not see death; and was not found, because God had translated him: for before his translation he had this testimony, that he pleased God." (KJV)

> I ask no higher state;
> Indulge me but in this,
> And soon or later then translate
> To thine eternal bliss.

On many occasions John Wesley, who often edited Charles's hymns for publication, created hymns by combining various stanzas from diverse texts of his brother which had the same meter. Such is the case with this hymn, which John compiled for the 1780 *Collection* in the section entitled "For Believers Groaning for Full Redemption," though the hymn as originally edited by John included some lines which are not in the text printed above. John selected the stanzas from *SH* 1762, in which Charles essentially wrote a Bible commentary in poetical verse, basing his hymns on specific passages of Scripture, which he quoted in whole or in part at the beginning of each hymn. The hymn "O come and dwell in me" consists of selected stanzas from three different hymns by Charles Wesley based on the following passages of Scripture: 2 Corinthians 3:17; 2 Corinthians 5:17; and Hebrews 11:5.

Charles Wesley calls believers once again to prayer in these verses. The hymn opens with a plea for the indwelling of the Holy Spirit. This was his constant prayer throughout his life and ministry. He never arrived at a point where he thought it was fruitless to utter such a prayer. He yearned for the "Spirit of power within." Many years after his conversion in 1738, he wrote to his wife, "I thought I received the first grain of faith then, but what does that avail me, if I have not the spirit now?"[3]

Wesley perceives God's Spirit as the "Spirit of power within," because the Spirit liberates "from sorrow, fear, and sin." These three are among the most devastating forces in human life, and God's Spirit within frees us from them.

In the same 1762 volume from which the stanzas of this hymn are taken, Charles Wesley further amplified the liberating power of the Spirit in these lines:

---

3. Baker, *Charles Wesley As Revealed by His Letters*, 33; from a letter to his wife dated Whitsunday, 1760, from Westminster.

> Spirit of faith, come down on me,
> For where thou art is liberty;
> Thy presence looses all my bands,
> And melts the fetters from my hands,
> Consumes like flax the cords of sin,
> And burns up all my foes within.[4]

When the Spirit comes to dwell in us by faith, in the gift of love expressed in Jesus Christ (God among us in life, ministry, death, and resurrection), the Spirit's power is released and we are liberated from the tyranny of all opposing forces. No matter what our situation, it is God's *presence* in us which shatters all external and internal shackles or chains that bind us. Sorrow, death, and sin—these inner foes are vanquished before the Spirit's power. No inner or outer tyranny is a match for the Spirit of power and faith alive and dynamic in our lives.

Christians will struggle to free all people who are oppressed, because of their commitment to the reign of God's justice on earth; nevertheless, they know that if they are not liberated within—if the Spirit of power has not come to dwell within them—they shall never be free, even if liberated from the forces of worldly bondage.

In stanzas 2 and 3 Wesley longs for the evidence of God's liberation in his own life. How does one become the new creation of which the Apostle Paul speaks and for which Wesley longs? Our sins are consumed by the fires of the Spirit. We become so filled with God's Spirit that there is no longer room for sin within. When Wesley says that "old things shall be done away, / and all things new become," he is affirming in the spirit of Paul that we are the same persons that God created from the beginning of our lives, but we become new. The same persons change lifestyle, perspectives, ways of relating to others. Deceit is turned into integrity, lies are transformed into truth, hate and jealousy become love and care.

Wesley discloses something about himself in stanza 3 that is characteristic of all human beings:

> I want the witness, Lord,
> That all I do is right.

If he had stopped there, the result could have been self-serving egotism, but he did not. He continued that the test of whether he is right is, if it is

---

4. *SH* 1762, 1:132.

SECTION 3: GOD THE HOLY SPIRIT

> According to thy mind and word,
> Well-pleasing in thy sight.

How do we know whether we are right? By measuring what we think, say, and do by the mind of God revealed in Holy Scripture, the "mind of Christ," which is characterized by self-emptying, humble love. If we are willing to be vulnerable enough to let ourselves be judged by God's mind and Word, we shall know whether we are right.

The hymn concludes with the expression of the ultimate yearning within the heart and soul of the Christian, namely, for complete and final union with God throughout all eternity. Wesley is inspired by the example of Enoch in the Hebrew Scriptures and in the Book of Hebrews (11:5) which describes his "translation" into the presence of God. Eternal union with God is the epitome of the believer's hope. There is "no higher state" for which to pray.

What should the Christian desire above all else? The indwelling Spirit of power, transformation as a new creation, witness of God's Word and mind to what is right in one's life, and ultimate eternal union with God. This is not a prayer for special occasions, but a prayer for every day of one's life!

SECTION 4

Faith

Faith is the life of the soul.
CHARLES WESLEY

23.

What shall I do with my life?
Give me the faith which can remove[1]

> Give me the faith which can remove
>   And sink the mountain to the plain;
> Give me the childlike praying love,
>   Which longs to build thy house again;
> Thy love, let it my heart o'erpower,
> And all my simple soul devour.
>
> I would the precious time redeem,
>   And longer live for this alone,
> To spend and to be spent for them
>   Who have not yet my Savior known;
> Fully on these my mission prove,
> And only breathe, to breathe thy love.
>
> My talents, gifts, and graces, Lord,
>   Into thy blessed hands receive;
> And let me live to preach thy word,
>   And let me to thy glory live;
> My every sacred moment spend
> In publishing the sinner's Friend.

1. *HSP* 1749, 1:300–301.

SECTION 4: FAITH

> Enlarge, inflame, and fill my heart
>   With boundless charity divine,
> So shall I all my strength exert,
>   And love them with a zeal like thine,
> And lead them to thy open side,
> The sheep for whom the Shepherd died.

In *HSP* 1749, Wesley published a series of twelve "Hymns for a Preacher of the Gospel." This hymn consists of four of the original eight stanzas in hymn No. 12. The hymns have to do with the ministerial office in its many dimensions, but particularly the proclamation of the gospel. At this time in his life Charles Wesley had been preaching and ministering among people for eleven years, since his conversion on May 21, 1738. He had preached before that, having been ordained in 1735, just before his voyage to the colony of Georgia in the New World. But in 1738 his preaching ministry of the Word became imbued with an evangelical spirit. In the original opening stanza, not included in the above text, he looked back across those short years.

> O that I was as heretofore
>   When first sent forth in Jesu's Name
> I rushed through every open door,
>   And cried to all, "Behold the Lamb!"
> Seized the poor trembling slaves of sin,
> And forced the outcasts to come in.

Some have speculated that Charles may have written these lines in a moment of depression or setback. Indeed, he was a man of moods, but it was his constant desire to aspire to this evangelical fervor.

The selection of stanzas in the above hymn, which are stanzas 3, 5, 6, and 7 of the original, are Wesley's perpetual prayer for total commitment of himself—his time, talents, gifts, and graces—to the gospel and its proclamation. It is interesting that, though Charles Wesley is known primarily as a writer of hymns, he saw one of his main vocational tasks as improving the preaching of the clergy. One can imagine a church filled with ministers who lived the commitment reflected in this hymn. What preachers of the gospel they would be!

At the opening of the stanza beginning "Give me the faith" Charles recalls Jesus' words in Matthew's account of the man who brought to Jesus his possessed son, whom the disciples could not heal. After Jesus made him well, the disciples asked Jesus why they had not been able to heal the child.

He replied, "Because of your unbelief: for verily I say unto you, If ye have faith as a grain of mustard seed, ye shall say unto this mountain, Remove hence to yonder place; and it shall remove; and nothing shall be impossible unto you" (17:20 KJV).

There are two fundamental aspects of human experience which are essential to a meaningful and fruitful life: *faith* and *love*. It is for these which Wesley prays. He desires the faith that can move mountains and the love that longs to build God's house. The story in Matthew concerns possession of a child's soul by evil power, and Charles contrasts this with the desire for his soul to be overpowered by God's love. The Wesleys understood that it did not suffice for a "preacher of the gospel" to be gifted in preaching. As they recorded in the Conference Minutes: "For what avails *Public Preaching alone*, though we could preach like Angels?"[2] One must live only "to breathe [God's] love."

Charles expanded his prayer in the second stanza to the stewardship of time. Here is one of the most eloquent expressions of the mission of the individual Christian and the mission of the church. The mission is affirmed and validated in this way—living for this alone:

> To spend and to be spent for them
>   Who have not yet my Savior known;
> Fully on these my mission prove,
> And only breathe to breathe thy love.

Charles's lines recall the apostle Paul's words to the church at Corinth, "I will most gladly spend and be spent for you" (2 Corinthians 12:15a).

In stanza 3 Charles folds into six lines a summary of Christian vocational commitment. As an artist, a poet, he had come to understand that God had bestowed upon him the gift of language—the turning of a phrase, the eloquence of diction, the music and rhythm of speech. To commit oneself fully to Christ and the church, to the proclamation and living of the gospel, does not mean to bury one's talents, gifts, and graces. To the contrary, it means to pursue them along lines leading to excellence and their most creative use in the enhancement of God's work:

> My talents, gifts, and graces, Lord,
>   Into thy blessed hands receive.

---

2. *Minutes of Several Conversations Between The Reverend Mr. John and Charles Wesley*, 6.

SECTION 4: FAITH

This process is essential to the empowerment and enablement of persons to preach God's Word and to live to God's glory. The development and unfolding of one's talents, gifts, and graces in study, discipline, and practice is a vital part of spending "every sacred moment / in publishing the sinner's friend." One does not give one's talents, gifts, and graces into God's hands poorly prepared and carelessly refined. If one would publish the sinner's Friend with maximum effectiveness, one invests the time, effort, and practice toward the fullest perfection of the gifts with which one is bestowed.

Stanza 4 is a doxology of love, which is so characteristic of Charles Wesley's hymns and poems. Love is the most powerful force in the world, and this stanza reflects a recurrent theme in his poetry and in his life. What eloquence!

> Enlarge, inflame, and fill my heart
> With boundless charity divine!

God's love is boundless, it knows no boundaries, and has no end, and Wesley desires to be so overflowing with it, so set on fire, so extended beyond what he is of himself that he will exert all of his strength and love to others with the passion of a God who loves all and seeks their well-being. This overwhelming and all-encompassing expression of love is what he knows will lead others to Christ, the Shepherd, who gave his life for the sheep.

What shall I do with my life? Wesley says in this hymn: make it a doxology of Christ's love in every dimension of living.

24.

How are we to respond to God's call?
A charge to keep I have[1]

Leviticus 8:35: "You shall remain at the entrance of the tent of meeting day and night for seven days, keeping the Lord's charge so that you do not die; for so I am commanded."

> A charge to keep I have,
>   A God to glorify,
> A never-dying soul to save,
>   And fit it for the sky.
>
> To serve the present age,
>   My calling to fulfill;
> O may it all my powers engage
>   To do my Master's will!
>
> Arm me with jealous care,
>   As in thy sight to live,
> And oh, thy servant, Lord, prepare
>   A strict account to give!
>
> Help me to watch and pray,
>   And on thyself rely,
> Assured if I my trust betray,
>   I shall forever die.

1. *SH* 1762, 1:58–59.

SECTION 4: FAITH

Charles Wesley's counterpart to his brother John's *Explanatory Notes Upon the New Testament* was his own Bible commentary written in verse, *SH* 1762, from which this hymn comes. It is based on Leviticus 8:35.

In this hymn, as was often his practice, Wesley responds to specific words and/or ideas in the biblical text. It is the language of the second half of the Leviticus verse which surfaces in the hymn, specifically the words "charge" and "die."

Leviticus 8:35 comes at the conclusion of the story of the consecration of Aaron and his sons in the tabernacle of the congregation. After the sacrifice of the bullock and ram, Aaron and his sons receive this command: "And ye shall not go out of the door of the tabernacle of the congregation in seven days, until the days of your consecration be at an end: for seven days shall he consecrate you." (8:33, KJV)

Wesley is keenly aware that consecration is accompanied by God's call to obedience which requires responsible, disciplined response. God may command and call to obedience, but it is human beings who have the capacity and responsibility to respond. Wesley then translates God's summons to obedience in the Leviticus passage to Christian vocation and the personal practice of the divine presence, that is, the path of holiness. His focus is on personal nurture along this path.

First, *all receive a charge from God:* "A charge to keep I have." What is the charge? It is very personal, namely: "a God to glorify." Furthermore, one is the steward of God-given life which is to be claimed for God: "a never-dying soul to save." This charge carries with it the responsibility to nurture God's gift of life and to prepare for life eternal: "and fit it for the sky." Behind Wesley's words are years of recollection of his own hesitancy to follow God's charge for his life. He remembered that he had reluctantly entered Holy Orders, that he had preached and served as a clergyman for three years before he experienced God's full redemptive power in Christ, and that even after his conversion on Pentecost Day 1738, there were times when it was not so simple to fulfill God's charge. Still he could not escape responsibility before God, and he persevered.

Second, *God's charge is contemporary and holistic.* Wesley knew that he and all followers of Christ could not dwell in the past. Like him they are called "To serve the present age / [their] calling to fulfill." He may have been converted on May 21, 1738, but he wrote the words to this hymn over twenty years later. While the memory of that experience sustained him, he was called "to serve the present age," not to live in the past. God summoned him ever anew to fulfill his calling in the present moment. How? with the engagement of his full powers. God's summons is a call to commitment. All that we are, the very essence of our being, is called into God's service. "O may it all my powers engage / to do my Master's will."

Third, *God's charge awakens a keen awareness of God's presence.* Wesley prays that he will be ever aware that he lives in God's sight, for God has a clear view of every aspect of his life. The question for him is: Will he live with a constant awareness of God's presence? And his prayer continues: "and oh, thy servant, Lord, prepare / a strict account to give!" God's charge anticipates accountability. One must give account of one's life. The practice of the divine presence cannot be done in a *nonchalant* fashion. Disciplined response to God's charge requires "a strict account" of one's daily existence.

Fourth, *God's charge anticipates the disciplines of contemplation and prayer.* Hence Wesley prays: "Help me to watch and pray, / and on thyself rely." Reliance upon God is not an assumption one takes for granted. It is not a subconscious state of the Christian. Wesley's sequence is not coincidental—watchfulness and prayer, anticipate, affirm, and deepen reliance upon God. He knew the values of these disciplines even when they seemed meaningless. On one occasion he recorded in his *Journal* that he served the sacrament of Holy Communion but he did not feel the presence of Christ. Yet he did not cease to celebrate the sacrament. On another occasion, as he reflected on Christ's sacrifice for him in the midst of the liturgy, awestruck he wrote in his *Journal,* "Oh Love, Love!"[2]

The closing line of this hymn has occasioned much speculation about its theological meaning and it has troubled many interpreters: "assured, if I my trust betray, I shall forever die." This must be understood against the background of the Leviticus passage (8:35) on which the hymn is based. Wesley affirms that the breech of God's charge is not without consequences.

---

2. *MSJ,* 1:111.

25.

How can I know how to live each day?
Christ, whose glory fills the skies[1]

Christ, whose glory fills the skies,
   Christ, the true, the only light,
Sun of Righteousness, arise,
   Triumph o'er the shades of night;
Dayspring from on high, be near;
Daystar, in my heart appear.

Dark and cheerless is the morn
   Unaccompanied by thee;
Joyless is the day's return,
   Till thy mercy's beams I see;
Till they inward light impart,
Cheer my eyes and warm my heart.

Visit then this soul of mine;
   Pierce the gloom of sin and grief;
Fill me, Radiancy divine,
   Scatter all my unbelief;
More and more thyself display,
Shining to the perfect day.

---

1. *HSP* 1740, 24–25.

This is one of the most eloquent prayers for personal illumination to be found in English-language hymnody. When Wesley first published it in 1740, he gave it the title "Morning Hymn." Against the background of the darkness of night just passed, he uses the metaphor of "light" to stimulate the inner vision of human beings that they may be able to see the path they should follow during the day before them and every day.

Wesley opens the prayer (stanza 1) with four ascriptions for God: Light, Sun of Righteousness, Dayspring from on high, and Daystar. He turns once again to Holy Scripture and the Book of Common Prayer for the language for God in prayer. *Light:* of the incarnate Word of God John 1 declares: "the true light, which enlightens everyone, was coming into the world" (1:9). And 1 John 1:5 avers, God is light and embodies "no darkness at all." *Sun of Righteousness:* in expressing the hope of the Messiah, the prophet Malachi speaks of the "Sun of righteousness" who will "arise with healing in his wings" (4:2 KJV). *Dayspring:* Wesley moves back to the New Testament, namely to Luke 1:78–79 (KJV), for the ascription "Dayspring." Every time he read the daily office of Morning Prayer he said or sang the words "day-spring from on high" in the *Benedictus* (Luke 1:68–79), which follows the second lesson of Scripture:

> Through the tender mercy of our God:
>   whereby the day-spring from on high
>   hath visited us;
> To give light to them that sit in darkness,
>   and in the shadow of death: and to
>   guide our feet into the way of peace.

Daystar: 2 Peter 1:19 (KJV) provides Wesley with the fourth divine ascription, "Daystar," which is also connected with prophetic hope: "We have also a more sure word of prophecy; whereunto ye do well that ye take heed, as unto a light that shineth in a dark place, until the day dawn, and the day star arise in your hearts."

Wesley's plea in this part of the prayer is fourfold and is couched in four verbs: arise, triumph, be near, appear. The confidence that God, the Light of all Light, will arise as the sun to obliterate the darkness in our lives and to lighten our inner vision is summarized eloquently by Charles Wesley in four lines from his well-known Christmas hymn "Hark! the herald angels sing":

SECTION 4: FAITH

> Hail the heaven-born Prince of Peace!
> Hail the Sun of Righteousness!
> Light and life to all he brings,
> Risen with healing in his wings.[2]

In the opening stanza of the prayer Wesley prays for God's power to conquer the forces of darkness in his life and to illumine his heart. Stanza 2 prayerfully considers the day at hand. Here is vital reflection for the beginning and living of each day: unless God's light accompanies me throughout the day, the day will be dark and cheerless. If when I come to its close and cannot see it filled with the light of mercy and compassion, it will be joyless. My quest is not, however, merely a search for the mercy of God somewhere throughout the day. "Beams of mercy" are to impart inward light to my own eyes and heart. Therefore, I become a source of mercy and compassion through whom this same light goes out to others. If not, the day at its close is joyless.

Realizing that God can impart the light to overcome the darkness of life and to illumine my inner vision so that I am an instrument of mercy, I pray earnestly with Wesley stanza 3, seeking the visitation of my soul with divine Radiancy. It penetrates all sin and grief in my life and disburses "all my unbelief." I begin my day with these words on my lips: "more and more thyself display." In other words, throughout the day I want God's light increasingly to be displayed in me. As I make my pilgrimage toward the fullness of perfection, it is only divine light which can illumine my path and make clear my direction.

Wesley has given us the fitting prayer for the beginning of each day and a pattern for our own prayers at the outset of every new day: invoke God's power and light, reflect on the day before us and how we may be instruments of illuminating mercy to others, and pray that God will impart such light to our daily paths and to our hearts that sin, grief, and unbelief disappear and we become sources of God's light to others. This is how we can know how to live each day.

---

2. *HSP* 1739, 206.

26.

Can We Prove Faith?
Ye different sects who all declare[1]

> Ye different sects who all declare,
> "Lo! Here is Christ!" or "Christ is there!"
> Your stronger proofs divinely give,
> And show me where the Christians live!

The Flemish Quietist, Antoinette Bourignon, tells a childhood story in her autobiography in which she relates her dissatisfaction with life around her after reading the Gospels. She realized that the environment in which she lived was not modeled after Jesus' example of love and selflessness. Therefore, she asked her parents, "Where are the Christians? Let us go to the country where the Christians live." Wesley is thought to have recalled her words when he wrote these powerful lines.

There is no age of Christianity which has not been riddled with dissension. Throughout history, councils of the church have sought to make decisions on what constitutes authentic doctrinal statements of the Christian faith and the Christian church. One need only list the primary emphases of major branches or churches of Christianity to grasp what have been seen traditionally as its "stronger proofs." Nevertheless, often over-emphasis on such "proofs" has led to the division of the church. One need only think of common misconceptions Christians sometimes have of one another.

---

1. *HSP* 1749, 2:334. Stanza 9 from Part 1 of a fourteen-stanza poem in two parts titled "Primitive Christianity."

SECTION 4: FAITH

"Roman Catholics *believe* in relics." "Presbyterians *believe* in predestination." "Baptists *believe* in the evil of dancing." "Methodists *believe* you can fall from grace." "Christians do not imbibe alcohol." Unquestionably, all such misconceptions have their origin in an over-emphasis on some aspects of faith's expression.

Wesley tells us that we cannot prove the faith by what we affirm, but we can demonstrate its effectiveness by how we live. Our task is not to *show* others what Christians believe but where Christians *live!*

27.

How do we relate believing and doing?
Their earthly task who fail to do[1]

Romans 12:11: "Not slothful in business; fervent in spirit; serving the Lord." (KJV)

Their earthly task who fail to do
Neglect their heavenly business too,
Nor know what faith and duty mean,
Who use religion as a screen,
Asunder put what God hath joined,
A diligent and pious mind.

Full well the labor of our hands
With fervency of spirit stands;
For God, who all our days hath given,
From toil excepts but one in seven;
And laboring, while we time redeem,
We let the work our God esteem.

Happy we live, when God doth fill
Our hands with work, our hearts with zeal,
For every toil, if God enjoin,
Becomes a sacrifice divine,
And like the blessed spirits above
The more we serve, the more we love.

1. *SH* 1762, 2:285–86.

SECTION 4: FAITH

An uncle of mine once preached a sermon on faith and works entitled, "With Which Wing Does a Bird Fly?" Obviously the answer was, "With neither one or the other but with both." Likewise, for the Christian, faith and works are not self-exclusive, but rather mutually inclusive. Both are necessary to a balanced walk with Christ. Saying that we understand the meaning of faith without doing faith's duty means we make out of our religion a screen. The side others see may look beautiful and impressive, but behind it there is emptiness, disarray, and confusion. God does not intend that we make such breaches in our behavior, characters, and personalities. God does not intend that we separate diligence and piety, but that we mold them into an enduring unity.

Upon the death of Heinrich Boell, the German writer who received the Nobel Peace Prize for literature in 1972, one of his friends, a clergyman, said of him, "He was one of the very few persons I have ever known for whom belief and action were totally synonymous." Boell, who became extremely active after World War II in opposing oppression of people in any manner and was engaged in the peace movement, knew that the only test of belief is the arena of action.

We experience the viability and validity of faith only by acting on it, by doing the radical things faith demands—such as loving our enemies, doing good to those who use us spitefully, loving our neighbors as we love ourselves, going out in complete trust not knowing where we are going, aiding the poor, feeding the hungry, caring for the sick and dying. Faith offers no alternatives to fulfilling these demands of the gospel. Indeed, they are faith's duty.

The apostle Paul gave the church at Rome a three-fold formula for maintaining the balance of faith and works: (1) take responsible action in all you do, (2) be fervent in spirit, and (3) serve God. Utilizing a vocabulary of active verbs will do much for discovering faith's response. Faith may involve understanding, but faith is by no means a static noun or state. Faith is action. People of faith *serve* and *love* God and others. How true that "the more we serve, the more we love."

If we do not do faith's duty, we make of our religion a screen, hiding our emptiness, disarray, and confusion.

28.

What is eternal life?
Christ the Lord is risen today[1]

HYMN FOR EASTER-DAY

Christ the Lord is risen today,
Sons of men and angels say:[2]
Raise your joys and triumphs high:
Sing, ye heavens, and earth reply.

Love's redeeming work is done;
Fought the fight, the battle won;
Lo! our Sun's eclipse is o'er,
Lo! He sets in blood no more.

Vain the stone, the watch, the seal;
Christ has burst the gates of hell!
Death in vain forbids his rise:
Christ has opened Paradise!

---

1. *HSP* 1739, 209–11; stanzas 1–5, 10–11 of an eleven-stanza hymn.
2. Erik Routley suggests the effective inclusive phrase "all creation joins to say" for this line. See *Rejoice in the Lord*, No. 325.

SECTION 4: FAITH

> Lives again our glorious King;
> Where, O death, is now thy sting?
> Dying once, he all doth save;[3]
> Where thy victory, O grave?
>
> Soar we now where Christ has led,
> Following our exalted Head;
> Made like him, like him we rise,
> Ours the cross, the grave, the skies!
>
> Hail the Lord of earth and heaven!
> Praise to thee by both be given;
> Thee we greet triumphant now;
> Hail the Resurrection thou!
>
> King of glory, soul of bliss,
> Everlasting life is this:
> Thee to know, thy power to prove,
> Thus to sing, and thus to love!

This popular and powerful hymn on the resurrection of Christ was originally titled by Wesley, "Hymn for Easter-Day." When first published in 1739, it included eleven stanzas. The seven printed here are those which appear most frequently in hymnbooks, although often they have been edited and rearranged.

When we sing or read this hymn, we catch the spirit of the resurrection and go on a journey through a vast spectrum of emotions and thoughts which issue from and surround Christ's resurrection. All creation joins in the refrain:

> Christ the Lord is risen today.

All creation sings, for love has defeated death! The darkness which surrounded the crucifixion has vanished, and no more must blood be shed to redeem humankind (see stanzas 1 and 2).

No human effort can contain God's mighty act to open Paradise to all creation (stanza 3). Hence, Paul's questions in First Corinthians, "O death, where is thy sting? O grave, where is thy victory?" (15:55 KJV) are preceded by the following affirmations:

---

3. The manuscript Richmond Tracts shows this line in Charles Wesley's handwriting in the following (and probably later) version: "Once he died our souls to save." It appears thus in many subsequent hymnbooks.

WHAT IS ETERNAL LIFE?

> "Lives again our glorious King;
>
> ...
>
> "Dying once, he all doth save."

We too rise with Christ: "Soar we now where Christ has led." He has gone before us and shown us our destiny which is summarized in three words, "Ours the *cross*, the *grave*, the *skies*." We suffer, die, and rise with Christ.

Unquestionably the church was born out of the resurrection faith and hope of life eternal. To be sure, this hymn eloquently proclaims that faith and hope. Wesley did not intend, however, to end the hymn merely on the note of hope in the resurrection faith and everlasting life, as many hymnbooks do by excluding the concluding two stanzas of the original hymn. They are stanzas 6 and 7 as printed here, but they are originally stanzas ten and eleven. The hymn ends as it has begun—in praise of the risen Christ. Yet there is more. It affirms that everlasting life is a present reality, not merely a future reward. Furthermore, it takes on a tangible form now.

> King of glory, soul of bliss,
> Everlasting life is this:
> Thee to *know*, thy power to *prove*,
> Thus to *sing*, and thus to *love*.

Wesley uses verbs to describe everlasting life because it is active life in the present. What is eternal life?

Thee to know. Wesley remembers Jesus' prayer in John 17:3, "And this is eternal life, that they may know you, the only true God, and Jesus Christ whom you have sent." Eternal life involves an active mental process. First John 5:20 expresses it this way: "We know that the Son of God has come and has given us understanding so that we may know him who is true; and we are in him who is true, in his Son Jesus Christ. He is the true God and eternal life."

Thy power to prove. Eternal life is proving God's power. Wesley does not mean we are to verify God's power; rather, we are to personify such power and be its proof, its testimony in a world which prefers to trust its own power.

Thus to sing. Eternal life is singing creation's hymn of praise to the Creator who has obliterated the force of death which would threaten creation. As Augustine once said, "The Christian must be an Alleluia from head to foot." That is the eternal song!

Thus to love. Eternal life is loving as Christ loved, even if it means sacrificing one's life. It is perpetual self-giving love, which goes in search of others and God at all costs.

Christians are active participants in everlasting life now. "Christ the Lord is risen today," and so are we! This is our hymn for Easter and every day of the year.

29.

What do we really want?
Jesu, lover of my soul[1]

IN TEMPTATION

Jesu, lover of my soul,
    Let me to thy bosom fly,
While the nearer waters roll,
    While the tempest still is high.
Hide me, O my Savior, hide,
    Till the storm of life is past:
Safe into the haven guide;
    O receive my soul at last.

Other refuge have I none:
    Hangs my helpless soul on thee.
Leave, ah leave me not alone,
    Still support and comfort me.
All my trust on thee is stayed,
    All my help from thee I bring;
Cover my defenseless head
    With the shadow of thy wing.

---

1. *HSP* 1740, 67–68.

SECTION 4: FAITH

Wilt thou not regard my call?
    Wilt thou not accept my prayer?
Lo, I sink, I faint, I fall!
    Lo, on thee I cast my care,
Reach me out thy gracious hand!
    While I of thy strength receive,
Hoping against hope I stand,
    Dying, and behold I live!

Thou, O Christ, art all I want;
    More than all in thee I find.
Raise the fallen, cheer the faint,
    Heal the sick, and lead the blind.
Just and holy is thy Name;
    I am all unrighteousness:
False and full of sin I am;
    Thou art full of truth and grace.

Plenteous grace with thee is found,
    Grace to cover all my sin:
Let the healing streams abound,
    Make and keep me pure within.
Thou of life the fountain art;
    Freely let me take of thee:
Spring thou up within my heart,
    Rise to all eternity.

The distinguished preacher Henry Ward Beecher once said, "I would rather have written 'Jesus, lover of my soul' than to have the fame of all the kings that ever sat on earth."[2]

Like many of Charles Wesley's poems, "Jesu, lover of my soul" takes on new meaning when understood against the backdrop of his own experience and the time in which he lived. While we do not know the specific date of its composition, we know it was published in 1740 at a time of great conflict in England and within the Church of England. The imagery of this poem grows out of the crises of the period. The Wesley brothers were often beaten, stoned, and run out of towns. By virtue of their affiliation with the university, they assumed an itinerant ministry and traveled from town to town, village to village, and parish to parish, which aroused the ire of many clergy and laity. In the face of violent opposition, Charles indeed hoped for

---

2. Robert McCutchan. *Our Hymnody*, 338.

a time when "the storm of life is past." Often in the midst of a riotous mob he knew that "other refuge have I none" and that he bore a "defenseless head" except God should cover it.

Stanza 3 does not appear in most hymnbooks. But it is most important, for it places before us Wesley's agonizing questions, so often a part of his most significant lyrics.

> Wilt thou not regard my call?
> Wilt thou not accept my prayer?

Wesley understood the anguish of rejection. At times he was called a Papist, a Jesuit, a Dissenter, and on one occasion was falsely accused of treason, a charge dismissed by a judge before whom Wesley eloquently defended himself. The agony of his thoughts as to whether God would reject him in the same manner human beings had done was overcome only by the confidence in his plea:

> Reach me out thy gracious hand!
> While I of thy strength receive,
> Hoping against hope I stand,
> Dying, and behold I live.

The sustenance of God's grace was Wesley's fountain of strength. In this poem he helps us to see that nothing but total commitment to Christ enables us to drink from that fountain. Here is how:

> All my trust on thee is stayed,
> All my help from thee I bring.

We may place our trust in others, families, nations, governments, lifestyles, laws, wealth, professions, vocations. It is God alone, however, who will sustain us in adversity, temptation, danger, and death.

> Lo, on thee I cast my care.

We may prefer to cast our cares on others because we are weak, irresponsible, apathetic, or spiteful. Only when we cast our cares on God, according to Wesley, do we find One who makes the burden bearable.

> Thou, O Christ, art all I want.

To know what we *want* is of primary importance every day we live. Perhaps the origin of much unhappiness, much paranoia, and many neuroses is that people have no idea what they want. Wesley focused on a singular *want*—Christ. There is the key. The question becomes not "*What* do we want?" but "*Whom* do we want?" Once we want only Christ, we begin to find out what we want to do in and with our lives.

It is understandable that the language of this hymn would become beloved by African-American Christians realizing the hopelessness of slavery and the pain of racism.

> Jesu, lover of my soul,
>   Let me to thy bosom fly,
> While the nearer waters roll,
>   While the tempest still is high.
> Hide me, O my Savior, hide,
>   Till the storm of life is past.

This is language an enslaved and suffering people could understand. Line after line speaks to one deprived of freedom. "Other refuge have I none." My soul is helpless. "Cover my defenseless head." "Let the healing streams abound." It is not surprising that this is a hymn for the ages.

30.

Where do we start?
Where shall my wondering soul begin?[1]

CHRIST THE FRIEND OF SINNERS

Where shall my wondering soul begin?
  How shall I all to heaven aspire?
A slave redeemed from death and sin,
  A brand plucked from eternal fire,
How shall I equal triumphs raise,
Or sing my great Deliverer's praise?

O how shall I the goodness tell,
  Father, which thou to me hast showed?
That I, a child of wrath and hell,
  I should be called a child of God,
Should know, should feel my sins forgiven,
Blest with this antepast of heaven!

And shall I slight my Father's love?
  Or basely fear his gifts to own?
Unmindful of his favors prove?
  Shall I, the hallowed cross to shun,

1. *HSP* 1739, 101–103.

SECTION 4: FAITH

Refuse his righteousness to impart
By hiding it within my heart?

Outcasts of men, to you I call,
    Harlots, and publicans, and thieves!
He spreads his arms to embrace you all;
    Sinners alone his grace receives:
No need of him the righteous have;
He came the lost to seek and save.

Come, all ye Magdalens in lust,
    Ye ruffians fell in murders old;
Repent, and live: despair and trust!
    Jesus for you to death was sold.
Though hell protest, and earth repine,
He died for crimes like yours—and mine.

Come, O my guilty brethren, come,
    Groaning beneath your load of sin!
His bleeding heart shall make you room,
    His open side shall take you in;
He calls you now, invites you home:
Come, O my guilty brethren, come!

Charles Wesley called this poem his conversion hymn. He wrote it just two days after a life-transforming encounter with Christ which he described in his *Journal*. "I now found myself at peace with God and rejoiced in the hope of loving Christ. . . . I saw that by faith I stood; by the continual support of faith" (May 21, 1738).[2] "At nine [on May 23] began an hymn upon my conversion, but was persuaded to break off for fear of pride. Mr. Bray coming encouraged me to proceed in spite of Satan. I prayed Christ to stand by me and finished the hymn."[3]

The following evening his brother John went to a society meeting at Aldersgate Street in London where, during the reading of Martin Luther's Preface to the Epistle to the Romans, he felt his heart strangely warmed and that he trusted Christ alone for salvation. After the meeting Charles records, "Towards ten, my brother was brought in triumph by a troop of our friends, and declared, 'I believe.' We sang the hymn ["Where shall my

2. *MSJ*, 1:108.
3. *MSJ*, 1:109.

wondering soul begin?"] with great joy, and parted with prayer. At midnight I gave myself up to Christ, assured I was safe waking or sleeping."[4]

Often so-called conversion hymns reflect a self-centered kind of assurance which Charles Wesley would have found displeasing. He helps us understand how to respond to such an experience.

First, be overcome with awe and wonder. Where do we begin once we have made a commitment to Christ? How can we aspire to heaven or even have the audacity to praise God when we know we are unworthy and weak? There is the beginning place—to admit our own unworthiness.

Second, desire to tell the story of redemption, but do so only after much soul-searching. Ask—How shall we tell of God's goodness? If we do not share this story, do we not slight God's love, prove ourselves unmindful of God's favor, and avoid the cross of Christ? Tell the story.

Third, begin with the most unlikely people: prostitutes, thieves, murderers. Christ "died for crimes like yours—and mine." So often the church has not begun its work among the most unlikely. It can learn from Christ, from its past, and from Wesley. Think of those persons, who would be the most unlikely to hear anyone tell and live out the story of redemption, and begin with them.

And finally, personify repentance, trust, and belief. We make our lives arguments for Christ by being repentant, by trusting, by showing our belief in what we think, say, and do. Then others may hunger for the love and forgiveness of God which they see in us.

---

4. *MSJ*, 1:111.

31.

For what shall we pray?
Let us plead for faith alone[1]

Ephesians 2:8–10: "For by grace you have been saved through faith, and this is not your own doing; it is the gift of God—not the result of works, so that no one may boast. For we are what he has made us, created in Christ Jesus for good works, which God prepared beforehand to be our way of life."

THE LOVE-FEAST

Let us plead for faith alone,
Faith which by our works is shown;
God it is who justifies,
Only faith the grace applies.

Active faith that lives within,
Conquers hell and death and sin,
Hallows whom it first made whole,
Forms the Savior in the soul.

Let us for this faith contend,
Sure salvation is its end;

---

1. *HSP* 1740, 183-4. The original first line reads, "Plead we thus for faith alone."

> Heaven already is begun,
> Everlasting life is won.
>
> Only let us persevere
> Till we see our Lord appear,
> Never from the Rock remove,
> Saved by faith which works by love.

On one occasion after his conversion, Charles Wesley recorded in his *Journal* that he was surprised that he had once thought the idea of justification by faith alone to be foreign to the Church of England, since it is found in its Articles of Religion.

On another occasion he was called before one of the bishops of the Church of England and accused of maintaining that the church was secondary to faith *alone*. Unquestionably Charles saw the church as the viable fellowship in which justification by faith is authentically expressed. But neither Charles nor John, after their life-changing encounters with God on May 21 and 24, 1738, respectively, was convinced that the church was a substitute for justification by faith alone, but rather it is the arena in which this experience is enabled, affirmed, and authenticated.

The text "Let us plead for faith alone" was published in *HSP* 1740 and based on Ephesians 2:8–10, one of the New Testament passages which has become a classical statement on the meaning of justification by faith alone. Charles probably wrote the hymn some time between his conversion on May 21, 1738 and the hymn's publication in 1740. Hence it was born out of his vibrant experience of Christ, which moved him to record in his *Journal* on that memorable day, "I knew that by faith I stood." He did not say by faith, good works, or anything else, only "by faith."

The title Wesley gave the hymn was "The Love-Feast." What does he mean by such a title? The key to an understanding of his intent is found perhaps in the last line of stanza 4: "saved by faith which works by love." Justification by faith is a work of love which works through love; hence justification by faith itself is a feast of love.

Unlike many of his other hymns, this text is not a prayer. It is an exhortation, an urging, an encouragement for all to plead for faith alone. Stanzas 1 and 2 describe such faith. It is active and by no means does "faith alone" mean an abandonment of good works. Faith shows itself by works. Nevertheless, works do not justify us before God. "God it is who justifies," says Wesley. By faith God's loving, justifying grace is "applied" in our lives through Jesus.

In stanza 2 Charles explains further that faith is a triumphant, conquering, inner experience. It overpowers the reign of hell, death, and sin within us. It also sanctifies or hallows those within whom it dwells. Stanza 2 concludes with one of the most powerful thoughts in the entire hymn, namely, faith "forms the Savior in the soul." The form of the Savior, Jesus Christ, within us shapes our personalities, characters, attitudes, and demeanors. The essence of the Savior is love and his love becomes the very essence of our being. It is an ongoing, life-transforming experience. In this text Wesley did not write in the past tense, however, as though the Savior were *formed* within the soul, but rather he wrote in the present tense: "*forms* the Savior in the soul."

In stanzas 3 and 4 Wesley adjures everyone to seek this faith, for it is the beginning of everlasting life in the present moment. Persevere and remain steadfast in faith: "never from the Rock remove." In the hymn "Ye servants of God, your Master proclaim" a stanza not included in most hymnals says:

> Men, devils engage, the billows arise,
> And furiously rage and threaten the skies;
> Their fury shall never our steadfastness shock;
> The weakest believer is built on a Rock.

Faith creates a community of loving workers, and justifying faith results in a constant love feast in earth and heaven.

32.

Why will you die for nothing?
Sinners, turn: why will you die?[1]

Ezekiel 18:31–32: "Cast away from you all the transgressions that you have committed against me, and get yourselves a new heart and a new spirit! Why will you die, O house of Israel? For I have no pleasure in the death of anyone, says the Lord God. Turn, then, and live."

> Sinners, turn: why will you die?
> God, your Maker, asks you why.
> God, who did your being give,
> Made you with himself to live;
> He the fatal cause demands
> Asks the work of his own hands.
> Why, you thankless creatures, why
> Will you cross his love, and die?
>
> Sinners, turn: why will you die?
> God, your Savior, asks you why.
> God, who did your souls retrieve,
> Died himself, that you might live.
> Will you let him die in vain?
> Crucify your Lord again?
> Why, you ransomed sinners, why
> Will you slight his grace, and die?

1. *HGEL* 1742, 2nd series, 43–46.

SECTION 4: FAITH

Sinners, turn: why will you die?
God, the Spirit, asks you why;
He, who all your lives hath strove,
Wooed you to embrace his love.
Will you not the grace receive?
Will you still refuse to live?
Why, you long-sought sinners, why
Will you grieve your God, and die?

You, on whom he favors showers,
You, possessed of nobler powers,
You, of reason's powers possessed,
You, with will and memory blest,
You, with finer sense endued,
Creatures capable of God;
Noblest of his creatures, why,
Why will you forever die?

You, on whom he favors showers,
You, possessed of nobler powers,
You, of reason's powers possessed,
You, with will, and mem'ry blest,
You, with finer sense endued,
Creatures capable of God,
Noblest of his creatures, why,
Why will you forever die?

You, whom he ordained to be
Transcript of the Trinity,
You, whom he in life doth hold,
You, for whom himself was sold,
You, on whom he still doth wait,
Whom he would again create,
Made by him, and purchased, why,
Why will you forever die?

You, who own his record true,
You, his chosen people you,
You, who call the Savior Lord,
You, who read his written word,
You, who see the gospel-light,
Claim a crown in Jesu's right,

> Why will you, ye Christians, why
> Will the house of Israel die?
>
> Turn, he cries, ye sinners turn,
> By his life your God hath sworn
> He would have you turn, and live,
> He would all the world receive;
> He hath brought to all the race
> Full salvation by his grace,
> He hath no one soul passed by
> Why will you resolve to die?
>
> Can you doubt, if God is love?
> If to all his bowels move?
> Will you not his word receive?
> Will you not his oath believe?
> See, the suffering God appears!
> Jesus weeps! Believe his tears;
> Mingled with his blood thy cry
> Why will you resolve to die?

This hymn summarizes a lifelong plea of the Wesleys to the world in which they lived. It is the ancient cry of the prophets of Israel to God's people—*turn, turn, turn!* There is a need to change the direction one is going, namely, *away from God,* and to set one's course *toward God* and the divine will for one's own life and all creation.

Wesley couches the summons *to turn* in the form of questions from the Holy Trinity: God the Maker, the Savior, and the Spirit: Sinners, turn: why will you die? The Holy Trinity has invested itself in every creature and all creation, and inquires of all mortals: Why will you choose the way of death, rather than the way of life which God offers?

The hymn originally has sixteen stanzas of which the following are included here: 1–3, 6–8, 13, and 16. A variety of stanza combinations have appeared in hymnals, and these stanzas that appear here are those most commonly used.

According to stanza 1, life itself is the ultimate divine gift that should convince all thankless creatures to redirect their paths. Life is a gift of love from the Creator. To choose hatred, deceit, deception, and greed in our relationships with others and creation is to "cross God's love," for such sin defiles that which the Creator loves.

God the Maker asks: "Sinners, turn: why will you die?" It is tempting to feel rather self-righteous about posing this question to others, as though it were the private mandate and message of those who have already "turned." But Wesley says this is not a mere human question, but rather God's constant query of all whom God has made. In stanza 6 the question is clearly directed to the community of believers. These are the ones who place faith in the truth of God's Word, are God's chosen, call Jesus "Lord," read the Scriptures, see the light of the gospel, and claim Christ! Why, says Wesley, will Christians and the house of Israel die?

Stanza 7 leaves no doubt that there can be *no* exclusive claims to God's redemption—it is for all: God "hath not one soul passed by." God has brought salvation by grace to "all the race."

The affirmation and fulfillment of the work of God's own hands in creation is what God asks, says Wesley. It is human sin which disestablishes the work of God in this world. It is sin which shakes the foundations of creation. One need only observe the misuse of rivers and forests and the devastation of nuclear disasters to see the groaning of God's creation within the grasp of human evil.

God the Savior asks also: "Sinners, turn: why will you die?" It is not only because God has given life that sinners should redirect their lives toward God, but also because God has reclaimed the world and all in it through love. Sin, however, drives God's love for all creation to a cross and crucifies it there. When Jesus died on the hill of crosses at Calvary, he showed us that God forgives even such a dastardly deed as crucifixion. In the midst of his agony Jesus uttered those words which defy all human justice: "forgive them; for they do not know what they are doing" (Luke 23:34). Human sin and evil send God's outpouring of love in the divine Son again and again to a cross, even though the very cross upon which Christ died reveals God's gracious forgiving love, poured out for all. If we do not turn from sin, we stay our course toward death and declare that there is no such thing as grace and love in the world God has made!

God the Spirit asks as well: "Sinners, turn: why will you die?" Throughout our lives, even when we are unaware, the Spirit of God is moving us to embrace divine love, which empties itself always for others. This Spirit never gives up. Throughout "all [our] lives" the Spirit strives with us. It is always there, inviting and yearning that we enfold God's self-giving love in all we think, say, and do—indeed, in our very being! It entreats us earnestly to personify love till we become love. Refusing this love, God's grace, is the refusal of life itself, says Wesley.

> Will you not his grace receive?
> Will you still refuse to live?

In stanza 4 Wesley returns to the theme of the gifts of the Creator to the created. How can inheritors of God's creation choose death over life? They are the noblest of God's creatures and possess unusual gifts: reason, will, memory, a finer sense. We are "creatures capable of God." All these gifts are expressions of our Maker's love. To exploit them merely for our own ends is to doubt the very love which bestowed them upon us.

The concluding questions of each stanza are constant reminders that those who will not turn from sin "cross [God's] love," "slight [God's] grace," "grieve . . . God," and choose death instead of life.

The Wesleys chose the life offered by God and emptied themselves of all but love for a world that enslaved Africans, slaughtered Native Americans, fought numerous wars, allowed forced labor of children, denied education to the masses, and refused to provide medical care for the poor. The Wesleys declared that such ways were evidence of the choice of death over life. In seeking to rectify such injustices through personal and social transformation, they went to their graves resounding the question of the Holy Trinity to all people in all ages: "Sinners, turn: why will you die?"

33.

How can I overcome the power of sin?
Depth of mercy! Can there be[1]

John 20:20a: "He showed them his hands and his side."

AFTER A RELAPSE INTO SIN

Depth of mercy! Can there be
Mercy still reserved for me?
Can my God his wrath forbear,
Me, the chief of sinners, spare?

I have long withstood his grace,
long provoked him to his face,
Would not hearken to his calls,
Grieved him by a thousand falls.

I my Master have denied,
I afresh have crucified,
Oft profaned his hallowed name,
Put him to an open shame.

---

1. *HSP* 1740, 82–84.

> There for me the Savior stands,
> Shows his wounds and spreads his hands.
> God is love! I know, I feel;
> Jesus weeps and loves me still.
>
> Now incline me to repent,
> Let me now my sins lament,
> Now my foul revolt deplore,
> Weep, believe, and sin no more.

Charles Wesley's hymns and poems so often are about one's personal spiritual pilgrimage and the struggle which one has with sin. This hymn was originally published with the title "After a Relapse into Sin" and included thirteen stanzas. In *HSP* 1740 in which it appears, it falls between two other poetical texts addressing the subject of sin. The preceding poem bears the title "A Prayer Against the Power of Sin" and opens with these three stanzas:

> O that thou would'st the heavens rent,
>   In majesty come down!
> Stretch out thine arm omnipotent,
>   And seize me for thine own.
>
> Descend, and let thy lightning burn
>   The stubble of thy foe,
> My sins o'erturn, o'erturn, o'erturn,
>   And let the mountains flow.
>
> Thou my impetuous spirit guide,
>   And curb my headstrong will.
> Thou only canst drive back the tide,
>   And bid the sun stand still.[2]

"Depth of mercy! Can there be" is followed in *HSP* 1740 by a poem which has the heading "Written in Stress of Temptation." Its second stanza reflects the spirit of the apostle Paul's conviction:

> Out of the deep on Christ I call,
>   In bitterness of spirit cry;
> Broken upon that stone I fall,
>   I fall,—the chief of sinners I![3]

---

2. *HSP* 1740, 79.
3. *HSP* 1740, 85.

SECTION 4: FAITH

Charles Wesley understood the power of sin in his own life and throughout humankind. It was a real and present power which evoked a daily struggle, even for the faithful. He knew that he could stumble and fall, yet God's mercy was sufficient to sustain him in the battle.

Many lines of his hymns are filled with deep, soul-searching questions. As he reflects upon his own "relapse into sin," he cries out, "Depth of mercy," and asks, "Can there be mercy still reserved for me?" He intensifies the question by a further query, "Can my God forbear wrath," and "me, the chief of sinners spare?" He is constantly awestruck by the possibility of divine mercy which forgives his sin. In the well-known hymn, "And can it be that I should gain," he asks, "Amazing love, how can it be / that thou my God shouldst die for me?"

Stanzas 2 and 3 stress the need for the confession of the soul. It is not always easy to acknowledge that one has "long *withstood*" God's grace and *provoked* God, *would not harken* to God's call, and *grieved* God by "a thousand falls." Even so, that is not the end of Wesley's confession. It continues in stanza 3. He admits that like Peter he has *denied* Jesus and *crucified* him afresh, *profaned* his name, and "*put him to an open shame.*" Notice the intensity of Wesley's confession, which is characterized by active verbs. Here is a key to grasping the fullness of God's mercy: confront the power of sin in one's life squarely and openly. Call one's sin what it is. Out of that experience comes the realization which characterizes the life of the Wesley brothers and the Wesleyan movement within the Church of England of the eighteenth century and, it is hoped, still today:

> There for me the Savior stands,
>   Shows his wounds and spreads his hands.
> *God is love! I know, I feel*;
> Jesus weeps and *loves me* still.

Wesley *knows* and *feels* that God is love and that divine arms of love embrace him. His intellect and the full spectrum of his feelings and emotions come to this realization. To *know* and *feel* were primary emphases of the evangelical movement of the Wesleys.

Confession of sin and confession of faith reflected in the first four stanzas of this hymn do not in themselves suffice. They lead to a life of repentance, free of sin.

> Now incline me to repent,
> Let me now my sins lament,

> Now my foul revolt deplore,
> Weep, believe, and sin no more.

A repentant spirit is the motivation for life without sin and hence, integral to one's struggle against it. Wesley does not say simply "believe, and sin no more." Those words are prefaced by *lament* and *weep*.

We will do more than we can imagine to resist sin in our lives by the practice and posture of a repentant spirit.

34.

How shall I approach my work?
Forth in thy name, O Lord, I go[1]

BEFORE WORK

Forth in thy name, O Lord, I go,
   My daily labor to pursue;
Thee, only thee, resolved to know
   In all I think or speak or do.

The task thy wisdom hath assigned,
   O let me cheerfully fulfill;
In all my works thy presence find,
   And prove thy good and perfect will.

Thee may I set at my right hand,
   Whose eyes mine inmost substance see,
And labor on at thy command,
   And offer all my works to thee.

For thee delightfully employ
   Whate'er thy bounteous grace hath given;
And run my course with even joy,
   And closely walk with thee to heaven.

---

1. *HSP* 1749, 1:246–47.

HOW SHALL I APPROACH MY WORK?

Charles Wesley was deeply concerned that the attitudes with which we approach the endeavors of each day reflect our Christian posture and character. Therefore, he wrote hymns and poems for numerous occasions of daily experience: "Hymns for those called to earn their bread," "For the traveller," "At the hour of waking," "At the hour of retirement," "Prayer for rain," "In temptation," etc.

"Forth in thy name" was published in 1749 with the title "Before Work." Here Charles reveals the Christian attitude toward work, which was extremely important to the Wesleys. They lived in eighteenth-century England, where working conditions were horrendous among the masses. There were no child labor laws, no regulations to prevent extended working hours in the damp darkness of the coal mines or in the suffocating blast furnaces of Newcastle. The Wesleys knew firsthand the despicable living conditions in the workhouses of London and other cities. The Wesleys reached out to the oppressed labor force, seeking to reshape attitudes toward work, which could not have been wholesome under adverse conditions.

They established reading classes for the illiterate, schools for coal miners' children, orphanages for homeless children, and even credit unions for borrowing and lending to enhance job opportunities and personal and family sustenance.

In this context Charles Wesley wrote in the spirit of the apostle Paul (that whatever we do should be done to God's glory):

> Forth in thy name, O Lord, I go,
> My daily labor to pursue;
> Thee, only thee, resolved to know
> In all I think or speak or do.

We *resolve to know* God in our work and everything we think, speak, and do. Here is the constant resolve of Christians at work, which underlies all that they do: *to know God.*

Stanzas 2 and 4 tell us further how Christians' attitudes toward work are shaped. Work has been assigned to them by a Wisdom that transcends human wisdom. Therefore, they approach their tasks *cheerfully, delightfully,* and *with joy.*

Do not think of this hymn in the context of affluent people who have the luxury of reflecting at length about their attitudes toward things in life. Think of it in terms of the daily worker, whose job may not leave time for reflection, and realize that Wesley is saying that in "all my works" I may find God's presence. In what I do I may discover God's good and perfect will.

SECTION 4: FAITH

In stanza 3 Wesley understands God to be present in the workplace "at my right hand." God is my companion at work and as I labor, what I do becomes an offering to God, not merely to labor management.

When we resolve to *know* God in our work and labor in the divine presence cheerfully and with delight, what we do will be characterized even by *joy* and a *close* walk with God. Charles Wesley does not say that our coworkers will experience *occasional* joy in us, but rather our joy will be constant!

Here is a hymn for singing and reflection before beginning the tasks of every day. It can redirect and reshape bad attitudes toward work and strengthen healthy ones. Above all, it will help us to labor everywhere and at all times with others in God's presence, even if they are unaware.

Without such attitudes toward work there are grave dangers, which await all as they pursue their diverse vocations.

> While they their calling here pursue,
> Nor keep eternity in view,
> How many to destruction run
> By lawful things alas, undone!
>
> They make themselves, not God, their end,
> Themselves, not God, to serve intend,
> They do not seek God's will alone,
> But live to gratify their own.
>
> They *will* be rich, whate'er betide,
> And Wisdom's warning voice deride,
> Their hope, by toils that never cease,
> To riot in luxurious ease.[2]

In another poem, however, Charles Wesley has summarized the joy evoked by the attitude toward work he has outlined in "Forth in thy name":

> None on earth can conceive
> How happy we live,
> Who our labor pursue,
> And do unto the Lord whatsoever we do.[3]

---

2. MS Misc. Hymns, 278–79; *UP*, 2:292.
3. MS Misc. Hymns, 274; *UP*, 3:289.

35.

What are the marks of faith?
How can sinners know they are forgiven?[1]

How can we sinners know
    Our sins on earth forgiven?
How can my gracious Savior show
    My name inscribed in heaven?

What we have felt and seen,
    With confidence we tell,
And publish to the ends of earth
    The signs infallible.

We who in Christ believe
    That he for us hath died,
We all his unknown peace receive
    And feel his blood applied.

We by his Spirit prove
    And know the things of God,
The things which freely of his love
    He hath on us bestowed.

---

1. *HSP* 1749, 2:220–22. The original stanza 1 reads, "How can a sinner *know* / His sins on earth forgiven? / How can my Savior *show* / My name inscribed in heaven?"

SECTION 4: FAITH

> The meek and lowly heart
> That in our Savior was,
> To us that Spirit doth impart
> And signs us with his cross.
>
> Our nature's turned, our mind
> Transformed in all its powers,
> And both the witnesses are joined,
> The Spirit of God with ours.

Self-awareness is an essential aspect of meaningful living, and we spend much of our lives in fulfilling the mandate of Socrates, the ancient Greek philosopher: *know yourself.* But we often understand more about knowing others than knowing ourselves. Self-knowledge which enables true self-understanding requires a willingness to be vulnerable, to see ourselves as we really are: our liabilities, assets, gifts, and inabilities. According to the world of reality revealed in Holy Scripture, we are to see ourselves as sinners in need of forgiveness. This is vital to being fully aware of who we are.

The idea of human beings as sinners remains a stumbling block to many, who prefer to stress human goodness. Unquestionably the potential for good is personified throughout history in hosts of people. Nonetheless, human history is a testimony to the carnage of sin and the desperate need for its forgiveness. Every age witnesses the inhumanity of God's own creatures toward one another. Given the perpetual recurrence of such inhumanity and constant displays of human sin, can mortals hope for forgiveness?

Perhaps you have experienced someone's forgiveness or have personally felt what it means to say, "I forgive you." Perhaps you have known what it means to forgive and to be forgiven. When you say these words or they are said to you, when you embrace another at the moment of their utterance, you *know* and *feel* forgiveness. But an age-old question remains, and Wesley raises it again in this hymn: How can sinners *know* they have been forgiven by God?

Two key words for Wesley in the experience and understanding of sin and forgiveness are *know* and *feel.* Forgiveness is experienced intellectually—through our minds, and emotionally—through our feelings. We can *know* we are forgiven, we can *feel* we are forgiven.

> What we have *felt* and seen,
> With confidence we tell,
> And publish to the ends of earth
> The signs infallible.

WHAT ARE THE MARKS OF FAITH?

There are signs of this *knowing* and *feeling* that our sins are forgiven. The first signs are ones we bear inwardly: "we all his unknown peace receive / and *feel* his blood applied." We alone sense whether we have received inner peace. We alone know whether or not we sense in our innermost being that someone else has done for us what we could not do for ourselves, namely, emptied himself fully with his life on our behalf in order to shape us in self-emptying living and love.

We *know* and *prove* (test) this experience by the divine Spirit of Love which overcomes us, as Wesley so eloquently states in the fourth stanza.

> We by his Spirit *prove*
> And *know* the things of God,
> The things which of his love
> He hath on us bestowed.

How do others know that this has transpired in our lives? There are outward signs, marks of faith, which are also a means by which we "publish to the ends of earth" what we have *felt* and *known*. The first sign is "the meek and lowly heart." In stanza 5 Wesley avers that it is imparted to us by God's Spirit. But is this not also an inward sign? Yes, but it is more. "The meek and lowly heart" is how we are signed by the cross. It is the divine signature in our lives. Others know we are forgiven sinners and bearers of love, if we are meek and lowly in heart.

The second outward sign is: "Our nature's turned, our mind / transformed in all its powers." Others see that we no longer live by the law of sin which places self-interests above all others. We know we are forgiven when we are transformed from personifying self-service, self-esteem, avarice, envy, enmity, and hate, and become testimonies of peace and love. Then our witness becomes one with the witness of God's Spirit to all ages.

If we do not bear the signs of meek and lowly hearts, turned natures, and transformed minds, we raise serious doubts with all around us as to whether we have ever known the meaning of forgiveness.

St. Paul reminds us in his eloquent canticle of Christ's obedience:

> "Let this same mind be in you that was in Christ Jesus,
>   who, though he was in the form of God,
>   did not regard equality with God
>   as something to be exploited,
>   but emptied himself,
>   taking the form of a slave,
>   being born in human likeness.

SECTION 4: FAITH

> And being found in human form,
> > he humbled himself
> > and became obedient to the point of death—
> even death on a cross" (Philippians 2:5–8).

This is the *turned* nature, the *transformed* mind in all its powers of which Wesley speaks in this hymn. Let this mind be in you!

When you are humble, when you have taken on the form of a servant, when you have emptied yourself for others, as did Christ, you will know, and others will know, that you are forgiven.

SECTION 5

Others and the World

> It is then the best time
> to labor for our neighbor,
> when we are most cast down,
> and most unable to keep ourselves.
>
> CHARLES WESLEY

36.

Do we care about others?
Your duty let the apostle show [1]

Acts 20:35: "I have showed you all things, how that so laboring ye ought to support the weak, and to remember the words of the Lord Jesus, how he said, 'It is more blessed to give than to receive.'" (KJV)

> Your duty let the apostle show
> Ye ought, ye ought to labor so,
>   In Jesus' cause employed.
> Your calling's works at times pursue,
> And keep the tent-maker in view,
>   And use your hands for God.
>
> Work for the weak, and sick and poor,
> Raiment and food for them procure,
>   And mindful of God's Word,
> Enjoy the blessedness to give,
> Lay out your gettings, to relieve
>   The members of your Lord.
>
> Your labor which proceeds from love,
> Jesus shall graciously approve,
>   With full felicity,
> With brightest crowns your loan repay,
> And tell you in that joyful day,
>   "Ye did it unto me."

1. *UP*, 2:403–404.

SECTION 5: OTHERS AND THE WORLD

As Paul bids farewell to the elders of Ephesus, he makes clear to them that his work among them was not for personal gain: "I coveted no man's silver, or gold, or apparel. Yea, ye yourselves know that these hands ministered unto my necessities, and to them that were with me" (Acts 20:33–34, KJV). Then he reminds them that they should support the weak in their labors, remembering Jesus' words, "It is more blessed to give than to receive."

Using our hands for God is part of the Christian's calling. How often we seek other ways to work for God than manual labor! It is often easier to give our money, lip-service, or even lend our names to support some cause. Wesley says to keep Paul, the tent-maker, in mind as your example of a servant of Jesus, "and use your hands for God." It is one thing to donate funds to buy food for a soup kitchen for the needy. It is quite another to go and pour the soup into the bowls for them. Both are necessary, and neither excludes the other.

Service to others was the foundation of the Wesleys' lifestyle from their days at Oxford, when they began taking food for body and spirit to prisoners, a practice they continued throughout their lives. Whether it was founding an orphanage or beginning a school for children of poor coal miners, the Wesley brothers sought to follow the example of Christ and the apostle Paul by laboring for the unfortunate. John even founded a medical dispensary for those who could not afford proper medical care.

It is a mandate of the gospel: "Support the weak!" It is not an option for the Christian; it is a duty. When we are mindful of Jesus' words about giving, we will enjoy the blessedness which accompanies it.

In stanza 3 Wesley points out the origin and focus of our labor—it "proceeds from love." It is love which necessitates, motivates, and precipitates our work for ourselves and others. When we give of our labor to the weak, sick, and poor, we give it to Christ. When we withhold it, we withhold it from Christ. "If you are ashamed of poverty, you are ashamed of your Master,"[2] says Charles Wesley.

If we begin each day with the same feeling once expressed by Charles, laboring for others will be the natural and joyous course of each day. "Thanks be to God, the first thing I felt today was a fear of pride, and desire of love."[3]

---

2. John Telford. *Charles Wesley*, 14.
3. *MSJ*, 1:128.

37.

Do we care about God's creation?
Author of every work divine[1]

> "O Lord, how manifold are thy works!
>   in wisdom hast thou made them all:
>   the earth is full of thy riches.
> So is this great and wide sea,
>   wherein are creeping things innumerable,
>   both small and great beasts.
> There go the ships,
>   There is that Leviathan whom thou hast made
>   to play therein.
>
> "These wait all upon thee;
>   that thou mayest give them their meat in due season.
> That thou givest them, they gather:
>   thou openest thine hand,
>   they are filled with good.
> Thou hidest thy face, they are troubled;
>   thou takest away their breath, they die,
>   and return to their dust.
> Thou sendest forth thy spirit, they are created:
>   and thou renewest the face of the earth."
>
> Psalm 104:24–30 (KJV)

---

1. *WH* 1746, 31–32; stanzas 1, 4–5, of a six-stanza poem.

> Author of every work divine
> Who dost through both creations shine,
>   The God of nature and of grace!
> Thy glorious steps in all we see,
> And wisdom attribute to thee,
>   And power, and mystery, and praise.
>
> Thou dost create the earth anew,
> (Its Maker and Preserver too,)
>   By thine almighty arm sustain:
> Nature perceives thy secret force,
> And still holds on her even course,
>   And owns thy providential reign.
>
> Thou art the *universal* Soul,
> The Plastic Power that fills the whole,
>   And governs earth, air, sea, and sky:
> The creatures all thy breath receive:
> And who, by thy inspiring, live,
>   Without thy inspiration die.

Without question the earth has been sacrificed to an emphasis on human redemption, be it religious or secular. The salvation of one soul or many at all costs *and* the "reclaiming" of humankind through "civilized industrialization" have both permitted the rape of God's earth. Now nature and its creatures, including human beings, face destruction. Streams, rivers, oceans, forests, plant and animal life are threatened by "technological progress," which has brought with it a host of new human diseases that cause premature death and sickness to people daily, and numerous environmental threats to the earth and all creation. God's creation is under attack.

Wesley affirms the spirit of the Scriptures that God shines "through both creations": the world of nature and the world of humankind. God's wisdom, power, and majesty are seen in *all* creation, not just in human beings.

How often Christians hail the importance of persons becoming new creations in Christ without having a like concern for God's new creation of the earth. We are to be a part of that too!

> Nature perceives thy secret force,
> And still holds on her even course.

There is a divine wisdom in nature that perceives when leaves turn multicolored and fall, when grass turns green after the winter, when salmon spawn, when bears hibernate. On and on nature perceives the secret force. Unfortunately, human beings can thwart such natural perception and the rhythm of nature by exploiting nature's resources and creating natural and chemical imbalances which threaten all life. Wesley bids us, like nature, to own God's providential reign and secret force in the spirit of Psalm 104.

In an age utilizing plastic power to venture beyond this planet and others, we turn to Wesley's verse of over two hundred years ago and find him addressing God as "the Plastic Power that fills the whole." In a nuclear age when plastic power has been produced in almost unimaginable proportions, Wesley calls us back to the Scriptures with the words: "The creatures *all* thy breath receive."

All creation has life from God. Plants and animals receive God's *nephesh* and are alive. Some English translations have misleadingly translated this Hebrew word in Genesis 2:7 as "soul," but *nephesh* is the "life principle" which distinguishes the living from the dead. According to the Scriptures, in God's creation plants as well as animals have *nephesh*. Both have God-given life. Interestingly, nature, its plants and animals, somehow perceives the divine "secret force" in creation and submits to its cycle of renewal. Human beings, however, often devise means of exerting their own force against the secret force of God. Nature has not been created to satisfy human whims but for the sustenance and glory of God's creation. Nonetheless, through the centuries, men and women, God's creatures, have exploited nature for their own advantage, forgetting that the whole of creation is imbued with the creative Spirit of God. Furthermore, the church often has placed a premium on human redemption and hence has not heard the rest of creation groan and wail for salvation and renewal.

Veni creator spiritus, come, Creator Spirit, is a powerful plea not only for human beings but also for all of creation. Indeed, to live by the inspiration of this Spirit is life, but not at the expense of the rest of God's creation. We must live by the Spirit with a concern for God's renewal of all creation.

> "Thou sendest forth thy spirit, they are created:
> and thou renewest the face of the earth."

38.

Can there be peace on earth?
Hark! the herald-angels sing[1]

HYMN FOR CHRISTMAS-DAY

Hark! the herald-angels sing,
Glory to the new-born King.
Peace on earth, and mercy mild,
God and sinners reconciled.
Joyful, all ye nations, rise,
Join the triumph of the skies;
With th'angelic host proclaim:
"Christ is born in Bethlehem."

Christ, by highest heaven adored,
Christ the everlasting Lord,
Late in time behold him come,
Offspring of a virgin's womb.
Veiled in flesh the Godhead see!
Hail, the incarnate Deity!

---

1. *HSP*, 1739, 206–208, stanzas 1–6 of a ten-stanza hymn of four lines each. The original opening two lines read: "Hark how all the welkin rings / Glory to the King of kings." These lines were changed by George Whitefield in his volume *Hymns for Social Worship* (1753), 24, to: "Hark! The herald angels sing / Glory to the new-born King!" Whitefield introduced several other small changes throughout the hymn.

> Pleased as man with men to dwell,[2]
> Jesus, our Immanuel.
>
> Hail, the heaven-born Prince of Peace!
> Hail, the Sun of Righteousness!
> Light and life to all he brings,
> Risen with healing in his wings.
> Mild he lays his glory by,
> Born that man no more may die,
> Born to raise the sons of earth,[3]
> Born to give them second birth.

Unquestionably this hymn is one of Wesley's best known and loved throughout the English-speaking world. It is traditionally sung to a melody by the German composer Felix Mendelssohn-Bartholdy. How appropriate, since a German branch of Christianity, namely, the Moravians, had such a profound influence on the Wesleys' spiritual growth. This international connection is most fitting to a hymn which is an outcry for peace around the world and is one of Wesley's greatest legacies to people everywhere. "Hark! the herald-angels sing" is, in the truest sense, the song which he sang throughout his life and ministry.

Eighteenth-century England was a time of unrest, war, and injustice. This poem was born out of the crises, conflicts, violence, and oppression of the day and is still timely. It will never be out of date as long as there is no peace on earth.

> When nations rage with hatred and war, and innocent people are slaughtered for no cause; when humans terrorize one another in body and spirit and the clamor from the streets is but a massive cry of despair and groans of hunger; when there appears no reason for child to be born to endure the insensibility of life; when it seems that all *is* lost and there *is* no hope; *there is still a song to be sung, a song which unites the music in every soul.*[4]
>
> Hark! the herald-angels sing,
> Glory to the new-born King.
> Peace on earth, and mercy mild,
> God and sinners reconciled.

---

2. Erik Routley, *Rejoice in the Lord*, No. 196, suggests: "pleased in flesh with us to dwell."
3. Ibid., born that we no more may die,
   born to raise us from the earth.
4. S T Kimbrough, Jr., *Sweet Singer*, 25.

SECTION 5: OTHERS AND THE WORLD

Let us pray daily two lines from a stanza of this hymn often not included in hymnbooks.

> Come, Desire of nations, come,
> Fix in us thy humble home.

39.

How does love for others grow?
Love divine, all loves excelling[1]

Love divine, all loves excelling,
    Joy of heaven, to earth come down;
Fix in us thy humble dwelling,
    All thy faithful mercies crown:
Jesus, thou art all compassion,
    Pure, unbounded love thou art;
Visit us with thy salvation,
    Enter every trembling heart.

Breathe, O breathe thy loving Spirit
    Into every troubled breast,
Let us all in thee inherit,
    Let us find that second rest:
Take away our power of sinning,
    Alpha and Omega be
End of faith as its beginning,
    Set our hearts at liberty.

Come, almighty to deliver,
    Let us all thy life receive;
Suddenly return, and never,
    Never more thy temples leave:

1. *RH* 1747, 11–12.

SECTION 5: OTHERS AND THE WORLD

> Thee we would be always blessing,
>   Serve thee as thy hosts above,
> Pray, and praise thee, without ceasing,
>   Glory in thy perfect love.
>
> Finish then thy new creation,
>   Pure and sinless let us be;
> Let us see thy great salvation,
>   Perfectly restored in thee;
> Changed from glory into glory,
>   Till in heaven we take our place,
> Till we cast our crowns before thee,
>   Lost in wonder, love, and praise.

Shortly before they married (February 1749), Charles Wesley wrote to his bride-to-be, Sally Gwynne:

> You have heard me acknowledge that at first sight 'My soul seemed pleased to take acquaintance with thee'. And never have I found such a nearness to any fellow-creature as to you. O that it may bring us nearer and nearer to God, till we are both swallowed up in the immensity of His love![2]

Above all else, Wesley wanted to be "swallowed up" in God's love, for all loves begin, end, and are fulfilled in that love. With this confidence he wrote one of the most meaningful and eloquent prayers for a love-filled life ever written, "Love divine, all loves excelling."

If we wish to grow in love, this prayer-hymn should be our daily guide. It directs us how to pray and grow in God's love. Acknowledge God as the source of unbounded, limitless love (stanza 1). Pray to be the dwelling-place of God's love; pray also for the indwelling of Christ.

Pray in the plural, not just in the singular (stanza 2). Pray that the Holy Spirit will enter the lives of *others* also, so that every troubled breast will be set at liberty. Through the power of the Holy Spirit we can be freed from the desire to do what is wrong and can be set free to love. Charles prays, "Take away our power of sinning," realizing appropriately that sin has power in our lives.

Pray for the reception of God's grace (stanza 3) which enables us to live the self-giving love expressed in Jesus Christ. When we receive God's grace, we recognize that God does for us what we cannot do for ourselves.

---

2. Baker, *Charles Wesley As Revealed by His Letters*, 55.

God reclaims our sinful lives and makes them new through Christ. When we live renewed lives, we begin to learn what it means to mature in love. Love takes priority over everything in our lives. There is no compromise.

Pray to be created new (stanza 4) and to continue in the creative process toward maturity in love. Wesley understood that to finish the new creation means lifelong spiritual growth. The ongoing process is defined by the world *till,* which designates the time between what has been and what will be, between *no longer* and *not yet.* He anticipates the time when we shall meet God in glory and be matured, new creatures in God's perfect love. We do not have to wait, however, for a "heavenly reward" to mature in love. In Christ we are new creations now. The great salvation perfectly restored in heaven is the fulfillment of the salvation we receive on earth.

For followers of Christ who want to grow in love, the continuing creative process within us is vitally important. There is no one who does not need to grow in love. If we use the guidelines of this hymn for our prayer life, we will live lives that are "lost in wonder, love, and praise."

40.

Do we give unbelievers a chance?
Can we in unbelievers find[1]

Acts 17:11–12: "These Jews were more receptive than those in Thessalonica, for they welcomed the message very eagerly and examined the scriptures every day to see whether these things were so. Many of them therefore believed, including not a few Greek women and men of high standing."

> Can we in unbelievers find
> That noble readiness of mind
> To hear, investigate, and prove
> The truth of Jesu's pardoning love?
> Yes, Lord; through thy preventing grace,
> There are who cordially embrace
> The joyful news of sin forgiven,
> With God himself sent down from heaven.

How readily the world often is divided into "believers" and "unbelievers." And it is easy for believers to view themselves as much better off than those who have not yet believed. The above verses from the Book of Acts remind us that unbelievers have a nobility all their own which may prepare them to receive God's word with an open mind. Wesley affirms the divine purpose which embraces unbelievers. We find an example of this in the Old Testament, when the prophet Isaiah calls the Median King Cyrus a *messiah*.

1   SH 1762, 2:272–73; stanza 1 of a four-stanza poem.

Cyrus was neither one of the Israelites nor a follower of their God. He decreed that the Israelites in Babylonian exile could return to their homeland, and Isaiah viewed him as "anointed," a *messiah*, the same title used for Jesus.

The believing community can build bridges to those who do not believe by fostering a spirit of free inquiry affirmed by the Scriptures. There are no exclusive rights to God's word. Our attitudes, however, may in fact exclude others from the gospel. The Scriptures plead: Keep an open mind toward everyone.

Wesley continues in stanza 3 of the same poem:

> What then are they that dare forbid
> The unconvinced thy Book to read,
> Who take the sacred key away,
> Damp their desire to search and pray,
> Conceal thy records from their view;
> "The Scriptures were not wrote for you:
> Accept your more unerring guide,
> The Church, the Catholics—the Bride!"

Will another believe because believers are open-minded?

41.

Is the church really for everyone?
O for a thousand tongues to sing[1]

ON THE ANNIVERSARY-DAY OF ONE'S CONVERSION

O for a thousand tongues to sing
  My great Redeemer's praise!
The glories of my God and King,
  The triumphs of his grace.

My gracious Master and my God,
  Assist me to proclaim,
To spread through all the earth abroad
  The honors of thy name.

Jesus! the name that charms our fears,
  That bids our sorrows cease;
'Tis music in the sinner's ears,
  'Tis life, and health, and peace.

He breaks the power of canceled sin,
  He sets the prisoner free:
His blood can make the foulest clean;
  His blood availed for me.

1. *HSP*, 1740, 121–22; stanzas 7–12 of an eighteen-stanza hymn."

> He speaks, and listening to his voice,
> > New life the dead receive,
> > The mournful, broken hearts rejoice,
> > The humble poor believe.
>
> Hear him, ye deaf, his praise, ye dumb,
> > Your loosened tongues employ,
> > Ye blind, behold your Savior come,
> > And leap, ye lame, for joy.

The inspiration for this hymn is believed to have come from the words of the Moravian Christian Peter Böhler, whom Wesley taught English in London. Böhler is reported to have said to Charles that if he had a thousand tongues, he would use them all to praise God. Charles had heard Christian worship in other tongues. He remembered throughout his life the inspirational German hymns sung by the Moravians on board the ship *Simmonds* on the voyage to America. He had read the fathers of the church in Latin and the New Testament in Greek. He and his brother John even learned to converse in Latin. In addition, Charles also practiced French by copying portions of Fénelon's writings and by exchanging communiqués with his friend John Fletcher, who had been born in the French-speaking part of Switzerland. Charles knew there are many tongues with which to praise God, and it is not surprising that the impetus for this great hymn, which was written for the anniversary-day of his conversion, should come from someone whose mother tongue was other than English, namely German, and who was extremely influential in his own quest for authentic faith.

The hymn originally had eighteen stanzas, although most hymnbooks usually include only those quoted here, which are original stanzas seven through twelve. The first six tell of a powerful life-transforming experience. For example, stanza five:

> I felt my Lord's atoning blood
> > Close to my soul applied;
> > *Me, me* he loved, the Son of God
> > For *me*, for *me* He died!

The familiar stanzas quoted above are a universal appeal to praise God. Original stanzas 15 and 16 of this text are often omitted from most hymnbooks, but are extremely important since they link praise with mission and remind us of the inclusiveness of the gospel:

> Harlots, and publicans, and thieves
>   In holy triumph join!
> Saved is the sinner that believes
>   From crimes as great as mine.
>
> Murderers, and all ye hellish crew,
>   Ye sons of lust and pride,
> Believe the Savior died for you,
>   For me the Savior died.

How many churches consciously seek out prostitutes, thieves, criminals of all sorts, murderers, and hell-raisers? Yes, Jesus sought them.

How many churches seek to make the following affirmation a reality?

> Hear him, ye deaf, his praise, ye dumb
>   Your loosened tongues employ,
> Ye blind, behold your Savior come,
>   And leap, ye lame, for joy.

How many churches make their worship experiences accessible to the deaf, blind, and lame? Are sign language, hearing aids, braille, ramps, lifts, wheelchairs, and vehicles with hydraulic lifts available to those in need? Are there classes for persons with learning disabilities? If not, the church is saying to persons with such needs, "You are not welcome to participate in our worship and church programs." Wesley's metaphors of impairment emphasize inclusive ministry, and they point to a deeper reality; when our tongues are not loosed to praise God and we do not acknowledge that the Savior has come, we are impaired.

"O for a thousand tongues to sing" stresses not only the need for a global outcry of praise to God, but calls the church and individual Christians to fulfill their mission: praise God *and* reach out to all.

42.

Can people be united?
No, they cry, it cannot be![1]

Jeremiah 32:39: "I will give them one heart and one way, that they may fear me for all time."

> No, they cry, it cannot be!
> Christians never will agree.
> All the world thy word deny;
> Yet we on the truth rely.
> Sure, in that appointed day,
> Thou wilt give us all one way.
> Show us each to other joined,
> One in heart, and one in mind.
>
> Hasten then the general peace,
> Bid thy people's discord cease;
> All united in thy Name,
> Let us think and speak the same.
> Then the world shall know and own
> The Divine hath made us one;
> Thee their Lord with us embrace,
> Sing thine everlasting praise.

1. *SH* 1762, 2:33–34.

SECTION 5: OTHERS AND THE WORLD

The promise of one unified heart and a singular path of life was not fulfilled for God's people in Jeremiah's time, nor during Wesley's eighteenth-century England. We still await realization in our day. God, who does not flag in faithfulness to the divine covenants and promises made throughout the Scriptures, is ever ready to fulfill this ancient promise to Jeremiah. It remains unfulfilled, because Christians themselves seem to have decided that they never will agree. This is a blatant repudiation of God's word, and a signal to the world that Christians deny its validity by their fragmented community.

Wesley knew what it meant to experience such fragmentation firsthand. On one occasion he was refused Holy Communion at Temple Church and recorded the incident in his *Journal*.

> The clerk came to me and said, "Mr Beacher bids you go away, for he will not give you the sacrament." I went to the vestry door and mildly desired Mr Beacher to admit me. He asked, "Are you of this parish?" I answered, "Sir, you *see* I am a clergyman." Dropping his first pretence, he charged me with rebellion in expounding the Scriptures without authority, and said in express words, "I repel you from the Sacrament." I replied, "I cite you to answer this before Jesus Christ at the day of judgment." This enraged him above measure. He called out, "*Here, take away this man!*" ... but I saved them the trouble ... and quietly retired.[2]

> Hasten then the general peace,
> Bid thy people's discord cease.

The lines of this couplet are not pious platitudes of a clergyman comfortably entrenched in denominationalism yet somehow compelled to speak of things beyond realization in this world. No! They are the agonizing outcry of Wesley's soul, for he knew that only if Christians *personify* oneness and unity will others know God has united them. Such unity will bring them to God. In other words, the unity of Christians is *ongoing* evangelism.

---

2. *MSJ*, 1:275.

43.

What shall be our covenant with God?
Come, let us use the grace divine[1]

Jeremiah 50:4–5: "In those days, and in that time, saith the Lord, the children of Israel shall come, they and the children of Judah together, going and weeping: they shall go, and seek the Lord their God. They shall ask the way to Zion with their faces thitherward, saying, Come, and let us join ourselves to the Lord in a perpetual covenant that shall not be forgotten." (KJV)

> Come, let us use the grace divine,
>   And all with one accord,
> In a perpetual covenant join
>   Ourselves to Christ the Lord;
> Give up ourselves, thro' Jesus' power,
>   His name to glorify;
> And promise, in this sacred hour,
>   For God to live and die.
>
> The covenant we this moment make
>   Be ever kept in mind;
> We will no more our God forsake,
>   Or cast his words behind.
> We never will throw off his fear
>   Who hears our solemn vow;
> And if thou art well pleased to hear,
>   Come down, and meet us now!

1. *SH* 1762, 2:36–37.

SECTION 5: OTHERS AND THE WORLD

> Thee, Father, Son, and Holy Ghost,
> Let all our hearts receive,
> Present with thy celestial host
> The peaceful answer give;
> To each the covenant-blood apply
> Which takes our sins away,
> And register our names on high
> And keep us to that day!

This hymn of Charles Wesley is sometimes called "The Covenant Hymn" and has traditionally been a part of the Covenant Service which John Wesley appropriated from other sources and initiated for use in the Methodist societies, usually on the first Sunday of January every year.

The hymn is based on Jeremiah 50:5 and comes from Charles Wesley's lyrical Bible commentary, *SH* 1762, written throughout in a poetical format. The biblical background is important for the understanding of Wesley's verse. The people of Israel were in exile and longed to return to Palestine, to Zion. The Jeremiah text says that the children of Israel and the children of Judah shall come together, weep, seek the Lord, ask the way to Zion, and join in a perpetual covenant with God. This is a power-filled statement!

At the death of King Solomon in 922 B.C.E. Israel and Judah were formed as two separate kingdoms—one in the north (Israel) and one in the south (Judah) with their own rulers. They often were hostile and violent opponents until Israel fell in 722 B.C.E. to Assyria, and Judah fell in 596 B.C.E. to the Neo-Babylonian empire. The majority of both populations was then forced into exile.

The passage upon which Charles Wesley reflects for this hymn recalls the anticipation of the return of God's people to Palestine. The picture painted in the words of the prophet is a powerful one—the broken, exiled people of God, who had divided themselves against one another, long to come together, weeping, seeking the Lord, asking the way to Zion, and joining themselves to God in an unbreakable, perpetual covenant.

Like the ancient Near East of Jeremiah's day, eighteenth-century England was also filled with division, strife, and thousands of people who had been forced into the exile of poverty, dispossession, and ignorance. To them, to everyone, Wesley extends the ancient prophetic call to unite, seek the Lord, and make a perpetual covenant with God that shall never be forgotten.

Wesley opens the hymn in stanza 1 with a summons to the covenant:

WHAT SHALL BE OUR COVENANT WITH GOD?

> Come, let us use the grace divine
> And all with one accord.

This is a summons to active participation in the covenant, not passive reception of it. The preface to covenant-making is unity—all are to come *with one accord*. The alienated, estranged, and exiled now are to come together as one people to make a covenant with God, which Wesley then translates to a New Testament context. Of what does the covenant consist?

(1) total commitment to Jesus Christ:

> Give up ourselves through Jesus' power
> His name to glorify;

(2) a promise or vow:

> For God to live and die.

There follows in stanza 2 the declaration of the covenant, which asserts:

(1) we will not forget the covenant; it will be ever kept in mind;

(2) we will not forsake God again;

(3) we will not cease to fear (in the sense of worshiping in awe) God;

(4) we will be open to God's presence:

> Come down and meet us now.

Wesley concludes the hymn with a doxological praise of the Holy Trinity and a final plea that the covenant-blood, the effectual sacrifice of Christ for all humankind, become the life force of every person, namely, self-emptying, caring love.

The singing or reading of this hymn should not be reserved only for the first Sunday of every year, but rather it is worthy of our daily recollection and voicing! Thus, our covenant with God will "Be ever kept in mind"!

44.

Can there be unity among God's people?
All praise to our redeeming Lord[1]

Ephesians 4:4–5: "There is one body and one Spirit, just as you were called to the one hope of your calling, one Lord, one faith, one baptism, one God and Father of all, who is above all and through all and in all."

AT MEETING OF FRIENDS

All praise to our redeeming Lord,
  Who joins us by his grace,
Who bids us, each to each restored,
  Together seek his face.

He bids us build each other up;
  And, gathered into one,
To our high calling's glorious hope
  We hand in hand go on.

The gift which he on one bestows,
  We all delight to prove,
The grace through every vessel flows
  In purest streams of love.

1. *RH* 1747, No. 32, 43.

> E'en now we think and speak the same,
>   And cordially agree,
> Concentered all, through Jesus' name,
>   In perfect harmony.
>
> We all partake the joy of one;
>   The common peace we feel,
> A peace to sensual minds unknown,
>   A joy unspeakable.
>
> And if our fellowship below
>   In Jesus be so sweet,
> What height of rapture shall we know
>   When round his throne we meet!

The title of the hymn, "At the Meeting of Friends," was often used by Charles Wesley. His *Journal* and letters reveal his awareness of the divisions within the body of Christ, the Church: the Church of Rome, England, Luther, Zinzendorf, dissenting groups, etc. God's people have a long history of dissension, and the Scriptures are filled throughout with pleas from prophet, priest, and rabbi for peace among the people.

The psalmist's plea, "Pray for the peace of Jerusalem" (Ps. 122:6), can but be uttered perpetually for the community of faith. It has no peace! But Charles's hymn expresses the Scripture's hope for peace and harmony among God's people by describing the path to unity in the first four lines. Firstly, common praise to God is the beginning of unity. Secondly, God joins us by grace, which is God's love expressed in Jesus Christ. Thirdly, we are corporately summoned by the Almighty to seek God's face. The psalmist reminds us that we are to seek God's face continually, that is, God's presence in our lives (Psalm 105:8; see also 2 Chronicles 6:11). We are to seek God's face together, as the people of God, "each to each restored." The unity to which we are called is a process of restoration.

What is our "high calling's glorious hope" of which Charles speaks? It is the same which Paul addresses in Ephesians 4:4-5, "There is one body, and one Spirit, even as ye are called in one hope of your calling; One Lord, one faith, one baptism" (KJV). There is one God of all. Our "high calling's glorious hope" is that in Christ we become one and can "hand in hand go on." This is why we are called to "build each other up."

In stanza 3 Wesley turns to the word central to Christian unity: grace. He has already stated in stanza 1 that it is the grace of God which enables

SECTION 5: OTHERS AND THE WORLD

unity. Now he turns to the idea of grace as a gift to every individual, as emphasized by Paul in Ephesians 4:7, "But unto every one of us is given grace according to the measure of the gift of Christ" (KJV). The evidence of God's grace in the world, in the body of Christ, is love. Everyone becomes a vessel through which streams of love flow, that is, God's reconciling, restoring, healing love. Where there is disunity, people often refuse to be vessels of God's grace-filled love in the world.

Stanza 4 is a call to be the fulfillment of Paul's plea to the church at Corinth: "Now I beseech you . . . by the name of our Lord Jesus Christ, that ye all speak the same thing, and that there be no divisions among you; but that ye be perfectly joined together in the same mind and in the same judgment" (1 Corinthians 1:10, KJV). What can it mean for Christians to be united in "perfect harmony"? Perhaps Wesley assists us with the word *concentered*, which means "directed to a common center." The unity of Christians exists in the common center, namely, Christ. Only as they think and speak this common name can they "cordially agree." Wesley bids the diverse communities of the global church of Christ to see themselves as a series of concentric circles, all of which have the same center, Jesus Christ. Only this self-understanding of the church leads to "perfect harmony" of the whole.

In stanza 5 Wesley introduces another word vital to unity: *peace*. It is a word common to the Old and New Testaments. The psalmist pleads: "Depart from evil, and do good; seek peace, and pursue it" (Ps. 34:14). The angels announce Jesus' birth proclaiming a message of "peace on earth and good will." Paul adjures the church of Corinth "be of one mind, live in peace" (2 Corinthians 13:11, KJV) and reminds the church of all ages that "he [Christ] is our peace" (Ephesians 2:14). The message of Holy Scripture from beginning to end is that we are to live at peace among ourselves.

In stanza 5 of this hymn we find the Wesleyan imprimatur, when Charles says, "the common peace we feel." It is not merely that in Christ we have peace, that we are given peace, but that "we *feel*" the common peace, that is, peace becomes a part of our experience, not merely something we think about and to which we give intellectual assent. We make peace a reality, we become peacemakers, we make peace, we experience it, we feel it! It is not a matter of knowing what peace is, for it is unknown to sensual minds, says Charles, but rather it is a matter of personifying peace in all our senses, all our being.

Finally, Wesley resounds that the peace we feel among ourselves is the sweetest fellowship we can know on earth and, if that unity be so sweet, we cannot imagine what unity with our Lord and the saints in heaven shall be like.

45.

Can all be one?
Blest be the dear uniting love[1]

1 Corinthians 2:2: "For I decided to know nothing among you except Jesus Christ, and him crucified."

AT PARTING

Blest be the dear uniting love
   That will not let us part;
Our bodies may far off remove,
   We still are one in heart.

Joined in one spirit to our Head,
   Where he appoints we go,
And still in Jesus' footsteps tread,
   And do his work below.

O may we ever walk in him,
   And nothing know beside,
Nothing desire, nothing esteem,
   But Jesus crucified!

---

1. *HSP* 1742, 159–60, based on 1 Corinthians 2:2.

> We all are one who him receive,
>   And each with each agree,
> In him the One, the Truth, we live;
>   Blest point of unity!
>
> Partakers of the Savior's grace,
>   The same in mind and heart,
> Nor joy, nor grief, nor time, nor place,
>   Nor life, nor death can part.

Charles Wesley understood divisiveness well. He began his ministry in a radically divided world—a world of "haves" and "have nots." It was precisely in the breech of this division that he began his pastoral office. His first priestly assignment was in the American Colony of Georgia, which was reeling with divisions: colonial officials trying to bridle the ways of prisoners freed from horrid, English debtor prisons sent to colonize the New World; there were the English versus the Spanish; there were whites against African slaves and Native Americans; and there were the local bickerings and divisions which riddled the little Georgia colony with constant strife. Even Governor Oglethorpe, whom Charles Wesley officially served as secretary, became divided against the young clergyman for a time, when he unjustly believed a false and malicious report that Wesley had seduced one of the women in the colony.

Charles Wesley's return to England thrust him into a world radically divided between the wealthy and the poor. At the beginning of the Wesley brothers' ministry there was essentially no middle class in England. John and Charles stood in this chasm between wealth and poverty and proclaimed the gospel of Christ, a message of oneness and wholeness. They declared from Scripture that in God's world all are one. Yet Charles knew what it was like to preach in the marketplace or on a street corner and be confronted by a divisive mob calling him: Papist, Jesuit, Presbyterian, Methodist, dissenter, traitor. These labels were used in derision for one who did not fit neatly into all aspects of the established Church of England, which Charles so faithfully supported. Like St. Paul, he knew what it was like to be attacked by a vicious mob and run out of town.

Against this background of experience, it is not surprising that the brilliant poet-priest of eighteenth-century England became the author of great songs of unity, songs one should sing "At Parting," the original title of the above hymn, to call the community to remember and to practice unity.

SECTION 5: OTHERS AND THE WORLD

In the first stanza of "Blest be the dear uniting love" he declared that there is a unity which transcends physical presence.

> Our bodies may far off remove,
> We still are one in heart.

What a welcome message to the uneducated, destitute masses of England, who were denied education, health care, justice, and English culture. A worker in the blast furnaces of Newcastle might never journey to London during his lifetime, yet he heard a heartening message in Wesley's hymns that he can be united with brothers and sisters in that city and elsewhere, yes, anywhere, through the most powerful uniting force on earth—love, God's love revealed in Christ. All become one people in him.

Stanza 2 of the hymn envisions a very practical unity for daily life. It points one in the right direction. It sets one on a daily path. One is to go Jesus' way and to do his work: loving, healing, caring, mending.

Stanza 3 points to the pattern for one's whole life—cruciform. How does one live each day? It is a unified pattern for all, the pattern of the cross: a constant self-emptying of oneself for God and others. This common vocation unites all who follow it.

Stanza 4 is the Christian manifesto of unity: "We all are one who him receive." This is the reality which does not have to be achieved, even by diverse churches, if they simply live the reality: oneness is received in Christ.

When Wesley says "each with each agree," he is referring to our common assent that Christ is "the way, the truth, and the life." But note how he turns the phrase: "in him the One ["way" implied], the Truth, we live." It is in Christ's life that we live. We live the Christ-life. Here, says Charles Wesley, is where and when we discover "the blest point of unity." We cannot receive Christ into our lives and propagate divisiveness.

Wesley concludes the hymn reminding all that it is God's grace which is the mortar of unity. It is by and through God's grace that we become one with each other. This is what "the Savior's grace" does—it transcends human barriers and solidifies human relationships through self-giving, self-emptying love. Nothing can divide those who are so joined.

46.

Who will sound the alarm of freedom?
Blow ye the trumpet, blow [1]

Leviticus 25:9–10a: "Then you shall have the trumpet sounded loud; on the tenth day of the seventh month—on the day of atonement—you shall have the trumpet sounded throughout all your land. And you shall hallow the fiftieth year and you shall proclaim liberty throughout the land to all its inhabitants."

THE YEAR OF JUBILEE

Blow ye the trumpet, blow!
   The gladly solemn sound.
Let all the nations know,
   To earth's remotest bound;
The year of jubilee is come!
Return, ye ransomed sinners, home.

Jesus, our great high Priest,
   Hath full atonement made;
Ye weary spirits, rest;
   Ye mournful souls, be glad:
The year of jubilee is come!
Return, ye ransomed sinners, home.

1. *HNYD* 1749 [1750], 6–7.

SECTION 5: OTHERS AND THE WORLD

> Extol the Lamb of God,
>   The all-atoning Lamb,
> Redemption in his blood
>   Throughout the world proclaim:
> The year of jubilee is come!
> Return, ye ransomed sinners, home.
>
> Ye slaves of sin and hell,
>   Your liberty receive,
> and safe in Jesus dwell,
>   And blest in Jesus live:
> The year of jubilee is come!
> Return, ye ransomed sinners, home.
>
> Ye who have sold for nought
>   Your heritage above
> Shall have it back unbought,
>   The gift of Jesus' love:
> The year of jubilee is come!
> Return, ye ransomed sinners, home.
>
> The gospel trumpet hear,
>   The news of heavenly grace;
> And saved from earth, appear
>   Before your Savior's face:
> The year of jubilee is come!
> Return to your eternal home.

This great hymn of liberation, published originally with the title "The Year of Jubilee," was written not only against the background of Scripture, as was Charles Wesley's custom, but that of human experience as well. Here he lifts the message of economic liberation of the Leviticus passage, which celebrates the jubilee year when the land and people are to be freed from exploitation, to new spiritual heights in the spirit of Isaiah 61:1–2a: "The spirit of the Lord is upon me, because the Lord has anointed me; and has sent me to bring good news to the oppressed, to bind up the broken-hearted, to proclaim liberty to the captives, and release to the prisoners; to proclaim the year of the Lord's favor."

In this hymn Wesley declares that with the advent of Christ every year is a jubilee year! One must not wait until the fiftieth year to stop the exploitation of the land and to free those who are enslaved. Every year is a jubilee year, every day is a day of atonement. Now is the year of the Lord's favor. Now is the time of good news to the oppressed, to bind up the brokenhearted, to proclaim liberty and release to prisoners.

Wesley understood well the message of liberation and freedom from Leviticus and Isaiah out of his experiences in the American colonies. Before his departure for England from Charleston (South Carolina) in 1736, Charles Wesley recorded his personal encounter with the horrors of American slavery, a portion of which reads as follows:

> It were endless to recount all the shocking instances of diabolical cruelty which these men (as they call themselves) daily practice upon their fellow-creatures, and that on the most trivial occasions. I shall only mention one more, related to me by a Swiss gentleman, Mr Zouberbuhler, an eyewitness, of Mr Hill, a dancing-master in Charles-town. He whipped a she-slave so long, that she fell down at his feet for dead. When by the help of a physician, she was so far recovered as to show signs of life, he repeated the whipping with equal rigor, and concluded with dropping hot sealing wax upon her flesh. Her crime was overfilling a tea-cup.[2]

As a vehement opponent of slavery, Charles Wesley carried the plight of all enslaved peoples in his heart and in this hymn wrote an international anthem for liberation. It is not surprising that the record of an occasion at Bethel Church in Philadelphia on July 31, 1838, celebrating the freeing of slaves in the British West Indies, should feature Wesley's hymn.

> Pursuant to previous notice, a very large and respectable assemblage of colored citizens, convened at Bethel Church, on Tuesday evening, July 31st, at half past 11 o'clock.
>
> At a quarter before 12, one of the committee of arrangements announced the near approach of the joyful hour that would usher in the glorious morn that should burst the fetters off the hands of 500,000 oppressed people of the British West Indies. A breathless silence prevailed throughout the assembly for the space of fifteen minutes.
>
> At precisely 12 o'clock the choir, joined by the whole congregation, struck up the jubilee hymn—

---

2. *MSJ*, 1:47.

> Blow ye the trumpet, blow!
> The gladly solemn sound.
> Let all the nations know,
> To earth's remotest bound:
> The year of jubilee is come, &c.[3]

Wesley summons all to sound the alarm, blow the trumpet, and let the whole earth resound with the message of freedom. "Let all the nations know" that the year of jubilee is come. Notice the language he uses, that oppressed peoples readily understand: weary spirits, mournful souls, slaves, liberty, safe, sold, ransomed. But what jubilee is Wesley celebrating? Why should "weary spirits, rest," "mournful souls, be glad," "slaves of sin and hell" receive liberty, "ransomed sinners" return home, and people dwell "safe in Jesus"? The answer is found in the fourth line of stanza five: "the gift of Jesus' love." His gift of love transforms every year into a jubilee celebration of freedom from sin and oppression. This is the jubilee Wesley celebrates in this hymn.

No matter how lives have been violated and exploited, Jesus' love heals the violation and exploitation. His self-emptying, self-giving love makes free, and gives us back our heritage. Where people receive the gift of Jesus' love as the power and pattern for living, all injustice falls, all prisoners and slaves are freed.

All have not yet been freed, however, and therefore those who have received the gift of Jesus' love continue to sing the hymn, to sound the alarm of freedom—to make "The gladly solemn sound," to blow the trumpet, that peoples everywhere "The gospel trumpet hear, / The news of heavenly grace"!

---

3. *The Coloured American*. Saturday, August 25, 1838.

47.

What does a faith community do when it gathers?

And are we yet alive?[1]

Philippians 3:8-9: "More than that, I regard everything as loss because of the surpassing value of knowing Christ Jesus my Lord. For his sake I have suffered the loss of all things, and I regard them as rubbish, in order that I may gain Christ and be found in him, not having a righteousness of my own that comes from the law, but one that comes through faith in Christ, the righteousness from God based on faith."

AT MEETING OF FRIENDS

And are we yet alive,
   And see each other's face?
Glory and thanks to Jesus give
   For his almighty grace!

Preserved by power divine
   To full salvation here,
Again in Jesus' praise we join,
   And in his sight appear.

1. *HSP* 1749, 2:321-22.

SECTION 5: OTHERS AND THE WORLD

> What troubles have we seen,
>   What mighty conflicts past,
> Fightings without, and fears within,
>   Since we assembled last!
>
> Yet out of all the Lord
>   Hath brought us by his love;
> And still he doth his help afford,
>   And hides our life above.
>
> Then let us make our boast
>   Of his redeeming power,
> Which saves us to the uttermost,
>   Till we can sin no more.
>
> Let us take up the cross
>   Till we the crown obtain,
> And gladly reckon all things loss
>   So we may Jesus gain.

Wesley's original intention for the text is clear, for it is the third in a series of eight hymns in his *HSP* 1749 titled "At Meeting of Friends." The first act of followers of Jesus when they gather, when they "see each other's face," is to join in an act of praise to God. Charles opens this act with the corporate question "And are we yet alive?"

The hymn was published near the end of the 1740s, an extremely tumultuous time for the Wesleys, their followers, and the evangelical revival within the Church of England. During these years from many quarters there was mounting opposition to the Wesleys and the Methodist movement. Many Church of England clergy openly refused the Werleys and the Methodist Societies the use of their parish properties and encouraged the people to resist them. Some officials of the Church of England also opposed them. Charles was even brought before a bishop and accused of treason for having preached "the return of the banished," which some construed as support for the return of the banished Pretender to the English throne. Of course, Charles had preached on the theme of return of the banished to God. The charge of treason was dropped.

It was a miracle that the Wesleys were not killed as a result of the mob violence they often confronted. They were run out of towns and stoned, and houses in which they preached were sometimes razed to the ground by angry mobs. In addition, much of the countryside was not safe; there were few adequate roads; and the Wesleys knew what it meant to be accosted and robbed by highwaymen, as they rode the length and breadth of England on horseback.

Against this background of turmoil and conflict, the people of the early Methodist movement in England knew when they met each other that they had been "preserved by power divine." It was God who had saved them; God had sustained them. Though now they saw each other's face, they rejoiced first and foremost to appear in Jesus' sight and to join in his praise.

It is understandable why groups of Christians across two-and-a-half centuries since the Wesleys have rejoiced to sing this hymn at the beginning of annual meetings or on other occasions. One joins voices with the early Methodists and hosts of others, who, in the midst of conflict, division, strife, persecution, and oppression within and without the church, have sung and still sing words that apply to any period of the church's history:

> What troubles have we seen,
>   what mighty conflicts past,
> fightings without, and fears within,
>   since we assembled last.

The song Charles Wesley ever sings, the song of love, resounds here once again. It is the central theme throughout his life and hymns.

> Yet out of all the Lord
>   hath brought us by his love;
> And still he doth his help afford,
>   and hides our life above.

No matter how difficult the circumstances of life, God's love, as it is expressed in Jesus Christ, sustains. This love is the most powerful force known to Charles Wesley. Its power is constant! At no point in the hymn does Charles answer his opening question with a simple "yes" or "no," but rather the succeeding stanzas are themselves a resounding: "Yes!" We are indeed alive! The "we" is of course the community of faith, the church. Wesley paints a picture in this hymn of how such a community is to respond to the reality that it is alive and to the God who gives life.

Taken as a whole this hymn asks—What does a faith community do when it gathers? Wesley delineates a series of imperatives for the assembled church in all ages. They may be expressed in diverse forms of worship, but still they remain imperatives for a responsible worshiping community:

1. it gathers in full recognition of the bond of mutual friendship;
2. it raises the question of the vital signs of the community;
3. it sings praise to God;
4. it openly acknowledges its conflicts within and without;
5. it confesses God's love as the sole source of sustenance;
6. it commits itself to a cruciform life.

Wesley emphasizes the commitment to a cruciform life, the way of the cross, in stanzas 4 and 5. Here he describes the spiritual posture of the church: humility and self-sacrifice. "Let us take up the cross," says Wesley. In other words, let us take up Christ's way of self-giving, self-emptying love—a self-effacing way of life. Hence, the gathered community of faith does not boast of its own power, but rather in the redeeming power of God. It recognizes that it is not yet perfect and that it must pray continually that it be saved "to the uttermost / Till we can sin no more."

The concluding original eight lines of the hymn, which are not included here, stress the ongoing pilgrimage toward perfection. The hymn ends with this prayer to God:

> Apply the hallowing word,
> Tell each who looks for thee,
> "Thou shalt be perfect as thy Lord,
> Thou shalt be all like me."

48.

Are these really united as one: slaves, free, males, females, parties, sects?

Christ from whom all blessings flow[1]

John 17:20–21: "I ask not only on behalf of these, but also on behalf of those who will believe in me through their word, that they may all be one."

THE COMMUNION OF SAINTS

Christ, from whom all blessings flow,
Perfecting the saints below,
Hear us, who thy nature share,
Who thy mystic body are.

Join us, in one spirit join,
Let us still receive of thine;
Still for more on thee we call,
Thou who fillest all in all.

Move and actuate and guide,
Diverse gifts to each divide;

---

1. *HSP* 1740, 194–95.

SECTION 5: OTHERS AND THE WORLD

> Placed according to thy will,
> Let us all our work fulfill;
>
> Never from thy service move,
> Needful to each other prove;
> Use the grace on each bestowed,
> Tempered by the art of God.
>
> Many are we now, and one,
> We who Jesus have put on;
> There is neither bond nor free,
> Male nor female, Lord, in thee.
>
> Love, like death, hath all destroyed,
> Rendered all distinctions void;
> Names and sects and parties fall;
> Thou, O Christ, art all in all!

These are selected stanzas from part four of Wesley's extended and moving prayer for Christian unity entitled "The Communion of Saints," which was published in 1740, at a time in which disunity reigned in English society and greatly affected the Church of England and the nascent Methodist movement. The opening stanza of part one sets the tone for the entire prayer-poem.

> Father, Son, and Spirit, hear
> Faith's effectual, fervent prayer,
> Hear, and our petitions seal;
> *Let us now the answer feel.*
>
> Mystically one with thee,
> Transcript of the Trinity,
> Thee let all our nature own
> One in three, and three in one.[2]

Wesley did not pray abstract prayers which were to have no practical response among the people. He genuinely desired that Christ's prayer for unity in John 17:20–21, the Scripture Wesley placed at the heading of sections three and four of the prayer, would become a reality which people feel: "that they may all be one." Unity is not just something to talk and pray about but to feel.

---

2. *HSP* 1740, 188.

In this prayer Wesley teaches us how to pray for unity. (1) *Begin with the unity of God.* God is the source of wholeness and unity, and God's people are to mirror divine unity. In his prayer, "that all may be one," Christ explains, "The glory that you have given me I have given them, so that they may be one, as we are one, I in them and you in me, that they may become completely one, so that the world may know that you have sent me and have loved them even as you have loved me" (John 17:22–23).

(2) *Seek unity of spirit.* Humankind is marvelously diverse: culturally, ethnically, linguistically. Societies are radically different in sociological, political, and economic perspectives. Integrity before God as God's creatures, one and all, means that our differences are strengths to be cherished, and therefore, it is often only in spirit that we may seek and find unity. Wesley clearly understands this to be not merely a uniting of spirits, however.

> Join us, in one spirit join,
> Let us still receive of thine
> Still for more on thee we call,
> Thee, who fillest all in all.

The unity of our spirits comes in union with God's Spirit.

(3) *Transcend passivity and be a response to your own prayer.* Wesley prays for the active overcoming of the inertia often created by disunity, which does nothing to bring people together. He prays in the spirit of Paul's first letter to the Corinthians that "diverse gifts" will be divided among the people. And as God moves, actuates, and guides them, they will be motivated to fulfill God's work wherever they are. In other words, those who pray prayers for unity must be willing to be an answer to their own prayers.

(4) *Seek unity in the needs of others.* The Christian's vocation is one of service to others, and the pattern for practicing this vocation is found in being an instrument of God's grace, "tempered by the art of God." So often the church has sought unity in creeds, doctrines, structures, and organization, but this is not what it means to be tempered by God's art. What is the art of God? Is this an aesthetic, ethical, or pragmatic expression? Wesley's brilliant turn-of-the-phrase is multi-faceted and as mystical as our union with Christ and the church. But one thing can be said about the "art of God," as it is revealed through Scripture—it is always *grace-filled.* Whatever one's own art or lifestyle in relating to others, in painting the pictures of human experience, in creating the songs of healing and love—if it is marked and imbued with grace, it will be "tempered by the art of God."

SECTION 5: OTHERS AND THE WORLD

(5) *Acknowledge and live this reality:* in Christ all are one. Those who think they can "put on" Jesus and be divided, suffer under an illusion. *The grace-filled, self-emptying love of Jesus unites.* Through Christ's life, love, and experience, we see all persons and peoples as equals. The distinctions which human beings make between those who are free or enslaved, those who are female or male, no longer matter. God's love in Christ shatters all human distinctions:

> Love, like death, hath all destroyed,
> Rendered all distinctions void;
> Names, and sects, and parties fall;
> Thou, O Christ, art all in all!

49.

Why celebrate yet another feast?
Come, and let us sweetly join[1]

THE LOVE-FEAST

Come, and let us sweetly join,
Christ to praise in hymns divine;
Give we all with one accord
Glory to our common Lord.

Hands and hearts and voices raise,
Sing as in the ancient days;
Antedate the joys above,
Celebrate the feast of love.

Jesus, dear expected Guest,
Thou art bidden to the feast;
For thyself our hearts prepare;
Come, and sit, and banquet there.

Sanctify us, Lord, and bless,
Breathe thy Spirit, give thy peace;
Thou thyself within us move,
Make our feast a feast of love.

---

1. *HSP* 1740, 181–82.

SECTION 5: OTHERS AND THE WORLD

This hymn is composed of selected stanzas of an extended poem bearing the title "The Love-Feast." This communal gathering has its roots in the New Testament *agape* meal. The Love Feast was a popular practice among Moravians and was taken over by the Wesleys. It was usually an extended evening gathering of the faithful with the sharing of bread or plain cake and water, testimonies, prayer, and singing.

The stanzas here selected form a twofold invitation to the feast: (1) to the community of faith, and (2) to Christ. The invitation to the community is a summons to join in hymns of praise. From the Moravians the Wesleys had learned much about the power of music to unite people. Certainly, all could join voices to praise God's glory, for God is the God of all, "our common Lord."

The hymn opens in the spirit of Colossians 3:16, "Let the word of Christ dwell in you richly in all wisdom; teaching and admonishing one another in psalms and hymns and spiritual songs, singing with grace in your hearts to the Lord" (KJV), or "singing and making melody in your heart to the Lord" (Ephesians 5:19b, KJV).

The invitation is by no means to passive involvement, but rather to active engagement. Wesley beckons all to raise "hands and hearts and voices." The external and internal are intended here, in other words the whole person becomes involved. Some cultural and ethnic groups find it much easier to raise their voices than their hands. Others are very free to move their hands and bodies in praise of their Creator. One should not miss the point Wesley is making, however; this Love Feast is a feast of jubilation and celebration for it is a foretaste of the "joys above." If one truly feasts on love, the entire created being, the whole person, wants to be a part of the celebration. But Wesley knows that not all are prepared for such an occasion of joy. Therefore, the invitation to Christ is an imperative, for hearts must be made ready.

The invitation to Christ to be a Guest at the feast distinguishes it clearly from Holy Communion where Christ is the host. At the Love Feast he is invited to come and as a companion at the table prepare the hearts of all to share in the meal.

The invitation to Christ is also a prayer to Christ, the Love-Feast prayer. It is the prayer for an evangelical meal where Good News and the symbols of bread and water, symbols of the common sustenance of all humankind, form within us singleness of heart in the bond of love, Christ's love, that gives and gives and gives again. The invitation is a multi-faceted

WHY CELEBRATE YET ANOTHER FEAST?

plea for—sanctification, the indwelling of the Holy Spirit, the gift of peace, and a feast of love. These are precisely the characteristic emphases of the Love Feast.

The Wesleys took most seriously the scriptural admonition, "For I am the Lord your God: sanctify yourselves therefore, and be holy, for I am holy" (Leviticus 11:44). This is our lifelong quest, the pilgrimage of holiness. Hence Wesley prays the prayer we must pray daily, "Sanctify us, Lord!"

In the Love-Feast prayer we implore Christ to "breathe thy Spirit, give thy peace." But has he not already breathed the Spirit and given his peace? John 20:21–22, "Then said Jesus to them again, Peace be unto you: as my Father hath sent me, even so send I you. And when he had said this, he breathed on them, and saith unto them, Receive ye the Holy Ghost" (KJV). Yet the world in which we live seems to accentuate the absence of the Spirit, rather than the Spirit's presence. Did Christ breathe the Spirit on the disciples in vain? No, but the gift of the Spirit must be received anew in every age. He gave his peace, but there is no peace in the world! Was the imparting of his peace for nothing? If we are not the instruments of peace, our answer to that question is, Yes!

The Love Feast is precisely what its name describes—a feast of love! It is intended to bring people together in a common voice:

> Give we all with one accord
> Glory to our common Lord.

Two stanzas not included in many hymnals remind us why we come together again and again to feast on God's love.

> Sing we then in Jesus' name,
> Now, as yesterday the same,
> One in every age and place,
> Full for all of truth and grace.
>
> We for Christ our Master stand
> Lights in a benighted land;
> We our dying Lord confess,
> We are Jesus' witnesses.

The imperative of a continuing Love Feast is made a reality by the failure of the church, yes, those who follow Christ, to be "one in every age and place." Let us pray that our experience will be that of Charles Wesley recorded on

SECTION 5: OTHERS AND THE WORLD

June 26, 1748, in Bristol, "In the word, and Sacrament, and Love-feast, the Lord made our souls as a watered garden."[2]

---

2. *MSJ*, 2:530.

50.

How shall I cope with the death of a faithful friend?

If death my friend and me divide[1]

1 Thessalonians 4:13: "But we do not want you to be uninformed, brothers and sisters, about those who have died, so that you may not grieve as others do who have no hope."

> If death my friend and me divide,
> Thou dost not, Lord, my sorrow chide,
>   Or frown my tears to see;
> Restrained from passionate excess,
> Thou bidst me mourn in calm distress
>   For them that rest in thee.
>
> I feel a strong immortal hope,
> Which bears my mournful spirit up
>   Beneath its mountain load;
> Redeemed from death, and grief, and pain,
> I soon shall find my friend again
>   Within the arms of God.
>
> Pass a few fleeting moments more
> And death the blessing shall restore

1. *SH* 1762, 2:234–35.

SECTION 5: OTHERS AND THE WORLD

> Which death has snatched away;
> For me thou wilt the summons send,
> And give me back my parted friend
> In that eternal day.

The images of death and grief in the eighteenth century, which were a part of the experience of the Wesleys, are not so different from those in our time—a parent grieving over the death of a child from a dreadful disease, a wife stricken with sorrow over a son or husband fallen in war, ragged street children huddled around a small fire in the dead of winter while hunger wrenches their stomachs in pain, an elderly couple dies from malnutrition, a little child screams in terror beside the dead bodies of its mother and father slain in war. On and on the images go.

How shall we cope with the death of others, our own friends, and loved ones? The apostle Paul reminds the church at Thessalonica in the passage to which Charles Wesley referred in writing this hymn, that they do not mourn death as though they had no hope.

Christians have a posture or an attitude of hope regarding death. We do not mourn the death of our friends "that rest in thee" as hopeless. Our hope transcends the emptiness we often feel at the absence of such friends precipitated by death. Mourn though we may at such loss, as followers of Christ we are not overcome with a "passionate excess" of grief.

How is it that those who trust in God to sustain them in life and death learn to "mourn in calm distress"? Wesley offers a response to this question in stanza 2.

> I feel a strong immortal hope,
> Which bears my mournful spirit up
> Beneath its mountain load;
> Redeemed from death, and grief, and pain,
> I soon shall find my friend again
> Within the arms of God.

Those who trust in God have an "immortal hope." God does not promise, however, that those who follow Christ will have no grief, nor that the burden of grief will be removed when one loses a faithful friend. But God does promise hope and that our burdens will be lightened, when we know we have been redeemed by God from "death, and grief, and pain." As Paul says in chapter 4 of 1 Thessalonians, on which Wesley reflects in this hymn, "For if we believe that Jesus died and rose again, even so them also which sleep in Jesus will God bring with him" (4:14, KJV).

HOW SHALL I COPE WITH THE DEATH OF A FAITHFUL FRIEND?

Life is so short; it passes swiftly. Nevertheless, death for the Christian is a time of restored blessing, for the emptiness which overcomes us at the departure of a faithful friend, whom "death snatched away," is restored to a sense of fullness, wholeness, and union with God at death.

> Pass a few fleeting moments more
> And death the blessing shall restore
>   Which death has snatched away;
> For me thou wilt the summons send,
> And give me back my parted friend
>   In that eternal day.

Death is an ever-present reality. It is experienced in horror and in beauty. It was no stranger to the Wesleys. Death struck seven of John's and Charles's brothers and sisters at very early ages. It claimed five of the eight children of Charles and Sarah Wesley within the first year of infancy. They met the stench of death in the hovels of workhouses of large cities and felt its nearness in the cells of condemned prisoners.

We know, as did the Wesleys, that the summons to death comes to all, but faith in Christ changes completely how we greet the summons. When we trust in God, the Father, Son, and Holy Spirit, the triune God, we do not grieve as those who have no hope. We experience the emotional and spiritual undergirding of hope in this life and in life beyond death. We are strengthened by learning to "mourn in calm distress." Thanks be to God for life that cannot be diminished by death, but rather is made full by it.

51.

What is the true nature of the church?
Jesus, united by thy grace[1]

A PRAYER FOR PERSONS JOINED IN FELLOWSHIP

Jesus, united by thy grace
  And each to each endeared,
With confidence we seek thy face
  And know our prayer is heard.

Help us to help each other, Lord,
  Each other's cross to bear;
Let each his friendly aid afford,
  And feel each other's care.

Up unto thee, our living Head,
  Let us in all things grow;
Till thou hast made us free indeed
  And spotless here below.

Touched by the lodestone of thy love,
  Let all our hearts agree,
And ever toward each other move,
  And ever move toward thee.

---

1. *HSP* 1742, 83–87.

WHAT IS THE TRUE NATURE OF THE CHURCH?

> To thee, inseparably joined,
>   Let all our spirits cleave;
> O may we all the loving mind
>   That was in thee receive.
>
> This is the bond of perfectness,
>   Thy spotless charity;
> O let us, still we pray, possess
>   The mind that was in thee.

This hymn consists of a selection of stanzas from a lengthy hymn by Charles Wesley that is divided into four parts. The first stanza begins with the first line "Try us, O God, and search the ground," which appears in some hymnbooks. The original title given by Wesley to the original hymn is "A Prayer for Persons Joined in Fellowship." He addresses intentionally here the question of Christian unity. The selection of stanzas found here provides a clear and strong statement about Christian social responsibility and the unequivocal commitment to unity there must be among Christians.

These ideas are properly prefaced with the first line "Jesus, united by thy grace." With all that Christians may do in working for unity, they are united by God's grace. It is only when they realize that they have been loved by God, even when their lives seem to have demonstrated how undeserving they are of such love, that they can be endeared to one another. When individual Christians or groups of Christians seek God's face or presence with confidence that they are right and everyone else is wrong, disunity within the Christian community is usually the result. There is no grace at work in such action, for grace embraces the unloved who very often are those who do not share the same views and lifestyle as those who think that they have a "divine right" to God's love. *Grace* is the foundation of unity. Only as Christians seek to emulate God's grace among themselves and others can they hope to fulfill God's purpose and be united.

One might refer to stanza 2 as the *social manifesto* of the Wesleyan movement, for this plea of Wesley yearns for the community of believers who exist to help others. They bear each other's burdens and as friends they provide whatever assistance they can. In so doing they learn to feel each other's care. This means that the needs of others become a part of the believers' sensory and emotional life. They draw each other and each other's needs into their experience. There is perhaps no better description of the Wesleyan emphasis on social holiness than these four lines.

SECTION 5: OTHERS AND THE WORLD

Stanza 3, however, moves directly to growth in personal holiness, thus uniting the personal and social emphases of this Christian pilgrimage. As our lives are united with others in the experience of living, we grow into the likeness of our Maker and Redeemer. In this process we become "free indeed / And spotless here below." Growth toward spiritual maturity and purity inevitably bonds personal and social experience with others and God.

Stanza 4 is vital to the molding of Christian community in unity. If grace is the foundation of Christian unity, most certainly love stabilizes and holds the community together. Note, however, that Wesley does not pray that those who have been "Touched by the lodestone of thy love" will agree in *all things*, but rather he pleads "Let all our *hearts* agree." If we know and sense to the core of our being that God's love shapes our lives, we will know that to move toward God means to move toward each other and vice versa. Stanza 5 punctuates this two-way relationship to God and others by yearning for the inseparable unity with God which leads toward receiving "the loving mind" of God, that was revealed in Jesus Christ. The loving mind seeks unity with God and others.

If the church would discover its true nature, if Christians, who so often are more divided than united, would discover the true nature of being the body of Christ, the church, that for which Wesley prays in this hymn must become a reality. The Holy Scriptures are filled from Genesis to the Revelation of John with stories of the fragmentation of the community of God's people and tireless efforts to mend the brokenness and alienation within and without. Church councils, divisions in east and west, and contemporary conciliar movements reveal the need to pray Wesley's prayer and for it to become a reality.

> This is the bond of perfectness,
> Thy spotless charity;
> O let us, still we pray, possess
> The mind that was in thee.

The mind of God does not seek disunity, but rather a loving, caring, humble bond which bears the burdens of all and celebrates the joys of creation. Paul pleads for the church in all ages to seek this mind: "Let this mind be in you, which was also in Christ Jesus" (Philippians 2:5, KJV). Those who have this mind humble themselves and take on forms of servants. It is this loving mind which leads to unity.

52.

What is the path to peace, not war?
Our earth we now lament to see [1]

    Our earth we now lament to see
        With floods of wickedness o'erflowed,
    With violence, wrong, and cruelty,
        One wide-extended field of blood,
    Where men, like fiends, each other tear,
    In all the hellish rage of war.

    As listed on Abaddon's side,
        They mangle their own flesh, and slay;
    Tophet is moved, and opens wide
        Its mouth for its enormous prey;
    And myriads sink beneath the grave,
    And plunge into the flaming wave.

    O might the universal Friend
        This havoc of his creatures see!
    Bid our unnatural discord end,
        Declare us reconciled in thee!
    Write kindness on our inward parts
    And chase the murderer from our hearts!

---

1. *HIM* 1758, No. 2, 4.

SECTION 5: OTHERS AND THE WORLD

> Who now against each other rise,
> > The nations of the earth constrain
> To follow after peace, and prize
> > The blessings of thy righteous reign,
> The joys of unity to prove,
> The paradise of perfect love!

Charles Wesley is not widely known as the author of anti-war hymns. Indeed, his lengthy poem on the American Revolution occasionally leaves the impression that his Tory-oriented perspectives and support of the King of England and his homeland might well have affirmed, if not encouraged, an English victory over the colonies. Nonetheless, as this hymn so poignantly states, the earth, God's creation, can but lament to see the battlefield where enemies tear each other apart "in all the hellish rage of war." The earth is "overflowed" with violence, wrong, and cruelty. How graphic is Wesley's image: the earth is but "one wide-extended field of blood."

The descriptions of the horrors of war and violence in stanzas 1 and 2 are as up-to-date in the twenty-first century as they were in Wesley's day, for wars continue to rage. Television reports constantly show how humans "mangle their own flesh and slay," and "myriads sink beneath the grave" every day and "plunge into the flaming wave."

Wesley knew the horrors of war, for his century was filled with it. He experienced firsthand the Spanish, French, and English vying for land in the New World, and he saw the Native Americans routed from their lands by Europeans. He knew what it was like to live in a Europe threatened by war and strife. He remembered well the French threats to invade England during his own lifetime. Wesley was not writing from an abstract and theoretical viewpoint, but rather from the context of the world of reality.

Stanzas 3 and 4 form a powerful prayer for peace. Stanza 3 is an appeal to our creatureliness—that as God's creatures we recognize what havoc we make of creation. The path toward peace outlined in Wesley's prayer involves important realizations and transformations for followers of Christ. (1) Human discord is not a natural part of creation. It is *unnatural* and should end. (2) Reconciliation is God's way with us and, hence, our way with others.

> Declare us reconciled in thee!

(3) Make kindness an inner anchor of everyone's being.

> Write kindness on our inward parts.

WHAT IS THE PATH TO PEACE, NOT WAR?

(4) Drive out of individuals all enmity and the desire to destroy others:

> and chase the murderer from our hearts!

Replacing discord and enmity with reconciliation and kindness, says Wesley, is essential to the accomplishment of peace. This is precisely what the "universal Friend," Jesus Christ, enables. When his love reigns within, wars cease!

Finally, Wesley avers in stanza 4 that nations which oppose each other but would "follow after peace," will discover that if they turn from protecting their own destiny at the expense of others and prize the reign of God's righteousness, which is the reign of just love, they will discover the "joys of unity," and the "paradise of perfect love!"

Would that such a path to peace were the hallmark of contemporary world diplomacy!

SECTION 6

Ourselves

Oh, what am I if left to myself?
But I can do and suffer
all things
through Christ strengthening me.

CHARLES WESLEY

53.

How do we overcome trials and persecution?

Ye servants of God, your Master proclaim[1]

HYMNS TO BE SUNG IN A TUMULT

Ye servants of God, your Master proclaim,
    And publish abroad his wonderful name;
The name all-victorious of Jesus extol;
    His kingdom is glorious and rules over all.

The waves of the sea have lift up their voice,
    Sore-troubled that we in Jesus rejoice;
The floods they are roaring, but Jesus is here,
    While we are adoring, he always is near.

Men, devils engage, the billows arise,
    And horribly rage, and threaten the skies:
Their fury shall never our steadfastness shock,
    The weakest believer is built on a Rock.

---

1. *HTTP* 1744, 43.

SECTION 6: OURSELVES

God ruleth on high, almighty to save;
    And still he is nigh, his presence we have;
The great congregation his triumph shall sing,
    Ascribing salvation to Jesus our King.

"Salvation to God who sits on the throne!"
    Let all cry aloud and honor the Son!
Our Jesus's praises the angels proclaim,
    Fall down on their faces, and worship the Lamb.

Then let us adore, and give him his right:
    All glory and praise, all wisdom and might,
All honor and blessing, with angels above,
    And thanks never ceasing, and infinite love.

Since stanzas 2 and 3 of this hymn are omitted in most hymnbooks, the life situation out of which the hymn was born is easily overlooked. Charles knew the agony of severe persecution and the necessity of standing firm in the faith against all opposition.

The 1740s were extremely difficult times, filled with suspicion of those averred to be disloyal to the Crown and to favor the Pretender to the throne of England. Many seized the opportunity to oppose the followers of the Wesleys, who were slandered and violently attacked by unruly mobs on numerous occasions. Charles himself was labeled a rogue, rascal, villain, pickpocket, and even the representative of the Pretender to the throne, whom some thought to be his brother John disguised as a priest. Although the Wesleys persistently maintained their loyalty to the monarchy, opposition to them mounted. It is miraculous that they were not killed by the raging mobs. At Walsal, John was dragged by the hair from the steps of the cross down the main street, and Charles was attacked while preaching from the market steps.

"Ye servants of God" is a Christian pledge of allegiance to God for the faithful who serve One who is greater than all kings. God rules above all, and there are no Pretenders with any claims whatsoever to the throne upon which the Author of salvation sits.

Any struggle for an earthly crown involves conflicts over who shall have the right, glory, power, wisdom, might, honor, and blessing ascribed to a monarch's throne. Wesley ascribes all these to God, and his hymn leaves no doubt that although he may have been loyal to the English monarch, his ultimate allegiance was to God. The following account of an event at Sheffield on May 25, 1743, from his *Journal* reveals this allegiance.

> At six went to the Society house, next door to our brother Bennet's. Hell from beneath was moved to oppose us. As soon as I was in the desk with David Taylor, the floods began to lift up their voice. An officer (Ensign Garden) contradicted and blasphemed. I took no notice of him, and sang on. The stones flew thick hitting the desk and people. To save them and the house I gave notice I should preach out[side], and look the enemy in the face.
>
> The whole army of aliens followed me. The Captain laid hold on me and began reviling. I gave him for answer *A Word in Season, or, Advice to a Soldier*, then prayed, particularly for His Majesty King George, and preached the gospel with much contention. The stones often struck me in the face. After the sermon, I prayed for sinners as servants of their master, the devil, upon which Captain ran at me with great fury, threatening revenge for my abusing, as he called it, "The king his master." He forced his way through the brethren, drew his sword, and presented it to my breast. My breast was immediately steeled. I threw it open, and fixing mine eye on his, smiled in his face, and calmly said, "I fear God and honor the king." His countenance fell in a moment, he fetched a deep sigh, put up his sword, and quietly left the place.[2]

We live in an age filled with tensions, and followers of Jesus are called upon anew to stand firm in their faith as champions of "infinite love." Amid political, economic, and social injustices, Christians around the world are beckoned to turn the cries of agony and hatred into resounding praises of God and love for one another. The love of God in Jesus is so transforming that it can change discriminatory laws, rectify the exploitation of the poor by the rich, provide shelter for the homeless, and supply food for the hungry. And on it goes. Injustices fall before God's love!

"Ye servants of God" is an eighteenth-century cry of the soul against oppression and persecution, not unlike the twentieth-century civil-rights outcry against injustice in the song "We Shall Overcome." It is through faith that we have the power to overcome through God's justice for all people. Charles Wesley illustrated this not only with his pen but also with his life. God is ever calling the servants of Jesus to personify justice for all.

---

2. *MSJ*, 2:344–45.

54.

What are we really like?
Gentle Jesus, meek and mild[1]

HYMNS FOR CHILDREN

Gentle Jesus, meek and mild,
Look upon a little child,
Pity my simplicity,
Suffer me to come to thee.

Fain I would be as thou art;
Give me thy obedient heart;
Thou art pitiful and kind;
Let me have thy loving mind.

Let me above all fulfill
God my heavenly Father's will;
Never his good Spirit grieve,
Only to his glory live.

Loving Jesus, gentle Lamb,
In thy gracious hands I am;
Make me, Savior, what thou art;
Live thyself within my heart.

---

1. *HSP* 1742, 194–95; stanzas 1, 2, 11, 13, 14 of a fourteen-stanza hymn.

WHAT ARE WE REALLY LIKE?

> I shall then show forth thy praise,
> Serve thee all my happy days;
> Then the world shall always see
> Christ, the holy child, in me.

All of us have been children. Perhaps there are times when we long to return to our childhood, that is, to recapture those aspects of being a child which affirm life at its best and as God intended it to be. Charles Wesley once said, "Be a little child yourself and a child will be led by you into all that is right."[2] He and his wife Sally had eight children, but only three of them survived the plagues and illnesses of infancy and childhood: Charles, Jr., Sally, and Samuel. Therefore, the inner yearnings expressed in the above poem grew not only out of his own experience as a child, but also out of those of his children with all of the accompanying anguish of suffering and death. How could one long to be a child when one had lived on the brink of poverty and seen his own children suffer and die from illnesses not yet controlled in the eighteenth century, e.g. diphtheria, mumps, measles.

Being a child means maintaining our simplicity (stanza 1). Children have an ability to cut through the complexities of life in what they say and do. They often express and demonstrate insight free of logic and reasoning. As we sat at the breakfast table one morning with our four sons, the three youngest ages three, four, and six had spread marmalade on their faces, the table, the floor, and a little on the toast. Suddenly a piece of toast was also tossed across the table. My wife said quite sternly: "People do not eat like that!" to which the four-year-old replied: "Mommy, we're not people, we're children." His mother had seen in him the person he was to become, but he had seen himself as he was—a child. With those simple words of our son I realized as never before the importance of accepting people as they are and not as we want them to be.

Being a child means maintaining an obedient heart and a loving mind (stanza 2). Parents and guardians of children expect children to obey them, and they establish rules of behavior. Our relationship to God is like that. God is the Creator Parent with expectations of behavior for us, the children of creation. The order of creation has its own regulations we are expected to observe and honor. However, we do not observe God's order for the sake of rules. The obedient heart and the loving mind go together. We keep rules and regulations not for the sake of merely keeping them. We obey them out of love for God and others, and for the world God has created.

2. Telford, *Charles Wesley*, 44.

The loving mind of children gives them an ability to forgive, forget, and accept others as they are. According to the Scriptures, these are godlike qualities—ones which adults too often leave behind in their childhood.

Being a child means maintaining the desire to fulfill God's will (stanza 3). Children do not always find it easy to do what their parents desire. As children, however, they usually want to fulfill the will of their parents, because their parents have the authority to expect the same. As we grow to adulthood, God's expectation of our fulfillment of divine will does not diminish. But we often allow our wills to take precedence over God's will. For example, God wills life, peace, and love for all people, yet we live in a world of hate, prejudice, unrest, and war. As children of creation, we are to fulfill the desires of the Parent of parents, God the Creator.

Being a child means maintaining Christ in our hearts, God's praise on our lips, and service to God in all we do (stanzas 4 and 5). Being a Christian means being childlike. Perhaps we can learn more about being Christians and living the faith from children than we have ever imagined. This may have motivated Charles Wesley to write in his *Journal* these words: "I was glad to hear of one of our English brethren, lately brought back by a little child—who told his father something . . . and disturbed him, so that he could not sleep at nights, since they left off family-prayer."[3]

We cannot return to our childhood, but we can be a child in spirit throughout our lives. We can pray daily the following:

> God, I want to be a child always. Give me an obedient heart, a loving mind, and the desire to do what you want me to do for me, others, and the world you made. Live in my heart and make me what Jesus is—love—that I may serve you every day I live.
> In the name of your Holy Child. Amen.

---

3. *MSJ*, 2:388.

55.

What is our outlook on life?
Rejoice, the Lord is King![1]

Rejoice, the Lord is King!
    Your Lord and King adore;
Mortals, give thanks, and sing,
    And triumph evermore.
Lift up your heart, lift up your voice;
Rejoice! Again I say: Rejoice!

Jesus the Savior reigns,
    The God of truth and love;
When he had purged our stains,
    He took his seat above:

His kingdom cannot fail,
    He rules o'er earth and heaven,
The keys of death and hell
    Are to our Jesus given:

He sits at God's right hand
    Till all his foes submit,
And bow to his command,
    And fall before his feet:

---

1. *HLR* 1746, 12–13. The same refrain in italics is sung after stanzas 1–4. For stanza 5 Wesley wrote a different refrain.

SECTION 6: OURSELVES

> Rejoice in glorious hope;
>   Jesus the Judge shall come
> And take his servants up
>   To their eternal home:
> *We soon shall hear the archangel's voice:*
> *The trump of God shall sound: Rejoice!*

As an airport-bus, transporting passengers from one terminal to another, made its rounds, one passenger, who boarded at the first stop and was riding to the last, noticed something interesting taking place. Almost all who boarded were unpleasant and complaining about their trip, airline services, delays, etc. With every announcement of the next terminal, the bus driver prefaced the name of the stop by saying, "Hello, folks! This is your happy bus driver telling you how fortunate you are to be able to travel and to get on and off this bus. The next stop is . . . . " At the last stop there was not an unpleasant person on the bus. The driver had changed everyone's discontentment into joy. Happiness breeds happiness.

The hallmark of Christian behavior is joy. Christian life is the explanation of joy. "Rejoice! Again I say: Rejoice!" The first four stanzas of Wesley's hymn resound with the refrain:

> *Lift up your heart, lift up your voice:*
> *Rejoice! Again I say: Rejoice!*

The first and last word of the hymn is "Rejoice!" Do not be low-spirited, brokenhearted, downtrodden, or a complainer throughout life! Be joyous! Joy breeds joy!

Wesley summarizes the reasons why Christians should rejoice. The Lord is King. The Bible often speaks of God as King, the One who reigns over creation. Psalm 24:8 asks:

> Who is the King of glory?
>   The Lord, strong and mighty,
>   the Lord, mighty in battle.

The Revelation to John (11:15) declares, "The kingdom of the world has become the kingdom of our Lord and of his Messiah, and he will reign forever and ever." The Christian understands that God—not earthly rulers—is at the helm of existence.

"Jesus the Savior reigns." Jesus' rule is not one of deception and hatred but one of truth and love. As we look at world diplomacy and the secret intelligence agencies of nations worldwide, we see clearly that governments and their leaders have not yet fully grasped the reign of One who puts all relationships on the basis of truth and love. That is, however, the world's hope.

"His kingdom cannot fail." History often is written by reviewing the rise and fall of great empires such as those of Egypt, Greece, and Rome. While earthly kingdoms rise and fall, God's kingdom of earth and heaven endures, for it is built upon truth and love. Jesus has shown us in his death and resurrection that even death is turned into triumph and victory in God's realm.

"Jesus the Judge shall come." There is life and hope which are larger than earthly existence. God's creative process does not end with physical death but works out its purpose in earth and heaven; those who serve God will not have served in vain. Their destiny will be judged by the truth and love of Jesus which endures forever.

Christians have cause to rejoice indeed! When they are despondent and despairing: Rejoice! When others about them are unpleasant and depressed: Rejoice! Rejoicing breeds rejoicing! Today give someone's heart a change of mood. Rejoice!

56.

How do we deal with sickness?
And live I yet by power divine?[1]

AFTER A RECOVERY FROM SICKNESS

And live I yet by power divine?
    And have I still my course to run?
Again brought back in its decline
    The shadow of my parting sun?

Wond'ring I ask, is this the breast
    Struggling so late and torn with pain!
The eyes that upward looked for rest,
    And dropped their weary lids again!

My feeble flesh refused to bear
    Its strong redoubled agonies:
When mercy heard my speechless prayer,
    And saw me faintly gasp for ease.

The fever turned its backward course,
    Arrested by Almighty power;
Sudden expired its fiery force,
    And anguish gnawed my side no more.

---

1. *HSP* 1739, 82–84; stanzas 1–2, 5, 7–8, 11, 17 of a seventeen-stanza poem.

HOW DO WE DEAL WITH SICKNESS?

> God of my life, what just return
>   Can sinful dust and ashes give?
> I only live my sin to mourn,
>   To love my God I only live.
>
> Be all my added life employed
>   Thy image in my soul to see:
> Fill with thyself the mighty void;
>   Enlarge my heart to compass thee!
>
> Prepare and then possess my heart,
>   O take me, seize me from above;
> Thee do I love, for God thou art;
>   Thee do I feel, for God is love.

Charles Wesley did not always enjoy good health. More than once he recovered from what might have been a fatal illness. Any of us who have faced grave sickness and pain, who have been brought back from what seemed certain death, know what it means to ask ourselves: "And have I still my course to run?" Is everything not at an end? Do I really have a new lease on life? Yet Wesley prefaces the question with another: "And live I yet by power divine?"

Recovery brings with it a sense of wonder and awe that one's fevered, weak body has been restored to health and wholeness. When we have endured tremendous pain and longed for it to cease, we know its subsiding is mercy and grace in action. One of my sons lay in a hospital bed for weeks at the threshold of death. On one occasion, when his pain and bodily condition were gravest, he said to me, "I look forward to the time when I can look back on all this and say, I made it." About a year later after his amazing recovery from the hospitalization and loss of a leg, he said, "Dad, you know, I am a walking miracle!" Hold fast to the sense of wonder during and after recovery and live by the power divine!

Recovery brings with it a sense that we have a debt to pay for being spared. Although we are accustomed to incurring medical debts during illnesses, our only debt to God upon recovery is love.

> God of my life, what just return
>   Can sinful dust and ashes give?
> I only live my sin to mourn,
>   To love my God I only live.

SECTION 6: OURSELVES

Recovery often brings with it lengthened life and the choice of what we shall do with it. Wesley says the choice which governs all others is the decision to be filled with God's love. There is one type of enlarged heart which is healthy, the one enlarged to encompass God: "Enlarge my heart to compass thee." There is one type of seizure which is healthy, the seizure of love:

> Prepare and then possess my heart,
> O take me, seize me from above;
> Thee do I love, for God thou art;
> Thee do I feel, for God is love.

Recovery brings with it the renewed opportunity to love God and to be the embodiment of love. That is what it means to live by power divine.

57.

Are we bigots?
Forgive my partial selfishness[1]

Genesis 20:11: "Abraham said, 'I did it because I thought, There is no fear of God at all in this place, and they will kill me because of my wife.'"

> Forgive my partial selfishness,
>   My rash, censorious thought,
> "Among this people, in this place,
>   Surely the Lord is not!
> If strangers to my sect and name,
>   Strangers they are to thee:
> God is not feared, except by them
>   Who know and honor me."

The words of Genesis 20:11 are Abraham's explanation to King Abimlelech as to why he had deceived the king in saying that his wife, Sarah, was his sister. Trusting Abraham's word, Abimelech had taken Sarah to himself. How wrong and bigoted Abraham was! God *was* in that place and appeared to Abimlelech in a dream and revealed the truth about Sarah. The next morning the king was obedient to God's command and returned her to her husband Abraham.

---

1. *SH* 1762, 1:23.

The apostle Paul was aware of similar bigotry in the early church when he wrote to the Christians at Corinth and reproached them for their divisions into followers of Paul, Apollos, Cephas, and Christ (1 Corinthians 1:12). They had become certain that God was to be found only by following their specific leader.

The fragmented nature of global Christianity with its multiple and ever-growing denominations and sects reminds us that we and our ancestors in the faith are guilty of selfishness and rash, censorious thought.

The Church of the Holy Sepulcher in Jerusalem, a symbol of Christianity for centuries, at times has reflected more bigotry and hate than unity and love. It is jointly owned by a number of churches (Greek Orthodox, Roman Catholic, Armenian Apostolic, and a few more) whose relationships have not always been harmonious. Centuries ago the in-fighting among the churches in charge of separate holy places within deteriorated to such a point that a new solution was devised whereby two Muslim families would hold the key to open and close the door of the church each day. Both Omar (637) and Saladin (1187) stressed this tradition, which continues in the twenty-first century. Is this a historical parable that emphasizes that no one, no group, no place has a monopoly on faith or God? It does stress how easy it is to fall prey to the opinion that one is right and others are wrong.

The Scriptures warn that God is in the place we least suspect, and Wesley has provided us with the appropriate prayer of forgiveness for individuals and for the church. Would that it were prayed at the beginning of all denominational meetings. It is a prayer worthy of memorization and constant repetition in private and in public. In spite of its sarcasm, it can help us to be forgiving Christians even as we have been forgiven in and through Christ.

58.

Are we saints?

Though all the precious promises[1]

Job 9:20: "If I justify myself, mine own mouth shall condemn me: if I say, I am perfect, it shall also prove me perverse." (KJV)

> Though all the precious promises
> I had fulfilled in Jesus' love,
> If perfect I myself profess,
> My own profession I disprove.
> The purest saint that lives below
> Doth his own sanctity disclaim;
> The wisest owns, I nothing know,
> The holiest cries, I nothing am!

Perfection is the impossible ideal for which we untiringly strive in many areas of life. Those who claim to attain it affirm their imperfection through the claim itself. Athletes may pursue perfection in their respective sports; musicians in their singing, playing, or composing; writers and speakers in their mastery of language; scientists and academicians in their excellence and accomplishments in specific arenas of research and experimentation. Nevertheless, there is yet a higher quest for perfection which gives all these other pursuits deeper and fuller meaning—the quest of perfection in love. This is the love personified in Jesus, which gives of self for others and pours

---

1. *SH* 1762, 1:228.

out tenderness, understanding, healing, concern, friendship, reconciliation, and justice. It pursues and embraces all people regardless of intellectual, social, or economic status.

Sometimes people are designated as "saintly" by the church as well as by individuals. When someone says of another, "He or she is a saint," we know it is not because such a person has claimed sainthood but rather has disclaimed it.

Truly great musicians know that there is no such thing as a "perfect performance" of a musical work, because there will always be many varied and valid interpretations by diverse performers. Hence the claim, "That was a perfect performance!" is an illusion.

The hymn "I Sing a Song of the Saints of God" declares:

> For the saints of God are just folk like me,
> And I mean to be one too.[2]

This means that all of us should mold our lives as saints, but not in the sense of thinking we can *attain* perfection. We must, however, *pursue* perfection as faithful servants of Jesus who wish to be perfect in love. Two of the great virtues of a saint are *purity* and *wisdom*. Wesley affirms biblical truth in this short poem by making clear that we are purest when we disclaim being pure, and wisest when we disclaim being wise. This is the path to perfection.

---

2. *The Hymnal 1982*, Hymn 293.

59.

Are we ablaze with love?
See how great a flame aspires[1]

AFTER PREACHING TO THE NEWCASTLE COLLIERS

> See how great a flame aspires,
>   Kindled by a spark of grace!
> Jesus' love the nations fires,
>   Sets the kingdoms on a blaze.
> To bring fire on earth he came;
>   Kindled in some hearts it is;
> O that all might catch the flame,
>   All partake the glorious bliss!

There is something enchanting and terrifying about fire. It can bring us warmth and comfort or destruction and death. Many children play with fire, much to the despair of parents, guardians, and elders. How delightful, however, to sit before a fireplace to escape the shivering cold of a winter night, watching the flickering, dancing shadows of flames play about the room. Yet how horrifying to see homes and buildings melt, tumble, and be devoured by a devastating, overwhelming blaze of fire!

Charles Wesley's ministry took him to the coal miners of Staffordshire and the iron workers of Newcastle, where he felt the heat and saw the fires

---

1. *HSP* 1749, 1:315–16, stanza 1 of a four-stanza hymn.

common to such work. He knew they would understand the imagery of their own labor applied to the gospel. Hence he wrote this hymn, which includes an additional three stanzas. It is still up-to-date.

Every fire is begun by a spark. When the spark plugs in a motor function properly, the fuel is ignited, resulting in the needed power for motion. As Christians, we too are involved in an ignition process, namely, kindling the flame of God's love wherever we are. According to Wesley, it is the spark of grace with which we are to ignite the fire of Jesus' love. This is the fire Jesus brings on earth, not a fire of destruction. "Kindled in *some* hearts it is," but not in all. Peoples of many nations have not yet learned to shower their enemies with food, clothing, and medical supplies instead of weapons of war.

As followers of Jesus, our work is unfinished. We have more fires of love to ignite. "O that *all* might catch the flame!" This excludes no one and includes everyone!

Spark a fire of love every day in the hearts and lives of others. They will catch the flames of God's love which will spread, grow, and glow. It will consume the flames of hatred and destruction.

Be ablaze with love!

60.

Are we forgiving?
Forgive my foes? It cannot be[1]

Luke 6:37: "Forgive, and you will be forgiven."

Forgive my foes? It cannot be:
   My foes with cordial love embrace?
Fast bound in sin and misery,
   Unsaved, unchanged by hallowing grace,
Throughout my fallen soul I feel
With man this is impossible.

Great Searcher of the mazy heart,
   A thought from thee I would not hide,
I cannot draw th' envenomed dart,
   Or quench this hell of wrath and pride,
Jesus, till I thy Spirit receive,
Thou know'st, I never can forgive.

Come, Lord, and tame the tiger's force,
   Arrest the whirlwind in my will,
Turn back the torrent's rapid course,
   And bid the headlong sun stand still.
The rock dissolve, the mountain move,
And melt my hatred into love.

1. *SH* 1762, 2:215.

> Root out the wrath thou dost restrain;
>   And when I have my Savior's mind,
> I cannot render pain for pain,
>   I cannot speak a word unkind,
> An angry thought I cannot know,
> Or count mine injurer my foe.

Is forgiveness possible for human beings? With God's help, yes! To say, "I forgive" glides easily from the lips at times, but to take our foes in our arms, embrace them, and express love and forgiveness is much more difficult. It is especially difficult in a world where people and nations constantly guard their spaces, where people continue to be persecuted for racial, creedal, political, ethnic, and cultural backgrounds, where the industry of war provides massive global employment, and where murder, robbery, and conflict are the daily agenda in so much of the world. On a more personal level, people have their home-town enemies. Grudges, enmity, jealousy, and hatred devour the human sense of decency, integrity, respect, and concern for others.

Wesley understood that until we receive the Spirit of God expressed in Jesus we are incapable of true forgiveness. Without that Spirit we cannot "quench this hell of wrath and pride." There is a power within us which feeds enmity and hatred between us and others. It has the force of a tiger on the kill, the devastating strength of a whirlwind, the driving thrust of a torrentially raging river. God alone is able to quell this inner force of hatred. God's transformation of hate into love and forgiveness is what changes weapons of war into food for the hungry and needy of the world.

The Scriptures give no alternatives to "love your enemy." No exceptions are stated, i.e., that under certain circumstances this imperative does not apply. It says simply, "Love your enemies." In other words, this is a part of the Christian code of ethics. Christians are to love their enemies.

When we follow Jesus, we will not hate our enemies, for we will have the Spirit's mind. Hence we will not render pain for pain. We will not consider others as foes.

Wesley experienced the power of Christ's Spirit to turn hatred into love and forgiveness, as an incident in his *Journal* reveals.

Monday, October 1. Expounded Isaiah 35 with great freedom and power. In the hours of conference, the following persons[2] declared to me their faith in Him who justifies the ungodly:

Mary Brown, took with strong trembling last night at the Hall, was there set at liberty, both from fear and guilt. "I love all mankind," she said, (the best proof of faith) "and could die for my worst enemy."[3]

---

2. After Mary Brown, Charles goes on to name Sarah Gough, Sarah Norton, Eleanor Kitchinor, Judith Williams, and Joseph Black.

3. *MSJ*, 1:209.

61.

Are we hard-hearted?
How oft have I, like Pharaoh, proved[1]

Exodus 8:15: "When Pharaoh saw that there was a respite, he hardened his heart."

> How oft have I, like Pharaoh, proved
>   A penitent in vain,
> And when I saw the plague removed
>   Returned to sin again.
> Hardening my heart, I still rebel,
>   The worse for each reprieve:
> But try if grace cannot prevail,
>   And now, O Lord, forgive.

Exodus 9:12: "The Lord hardened the heart of Pharaoh."

> There needed, Lord, no act of thine,[2]
> If Pharaoh had a heart like mine:
> One moment leave me but alone,
> And mine, alas, is turned to stone.
>
> Thus if the blessing thou restrain,
> The earth is hardened by the rain.

1. *SH* 1762, 1:39.
2. *SH* 1762, 1:39–40.

ARE WE HARD-HEARTED?

> Withheld and thus, if God depart,
> Jehovah hardens Pharaoh's heart.

How can we relate our experience to that of an ancient Egyptian monarch? Wesley simplifies the matter. He internalizes Pharaoh's experience and mirrors his own in it. Therefore he discovers that the Pharaoh who oppressed the Hebrew people is very much up-to-date.

Like Pharaoh, we harden our hearts. We are often penitent with the hope of relief from evil, difficulty, pain, sickness, or even death. Yet when relief comes, we are sometimes no longer penitent and forget we have received a reprieve. Perhaps we even take our new lease on life for granted and lapse into the same sinful life we led previously. Worse still, this may become a pattern of our behavior, and we make our hearts harder each time we repeat it.

> Hardening my heart, I still rebel,
> The worse for each reprieve.

Our hearts are so hard that no action of God is needed to harden them. Wesley gives us a new perspective from which to view the Scriptures' claim that God hardened Pharaoh's heart. That is not an issue when we acknowledge that, left to our own devices, our hearts are harder than Pharaoh's.

> There needed, Lord, no act of thine,
> If Pharaoh had a heart like mine.

The act of God needed is the divine heart-surgery that replaces hearts of stone with hearts of flesh which are alive and beating with God's love.

The prophet Ezekiel gives us hope when he describes such surgery performed by a God who by grace forgives and gives new life. "A new heart also will I give you, and a new spirit I will put within you: and I will take away the stony heart out of your flesh, and I will give you an heart of flesh" (Ezekiel 36:26 KJV).

The heart is a central, unifying, life-giving force in us, and God will give it new life. The New Testament describes the experience for followers of Christ in these words:

> "I pray that according to the riches of his glory, he may grant that you may be strengthened in your inner being with power through his Spirit, and that Christ may dwell in your hearts through faith, as you are being rooted and grounded in love. I pray that you may

have the power to comprehend, with all the saints, what is the breadth and length and height and depth, and to know the love of Christ that surpasses knowledge, so that you may be filled with all the fullness of God" (Ephesians 3:16–19).

62.

Are we all alone?
Like him in piety's decay[1]

1 Kings 19:10: "I, even I only, am left." (KJV)

> Like him in piety's decay
>   I made my solitary moan:
> Thou heard'st thy desolate servant say,
>   I, even I, am left alone!
> But now with open heart and eyes
>   Thousands I in our Israel see
> Who idols hate, the world despise,
>   Its god renounce, and follow thee.

The agony and pathos conveyed through the musical setting for this verse from 1 Kings in the beautiful aria, "It is enough," in Felix Mendelssohn-Bartholdy's oratorio *Elijah*, evoke empathy for this prophet of God. Elijah is weary of his struggle for God against the Baalites, evil forces, and gods of the world. The worshipers of the god Baal have slain some of Israel's prophets, vandalized God's altars, and want to kill him. Wesley sees Elijah's "solitary moan," however, as a symptom of piety's decay.

    We tend to think of Elijah as a giant among the early prophets who performed extraordinary feats demonstrative of great faith. Yet in the moment of greatest despair, when he prays for his life to be taken away, he

---

[1]. *SH* 1762, 1:172.

SECTION 6: OURSELVES

suffers from piety's decay, according to Wesley. Why the cry, "I, even I only, am left"? It is self-centered and reflects the decline of his own faithfulness. Distress and anxiety have blurred his vision.

Like the prophet Elijah, Wesley knew what it means to confront the loneliness of a threatening mob, as he did in England during the 1740s. At times he was violently attacked by outraged crowds, for many of the clergy and laity of the Church of England opposed his itinerant preaching and teaching ministry, especially among the Methodist societies. He also knew the peril of self-centered moans of despair in the solitude of ridicule and threats of personal harm and death. Yet he discovered that it is faith which opens our hearts and eyes to see that we are not alone.

Times will come in the journey of faith when it seems that we stand alone. But if we commit ourselves fully to the hope of faith's promises, the soundness of our fidelity to God and others will not be shaken. Those promises are manifold, but two of the most powerful and sustaining are as follows. First, we are not alone! God is with us! Jesus says, "And remember, I am with you always, to the end of the age" (Matthew 28:20); "I will not leave you orphaned; I am coming to you" (John 14:18). Second, we are not alone! Others are with us! "Therefore, since we are surrounded by so great a cloud of witnesses, let us also lay aside every weight and the sin that clings so closely, and let us run with perseverance the race that is set before us" (Hebrews 12:1).

63.

Are we ministers?
O may I never take the praise[1]

Luke 8:56: "He ordered them to tell no one what had happened."

> O may I never take the praise,
>   Or my own glory spread,
> If made thine instrument to raise
>   A sinner from the dead!
> O may I never boast my own
>   Successful ministry,
> But sink forgotten and unknown,
>   And swallowed up in thee!

Charles Wesley records in his *Journal* the account of being confronted by a clergyman who complained of George Whitefield's criticism of the clergy.

> I told [him], if he himself was a carnal, worldly-minded clergyman, *I* might do what he would call railing: warn God's people to beware of false prophets. I did not *say* (because I did not know) that he *was* one of those shepherds that fed themselves, not the flock; of those dumb dogs that could not bark; of those greedy dogs that could never have enough. If he was, I was sorry for him, and must leave that sentence of Chrysostom with him, "Hell is paved with the skulls of Christian priests."[2]

1. *SH* 1762, 2:218.
2. *MSJ*, 1:223.

SECTION 6: OURSELVES

Authentic Christian ministry has no room for self-aggrandizement. When greed and success become primary motives for ministry, and obsessions with broadcasting one's accomplishments and focusing on oneself dominate the goals of ministry, one does nothing more than pave the streets of hell with the skull of another Christian clergyperson.

Authentic Christian ministry has two primary foci which are clearly articulated in Wesley's poem:

1. to bring life where there is death—

> O may I never take the praise,
> Or my own glory spread,
> If made thine *instrument to raise*
> *A sinner from the dead!*

2. to be swallowed up in God—

> O may I never boast my own
> Successful ministry,
> But sink forgotten and unknown,
> And swallowed up in thee!

Recently while reading a newspaper of a major denomination, I came across the "Winners Column," which contained a list of names of clergy and the numbers of persons they had brought into church membership on profession of faith during a specific period of time. While the dissemination of such information may be viewed as encouraging the growth of the church, it is in large measure contrary to the spirit of Jesus' words in Luke 8 and Wesley's understanding of them.

It is inevitable that people will respond to strong ministerial leadership and that churches will grow and thrive when their clergy and laity diligently apply themselves. If, however, one is instrumental in raising a single sinner from death through the gift of life in Christ, it is God alone who is worthy of praise.

Here are some simple rules for ministry which apply to both clergy and laity and convey the spirit of Wesley's poem:

1. In all things give God the glory.

2. Do not endorse your personal praise.

3. Do not boast of your successes.

4. Be willing to be forgotten and unknown.

64.

How do we do God's will?
Come, let us anew[1]

Come, let us anew
Our journey pursue,
Roll round with the year,
And never stand still, 'till the Master appear;

His adorable will
Let us gladly fulfill,
And our talents improve
By the patience of hope, and the labor of love.

Our life is a dream,
Our time as a stream,
Glides swiftly away,
And the fugitive moment refuses to stay,

The arrow is flown,
The moment is gone,
The millennial year
Rushes on to our view, and eternity's here!

O that each in the day
Of his coming might say

---

1. *HNYD* 1749, 9.

SECTION 6: OURSELVES

> "I have fought my way through,
> "I have finished the work thou didst give me to do!"
>
> O that each from his Lord
> May receive the glad word,
> "Well and faithfully done,
> "Enter into my joy, and sit down on my throne!"

A new year brings with it the hope of beginning again. Resolutions often express desires to avoid wrong directions of the past and fulfill new dreams of the future. Just as the early church lived with a sense of urgency and hope of a time fulfilled by the Messiah's return, we too live with that hope. It is this sense of urgency that gives us the momentum to pursue our journey anew. It is a messianic hope which sends us out each day. It is the hope of a Messiah who came, comes, and comes again to reconcile broken and divided humankind. Unlike the misguided Thessalonians, who misunderstood Paul's anticipation of the end of the age to mean that they should pool their resources and wait for the Messiah's return, we are to be active and not complacent in the time allotted to us.

Two directions for our journey remain constant regardless of how people and the world change with time. First, gladly fulfill God's will. Second, improve our talents. Both of these we do through the patience of hope and labor of love. In moments of serious doubt and despair it is patient hope which gives us the endurance to live with life's circumstances long enough to see the will of God worked out in them. To be sure, we will find it difficult to do God's will or improve our talents through impatience and despair.

Doing God's will and improving talents are accomplished through the labor of love. Love is a labor, not an inactive state. It is something we do! Love is our activity. Love is our full-time occupation. When we live out love as Jesus did in his life, ministry, and on the cross, by giving ourselves for God and others, we are doing God's will. When we love ourselves as God's creation and nourish our talents as God's children, they *will* develop and improve. This means that fundamental to doing God's will and improving our talents is an active life of love.

65.

Why is music important in our lives?
Thou God of harmony and love[1]

THE MUSICIAN'S [HYMN]

Thou God of harmony and love,
Whose name transports the saints above
   And lulls the ravished spheres,
On thee in feeble strains I call,
And mix my humble voice with all
   Thy heavenly choristers.

If well I know the tuneful art
To captivate a human heart,
   The glory, Lord, be thine.
A servant of thy blessed will
I here devote my utmost skill
   To sound the praise divine.

Suffice for this the season past:
I come, great God, to learn at last
   The lesson of thy grace.
Teach me the new, the gospel song,
And let my hand, my heart, my tongue
   Move only to thy praise.

---

1. *RH* 1747, 34–36; stanzas 1–2, 4–7 of a ten-stanza hymn.

SECTION 6: OURSELVES

> Thine own musician, Lord, inspire,
> And let my consecrated lyre
>   Repeat the psalmist's part;
> Thine only Son reveal in me,
> And fill with sacred melody
>   The fibers of my heart.
>
> So shall I charm the listening throng,
> And draw the living stones along
>   By Jesus' tuneful name.
> The living stones shall dance, shall rise,
> And form a city in the skies,
>   The new Jerusalem.
>
> O might I with thy saints aspire,
> The meanest of that dazzling choir
>   Who chant thy praise above!
> Mixed with the bright musician band
> May I an heavenly harper stand
>   And sing the song of love.

Although Wesley wrote this prayer for musicians before he was married and became a father, he may have prayed it often after his sons, Charles, Jr., and Samuel, demonstrated unusual musical gifts as children and later became distinguished musicians and composers. Letters to them and his wife are filled with admonitions for them to be faithful in their keyboard practice. Charles knew that the stewardship of talents, which are God's gifts, is an imperative for the faithful. Therefore in this poem he writes the Christian artist's manifesto.

> I here devote my utmost skill
> To sound the praise divine.

Wesley's poetry and life resound with the spirit of Johann Sebastian Bach's ascription to his compositions: *soli Deo gloria* (to God alone be glory).

> If well I know the tuneful art
> To captivate a human heart,
> The glory, Lord, be thine.

It is a custom in many churches for choir members, organists, and others involved in musical leadership to pray in preparation for worship.

Such prayers may be offered by clergy or laity. How appropriate is each of the above selected stanzas for such a purpose! Music is at the heart of worship. When we praise God with music, we blend our strains of exultation with the concert sounds of heaven and earth across the ages which laud the Author of all harmony: God the Creator.

Wesley succinctly stresses the vocational task and theological purpose for the use of music and all other talents:

> And let my heart, my hand, my tongue
> Move only to thy praise.

Composers, lyricists, arrangers, instrumentalists, and vocalists, all makers of music, are stewards or trustees of the sounds which are the gift of creation. Those sounds which are shaped into what is called music have special qualities which make music important in our lives.

Music teaches (stanza 3). Every musician knows the value of sound music lessons and training. Even after one no longer studies formally, one should continue to grow, learn, and mature as personal abilities and talents develop further. Attitudes as well as personal and psychological development are also vital to the musician's learning process. Wesley perceives that one of the most important growth experiences for the musician is "the lesson of grace" taught by the Author of harmony.

> Suffice for this the season past:
> I come, Great God, to learn at last
> The lesson of thy grace.

From the "lesson of grace" we learn that the song of life is God's gift, "the new, the gospel song." It is the song musicians sing, play, compose, and arrange all their lives—"the song of love!" Love alone, as God reveals in the life, death, and resurrection of Jesus, reclaims human life and makes it viable and meaningful. Musicians are involved in giving shape and form to life and its sounds. And if their task is to have meaning, it must be imbued with this sense of love.

Music inspires (stanza 4). It creates moods. It can make us happy, sad, melancholic, nostalgic, energetic. All about us are examples of the use of music to create atmospheres conducive to productive work, sound mental concentration, body and mind development, and healing. Unquestionably music has great therapeutic value. Consider the ancient example of David's soothing of King Saul's spirit with music from his lyre (1 Samuel 16:23).

SECTION 6: OURSELVES

In stanza 4, musicians pray with Wesley to be inspired by God so that their consecrated talents will "repeat the Psalmist's part." If musicians seek inspiration; if they want their music to be infused with a sense of awe and wonder; if they want to capture the colors and sounds of creation; if they want to catch the spirit of the gospel; if they want to be filled with sacred melody; they should read and sing the Psalms.

Music shapes destiny (stanza 5). In this stanza Wesley draws his imagery from 1 Peter 2:5, "Like living stones, let yourselves be built into a spiritual house, to be a holy priesthood, to offer spiritual sacrifices acceptable to God through Jesus Christ." Music as a part of creation and our lives participates in shaping destiny—in the building of a spiritual house. Hence musicians and those who listen to their music are the living stones which dance and rise

> And form a city in the skies,
> The new Jerusalem.

That which inspires them and shapes them for their labor is the tuneful name of Jesus. Therefore, the musician's noblest aspiration is to sing the song of love. That is the eternal song the Author of all harmony sings through the life of Jesus.

Music spreads love (stanza 6). Musicians who come from different linguistic, cultural, political, social, economic, and religious backgrounds can gather to play a symphony of Beethoven, Mendelssohn, Mahler, or Brahms, and suddenly all of their individual differences have little or no consequence. What matters is the music. Can they make harmonious and beautiful music together? This is a parable for musicians as followers of Jesus. What matters most is: Can they sing the song of love harmoniously in concert with the God of creation and all God's creatures, great and small?

The God of harmony and love of whom Wesley speaks desires that the music of creation resound with harmony and love.

66.

How do our hearts become pure?
O for a heart to praise my God[1]

Psalm 51:10: "Create in me a clean heart, O God; and renew a right spirit within me." (KJV)

MAKE ME A CLEAN HEART, O GOD

O for a heart to praise my God,
   A heart from sin set free,
A heart that always feels thy blood
   So freely spilt for me.

A heart resigned, submissive, meek,
   My great Redeemer's throne,
Where only Christ is heard to speak,
   Where Jesus reigns alone.

A humble, lowly, contrite heart,
   Believing, true, and clean,
Which neither life nor death can part
   From him that dwells within.

---

1. *HSP* 1742, 30–31.

SECTION 6: OURSELVES

> A heart in every thought renewed
>   And full of love divine,
> Perfect and right and pure and good,
>   A copy, Lord, of thine.
>
> Thy nature, dearest Lord, impart;
>   Come quickly from above;
> Write thy new name upon my heart,
>   Thy new, best name of Love.

Charles Wesley titled this hymn, which originally was published with eight stanzas, "Make me a clean heart, O God." His brother John included it in the section "For Believers Groaning for Full Redemption" in the 1780 *Collection*. It is a prayer in the spirit of the plea in Psalm 51 for the creation of a clean heart. Unquestionably, however, Wesley read the psalm and shaped the prayer from the perspective of a follower of Christ, the One who roots and grounds the human heart in love.

Wesley often took a central idea from a passage of Scripture and developed his poetry around it. Interestingly this hymn is connected specifically with Psalm 51:10. Nevertheless, it is the idea of God's steadfast love in verse 1 which pervades Wesley's description of the quest for the clean or pure heart:

> "Have mercy upon me, O God,
>   according to thy *lovingkindness* [or steadfast love]:
> according unto the multitude of thy tender mercies
>   blot out my transgressions." (51:1, KJV)

It is through the steadfast love of God that we are granted pure hearts. It is God's love that enables and sustains purity of heart. There is no way to purity and holiness without love!

Stanza 1 resonates the psalmist's yearning:

> "Wash me throughly from mine iniquity,
>   and cleanse me from my sin." (KJV)

Wesley prays for "a heart from sin set free." But he goes beyond the psalmist's affirmation, "I acknowledge my transgressions: and my sin is ever before me" (Psalm 51:3). Wesley unquestionably acknowledges his sinfulness, but he desires an experience of *liberation* from sin through "A heart that always *feels* thy blood / So freely shed for me." He constantly seeks the total experience of holiness, which is intellectual and emotional, the experience which unites head and heart. Just as one's adrenalin may so activate the human circulatory system that one actually feels the pulse of blood flowing through one's veins, so Wesley longs to *feel* throughout his whole human experience the pulsation of Christ's life-giving blood, which was "so freely shed for [him]." It is Christ's sacrifice that attests to and actuates the self-giving, steadfast, purifying love of God within human beings.

In stanzas 2–4 Wesley describes the nature and qualities of the pure heart for which he prays. It is first and foremost "a copy" of Christ's heart. It is resigned, submissive, and meek. It is the inner dwelling of Christ, and those in whom Christ dwells resound the words of Christ in their speech. It is "humble, lowly, contrite, believing, true, and clean" and is inseparable from Christ. It is renewed in every thought "and full of love divine." It is perfect, right, pure, and good. Only such hearts are "A copy, Lord, of thine."

How do we know whether such hearts have been created within us? We can never claim to "have" such hearts; we, like Wesley, can only pray that we shall be granted them. Yet we know that the pure heart exhibits the attributes described by him. Whose heart is "in *every* thought renewed / And *full* of love divine" but the heart of Christ? Can we hope for such a heart in this life? Wesley avers that yearning for the loving heart of Christ is the path toward holiness and perfection. It is the Christian's life journey.

Therefore Wesley concludes the prayer with a petition to be imbued with God's *nature*.

> Thy *nature*, gracious Lord, impart,
> Come quickly from above;
> Write thy new name upon my heart,
> Thy new, best name of Love.

He perceived that the best name for God is "love." That is the name Wesley desired to have written upon his heart. It is the name which 1 John 4:8 also declares best expresses what God at the center of existence means: "God is love!"

The prophet Jeremiah had spoken centuries before the coming of the Messiah, of the new covenant God would make with the house of Israel: "I will put my law within them, and I will write it on their hearts" (Jeremiah 31:33). Jesus came proclaiming the new law of love "that you love one another. Just as I have loved you, you also should love one another. By this everyone will know that you are my disciples, if you have love for one another" (John 13:34–5). When God's nature, "Love," forms our nature, all that we are in character, personality, and demeanor will reveal to others that God is present. "No one has ever seen God; if we love one another, God lives in us" (1 John 4:12), and this is the love Wesley knew and experienced that God can and will perfect in us.

67.

What will keep me from sin?
I want a principle within[1]

FOR A TENDER CONSCIENCE

I want a principle within
  Of jealous, godly fear
A sensibility of sin,
  A pain to feel it near.
I want the first approach to feel
  Of pride, or fond desire,
To catch the wanderings of my will,
  And quench the kindling fire.

From thee that I no more may part,
  No more thy goodness grieve,
The filial awe, the fleshly heart,
  The tender conscience give.
Quick as the apple of an eye,
  O God, my conscience make;
Awake my soul when sin is nigh,
  And keep it still awake.

1. *HSP* 1749, 2:230–1. Only three stanzas of a five-stanza poem appear here and stanza one has been moved to the third position.

SECTION 6: OURSELVES

> Almighty God of truth and love,
>   In me thy power exert,
> The mountain from my soul remove,
>   The hardness from my heart.
> O may the least omission pain
>   My well-instructed soul,
> And drive me to the blood again,
>   Which makes the wounded whole.

The original title given to this hymn text by Charles Wesley was "For a Tender Conscience." He yearned for a conditioning of his senses to the potential of sin in his life, and he desired to be a person of stalwart, inner principle. "Watchful, godly fear" recalls the psalmist's assertion that "the fear of the Lord is the beginning of wisdom" (Psalm 111:10a). But it is not fear in the sense of terror that the psalmist means, but rather awesome fear, in the sense of worship.

What characterizes the *tender conscience* according to Wesley? (1) *It has a sensibility of sin*. This means that the biblical realities of good and evil shape one's judgment. It means learning to distinguish the forces and acts of good and evil. (2) It is not merely an intellectual response; *it engages our feelings*. When we are aware of the nearness of sin, the conscience feels pain. (3) *It senses the first approach of sin*. This is not an incidental matter, for the more frequently one commits the same sinful act, be it stealing, cheating in business negotiations, or other deceitful acts, less and less one is aware of the "approach of sin" until the conscience no longer responds, and what one once may have thought to be an evil act or sin no longer seems so.

Wesley offers three things of which to be aware particularly in cultivating a tender conscience: pride, wrong desire, and a wandering will. Watchful awareness of conscience by no means stops here, but by sensitizing oneself to these with discipline the ability to feel the approach of sin in all facets of one's life will be greatly enhanced.

Wesley introduces the image of fire in stanza 1 very differently from its usage in many of his other hymns. Here he wants to quench the fire of sin which burns within his breast. This is a distinct contrast to his lines in another hymn:

> See how great a flame aspires,
>   Kindled by a spark of grace!
> Jesus' love the nations fires,
>   Sets the kingdoms on a blaze.

> To bring fire on earth he came;
> Kindled in some hearts it is;
> O that all might catch the flame,
> All partake the glorious bliss![2]

Wesley would burn with the fire of love instead of the fire of sin.

Stanzas 2 and 3 form a prayer for a tender conscience which we should always be praying. Such a conscience is vital to mental health and wholeness of being, for it keeps us ever vigilant of all that can turn us away from God and the divine way of self-giving, caring love.

The conclusion of this prayer reminds us that the power of truth and love can indeed remove overwhelming burdens to the human soul and soften the hardened heart.

Lest one think, however, that the tender conscience sensitizes us only to acts of sin we have committed or are on the verge of committing, Wesley reminds us that there are sins of omission also. Those who allow their consciences to be lulled to sleep by indifference or by constant submission to sin are the most vulnerable to sins of omission.

Stanza 3 points us to the vantage point from which our conscience may be renewed, revived, and re-sensitized: at the foot of the cross of Christ. It is there alone, before his loving, but agonizing, sacrifice of himself for all that the wounded are made whole. Isaac Watts expressed this eloquently in the familiar hymn:

> When I survey the wondrous cross
> On which the Prince of Glory died,
> My richest gain I count but loss,
> And pour contempt on all my pride.[3]

From the view of the cross the tender conscience will be nourished and kept ever awake, and it will keep one from sin.

---

2. *HSP* 1749, 1:315.

3. Watts, *Hymns and Spiritual Songs*, Book 3 with the title "VII. Crucifixion to the World by the Cross of Christ; Gal. 6:14."

SECTION 7

Daily Living

Thanks be to God,
the first thing I felt today
was a fear of pride
and desire of love.

CHARLES WESLEY

68.

What makes the impossible possible for us?

The table of my heart prepare[1]

Deuteronomy 6:6: "Keep these words that I am commanding you today in your heart."

> The table of my heart prepare,
>   (Such power belongs to thee alone)
> And write, O God, thy precepts there,
>   To show thou still canst write on stone,
> So shall my pure obedience prove
> All things are possible to love.

"These words that I am commanding you today" refers, of course, to the preceding two verses of the chapter. Deuteronomy 6:4–5, "Hear, O Israel: The Lord is our God, the Lord alone. You shall love the Lord your God with all your heart, and with all your soul, and with all your might." Verse 4 is known as the *Sh^ema Yisrael*, and in mainstream rabbinic Jewish tradition it is to be repeated twice daily and posted on the entrance to a dwelling. This is to fulfill the biblical commandment: "And write them [words of God] on

---

1. *SH* 1762, 1:91–92. The six stanzas examined in the following six studies are based on Deuteronomy 6:6–7. They originally appeared as single poems in sequence prefaced by verses from Deuteronomy 6.

the doorposts of your house and on your gates" (verse 9). These words are to be at the center of one's being and to accompany one each day and night.

What does the Book of Deuteronomy say to us in these words? It affirms that God alone is our God. It also says that we are to love God with our whole being. These are the fundamental precepts at the center of our relationship with God. Even if we have hardened hearts, God is able to leave the imprint of these words there. We are not told, "Make God your God, or else!" in a threatening manner. Rather, because God is God, we shall love God with all that we are: heart, soul, and strength.

The realization that God is our God alone opens to us the possibilities of love, for the Scriptures tell us that "God is love" (1 John 4:8). And we learn in Matthew 19:26, "With God all things are possible" (KJV). Therefore, all things are possible for love. King David, an adulterer, becomes a writer of eloquent psalms of praise to God. Moses, a murderer, is chosen by God to lead the Hebrew people out of Egyptian bondage. Saul, a persecutor of followers of Jesus, becomes Paul the apostle, an author of many books in the New Testament. With God the impossible becomes possible. We can never know what we might become unless we commit ourselves completely to love God with our whole being. No matter how hardened one's heart becomes, as Wesley says, God can still "write on stone."

69.

What can we learn?
Father, instruct my docile heart[1]

Deuteronomy 6:7: "You shall teach them diligently to your children." (RSV)

> Father, instruct my docile heart,
>   Apt to instruct I then shall be,
> I then shall all thy words impart,
>   And teach (as taught myself by thee)
> My children in their earliest days,
> To know and live the life of grace.

We spend the first few years of our lives being taught by others. At the outset we learn essential skills such as walking and talking. As our minds and bodies develop, we begin to appropriate and apply our skills and abilities to a variety of tasks. We learn that they can be used for good and evil. Therefore, what we are taught and by whom determines in large measure the path of life we will pursue in the future.

Reflecting on Deuteronomy 6:7, Wesley says that above all else children should be taught that God is the center of all life and to love God with all that they are. This means that from the earliest age children should learn that the main force in their lives, from which the energy and momentum

---

1. *SH* 1762, 1:92.

for all they do originates, is God, who is love. Hence, love is the most powerful force in life.

The primary responsibility for such instruction lies with parents or guardians. One of the most awesome responsibilities ever entrusted to a human being is to teach a child. This is no doubt why parents and other teachers of children must spend time in prayer, meditation, and Bible study to grasp the understanding of life shared by divine wisdom. Paul reminds us of the importance of divine instruction when he says that "the gospel that was proclaimed by me is not of human origin; for I did not receive it from a human source, nor was I taught it, but I received it through a revelation of Jesus Christ" (Galatians 1:11–12).

Christian education of children which seeks to impart knowledge *about* God without teachers who seek God's instruction may be well-meaning, but it is wrong-headed. Relationships to God are not established by merely communicating facts and ideas, as important as facts and ideas may be for the growth of one's spiritual journey. One must seek first the nurture of life through a lifelong pattern of behavior which involves prayer, study, self-examination, acts of faith, and acts of social outreach. The Wesleys would also add—regular attendance at the sacrament of Holy Communion.

Love is the focus of teaching as understood in Deuteronomy. If instructed in love, if taught love, if loved by their teachers, children will catch the spirit of love and will learn from their earliest days "to know and live the life of grace." "The life of grace" is one whose foundation, goal, and purpose is love. This is the heart of Jesus' life, ministry, death, and resurrection. Jesus personified self-giving love. We are to personify it as well.

70.

How can we grow?
When quiet in my house I sit[1]

Deuteronomy 6:7: "Thou shalt talk of them when thou sittest in thine house." (KJV)

> When quiet in my house I sit,
> Thy book be my companion still,
> My joy thy sayings to repeat,
> Talk o'er the records of thy will,
> And search the oracles divine,
> 'Till every heart-felt word is mine.

On the evening of March 25, 1736, while in the American colony of Georgia, Charles Wesley recorded in his *Journal*: "After spending an hour at the camp in singing such psalms as suited the occasion, I went to bed in the hut, which was thoroughly wet with today's rain."[2] This was almost two years before his conversion experience in May of 1738, although he was already an ordained clergyman of the Church of England. Both before and after his transforming encounter with Christ, Wesley was committed to daily time in quiet meditation and study, whether it was singing the Psalms and reading lectionary passages appointed by the Church of England for the day or reading other parts of the Bible.

1. *SH* 1762, 1:92.
2. *MSJ*, 1:13.

This stanza of the poem based on Deuteronomy 6:7 provides a simple and helpful design for daily personal growth as a servant of God.

Set aside a quiet time for yourself, God, and the Scriptures. Wesley has appropriated "these *words,* which I command thee this day," which are to be the object of constant reflection and living, in the larger sense of the entire Holy Scriptures. If we understand the purpose of the entire Bible to be summarized in Deuteronomy 6:4–5 ("Hear, O Israel: The Lord our God is one Lord: And thou shalt love the Lord thy God with all thine heart, and with all thy soul, and with all thy might" [KJV]), Wesley's appropriation of these words becomes very meaningful.

Repeat the sayings of the Scriptures as the source of great joy and wisdom. Listen to them over and over again. Memorize them and discuss them. They are indeed records of God's will and way with the people of the earth. The more intimate we become with God's will in the lives of sacred history, the better we will understand God's will for our own lives.

Study the Scriptures in depth. It has been claimed that most of the Bible could be reconstructed from the hymns and poetry of Charles Wesley. This is because he was committed to "search the oracles divine." The recitation, memorization, and reading of God's word takes on its full meaning *only* when we plunge into the depths of each book with the desire that "every heartfelt word" will increase our wisdom for living and become a part of our being.

Dietrich Bonhoeffer reminds us how important our immersion in God's word is:

> It is the divine intention that we find God in the entire Bible. That may seem like a very primitive matter. But you have no idea how happy we are, when we find our way back from the dead-end streets of some theologies to this primitive matter.[3]

---

3. Bonhoeffer. *Gesammelte Schriften,* 3:28, 30; English translation, S T Kimbrough, Jr.

71.

What is most important?
O might the gracious words divine[1]

Deuteronomy 6:7: ". . . and when thou walkest by the way." (KJV)

> O might the gracious words divine
>   Subject of all my converse be,
> So would the Lord his follower join,
>   And walk, and talk himself with me,
> So would my heart his presence prove,
> And burn with everlasting love.[2]

Wherever we go, the primary focus of our thought, behavior, and speech should be that God alone is our God and everything about us should express our love for God. This is the spirit of the words in Deuteronomy 6:4–5 and the spirit of the whole of God's word in the Scriptures. It was the force of Charles Wesley's life wherever he went. God was his partner in conversation through the word as his poetry and letters indicate. Although he was often riddled with doubt, no matter where he was or with whom he found himself, Wesley's chief concern was to embody God's presence and be aflame with the divine love he discovered in Jesus Christ. This was his passion, the fire that sparked his vibrant concern for others. It is perhaps nowhere more beautifully expressed than in a letter he wrote to Mr. John Kelway, the distinguished

---

1. *SH* 1762, 1:92.
2. See also Luke 24:15, 32.

music teacher of his gifted son, Charles, Jr. It was written after they happened to meet, having not seen each other for many years.

November 23, 1778

Dear Sir,—The joy I felt at seeing you on Monday somewhat resembled the joy we shall feel when we meet again without our bodies. Most heartily I do thank God that He has given you a longer continuance among us; and, I trust, a resolution to improve your few last precious moments. We must confess, at *our* time of life, that "one thing is needful," even to *get ready for our unchangeable eternal state*. But what is that readiness or meetness?

You are convinced of my sincere love for your soul, and therefore allow me the liberty of a friend. As such I write, not to teach you what you do not know, but to stir up your mind, by way of remembrance, and exhort both you and myself,

"Of little life the most to make,
And manage wisely your last stake."

When God came down from heaven to show us the way thither, you remembered his first words: "The kingdom of God is at hand: *repent* ye, and *believe* the Gospel." He himself declares, "The kingdom of God is within you; even righteousness, and peace, and joy in the Holy Ghost:" and assures us, every one that seeks, finds it; every one that asks, receives it.

"Him hath God exalted, to *give* both repentance and remission of sins:" faith also is the gift of God, through Jesus Christ, its Author and Finisher.

The true repentance is better felt than described. It surely implies a troubled and wounded spirit, a broken and contrite heart. It is what the publican felt when he could only cry, "God be merciful unto me a sinner;" what Peter felt when Jesus turned and *looked* on him; and what the trembling jailer felt when he asked, "What must I do to be saved?"

By this brokenness of heart our Saviour prepares us for divine faith and present pardon, sealed upon the heart, in peace which passes all understanding, in joy unspeakable and full of glory, and in love which casts out the love of sin, especially our bosom sin, our ruling passion, whether the love of pleasure, of praise, or of money.

Now, my dear Sir, this meetness for heaven is what I must earnestly wish [for] you and myself, even repentance, faith, and love: and all things are now ready for you. One look of Jesus Christ can break your heart this moment, and bind it up by faith. One day is with Him as a thousand years: and He is still the Man who receiveth sinners: "the same yesterday, to-day, and for ever."

"I will pardon those whom I receive," is His own promise; and for this gracious end He has reserved you, and held your soul in life for above seventy years; for this end He has delivered you in innumerable dangers, blessed you with innumerable blessings; and for this end, I humbly hope, His providence brought you acquainted with, dear Sir,

The faithful servant and friend of your soul,

C. W.[3]

---

3. Jackson, *The Journal of Charles Wesley*. 2:285–86. The journal ends on p. 139. Thereafter Jackson has included a variety of letters and papers of Charles Wesley wherein the Kelway letter appears.

72.

How do we prepare for the evening and rest?

Oft as I lay me down to rest[1]

Deuteronomy 6:7: ". . . when you lie down."

> Oft as I lay me down to rest,
>   O may the reconciling word,
> sweetly compose my weary breast,
>   while on the bosom of the Lord.
> I sink in blissful dreams away,
> and visions of eternal day.

In his letters and *Journal,* Charles Wesley often expressed the physical and mental fatigue which pursued him throughout his life. During his itinerant ministry, he traveled thousands of miles on horseback, preached sometimes more than a dozen times in a week, often was attacked by unruly mobs, and was possessed by an inner drive to express the breadth and depth of the Christian faith in poetry. After his marriage to Sarah Gwynne at the age of forty-two, came the additional responsibilities of husband, father, and parish priest. Charles Wesley was accustomed to lying on his bed to rest with his body exhausted, his composure taxed, and his strength spent.

1. *SH* 1762, 1:92.

HOW DO WE PREPARE FOR THE EVENING AND REST?

The sixth chapter of Deuteronomy helped him to understand that rest, sleep, and regaining physical and mental composure are a vital part of expressing love for God. Indeed, if we love God with our whole being, replenishing our strength is an essential part of that love and is requisite to faith and Christian service.

Wesley understood that God's word includes an interesting prescription for rest.

> Oft as I lay me down to rest,
> O may the reconciling *word*
> sweetly compose my weary breast.

During the third week of May 1738, the week of his conversion, Charles Wesley had wrestled with Martin Luther's commentary on the Book of Galatians, and he yearned to know the God whose love was poured out to him in Jesus Christ. After struggling to grasp such an overwhelming self-giving love, he recorded the following lines in his *Journal*:

> I laboured, waited, and prayed to see "who loved *me* and gave himself for *me*." When nature near exhausted forced me to bed, I opened the book upon, "For he will finish the work, and cut it short in righteousness, because a short work will the Lord make upon earth" [Romans 9:28]. After this comfortable assurance that he would come, and would not tarry, I slept in peace.[2]

Wesley followed the divine admonition of Deuteronomy 6:4, and when he laid down to rest, he focused his thoughts on God and God's word.

When we live lives of commitment to God, we may prepare ourselves for rest and composure as Charles did. With God's word on our minds and in our hearts and filled with God's love, we can rise on the morrow refreshed to meet the needs of each new moment.

---

2. *MSJ*, 1:104

73.

How do we prepare for the day?
Rising to sing my Savior's praise[1]

Deuteronomy 6:7: ". . . and when you rise."

> Rising to sing my Savior's praise
>   Thee may I publish all day long,
> And let thy precious word of grace
>   Flow from my heart, and fill my tongue,
> Fill all my life with purest love,
> And join me to thy church above.

The all-consuming passion for every day is the love of God. According to Deuteronomy, God's love is to pervade all that we are: body, mind, and spirit. Loving God totally is to be the subject of our conversation and action from the time we rise in the morning until we retire in the evening.

> Rising to sing my Savior's praise,
>   Thee may I publish all day long.

As he often does, Wesley moves beyond doctrinal and denominational boundaries in these lines and stresses three essentials for the Christian's daily walk with God. (1) "Thee may I publish all day long" emphasizes that the priority of the glad tidings of the gospel is not a specific set of doctrines, i.e., not acceptable formulations of faith language. Rather it is the constant

---

1. *SH* 1762, 1:93.

awareness that "in Christ God was reconciling the world to himself" (2 Corinthians 5:19). Therefore, the word that we have for those about us every day is God's "precious word of grace." In other words, we fill our hearts and tongues with thoughts and words of mercy, healing, compassion, reconciliation, tenderness, justice, goodness, kindness, and love.

(2) "Fill all my life with purest love." This is a constant theme of Wesley. Understanding that God's nature is love, he desires for his own nature to become that of God. There is a lifelong or ongoing transformation into God's nature, known as *theosis* among the early Church Fathers.

(3) "And join me to thy church above." Love does not exist in isolation. It is the matrix of community, of the body of Christ, the church. Thus the desire to be a part of God's loving community of the church does not wane.

Finally, it is never enough to have the intent of our hearts right and to speak words imbued with God's grace. We must ask God for the supreme gift: "Fill all my life with purest love."

Inspired by Deuteronomy 6:4–7, Wesley would rise each morning and resolve to be the evidence of God's praise, the vehicle of God's grace, and the vessel of God's love.

74.

How shall we spend our time?
At evening to myself I say[1]

Ruth 2:19: "Where hast thou gleaned today?" (KJV)

> At evening to myself I say,
> Soul, where hast thou gleaned today,
>   Thy labors how bestowed?
> What hast thou rightly said, or done?
> What grace attained, or knowledge won,
>   In following after God?

What have our souls gleaned from the day just past? Have we reaped a harvest of inner spiritual growth? Where have we been that would make this possible?

    Wesley transforms Naomi's question to her daughter-in-law Ruth into one of self-examination and introspection, as one reflects upon the day's course of events. Where we have been during the day determines in large measure what we can glean for our souls. Too often we are preoccupied with gleaning only the sustenance for our daily existence, as was the case with Ruth. We go to work to earn enough money to provide food, clothing, and shelter. Our internal sustenance, however, is as important as the external.

---

1. *SH* 1762, 1:140.

HOW SHALL WE SPEND OUR TIME?

Where have we been today? The surroundings and personal associations of the day are vital to the nurture of our inner life. Are the places we have been and those with whom we have associated conducive to spiritual growth? Wesley tells us there are some questions which will help set a daily course for spiritual growth.

How have we used our energies today? What are our jobs, professions, occupations? Are they honest and just ways to earn a living? How have we spent our energies at our places of work? Have we honored God and others, or have we used others for our own benefit or exploited them? Have we sought to feed our souls in our labors? Whether we are gainfully employed or not, how we spend our time and energy determines whether or not we will grow inwardly. Daily labor is an opportunity to grow spiritually.

What have we said or done today that is right? Speech and actions also influence inner growth. Speaking and acting rightly reflect who we are deep within. Gossip, harsh words, and constant profanity stunt spiritual growth, as do deceptive, belligerent, or self-serving actions. Every wrong word or deed denies the opportunity to grow inwardly.

What grace have we received today as children of God? Grace can be like unearned or undeserved food; that is, by the world's standards we deserve that for which we have labored. Giving food to persons in need who have expended no energy to procure or purchase it is grace in action. We grow spiritually by realizing what we receive from God each day and from those who also follow after God. God's unconditional love comes to us in many ways. We grow spiritually as we recognize it and thank God for it.

What knowledge have we received in following after God? Our minds have been given to us for growth. If we do not nurture them daily with study and diligence, we will not grow inwardly and intellectually. Body, mind, and soul make up the total person. If we do not grow in knowledge, we will be incomplete and only part of the person we should be. John Wesley believed in the importance of the universal knowledge of creation. One should want to learn as much as possible about the breadth of God's creation. Hence, it is not surprising to find him writing about electricity, world history, equestrianism, etc.

My paternal grandfather set a goal to learn a new English word each day. Imagine how his vocabulary and means of expressing himself expanded over the years. Similarly, if we consciously seek to follow after God each day, we will be unending in our quest for knowledge and the expansion of our minds, which are themselves gifts of grace.

SECTION 7: DAILY LIVING

Where have our souls been fed today? Where will they be fed tomorrow?

75.

Do we eat for the right reasons?
Death in the pot! 'Tis always there[1]

2 Kings 4:40: "There is death in the pot!"

> Death in the pot! 'Tis always there,
> The bane of all our food,
> When we partake it without fear
> Without an eye to God.
>
> Unless God sanctify the meat
> And bless us from the sky,
> Unless we to God's glory eat,
> Our souls by eating die.

According to 2 Kings 4:40, when Elisha came to Gilgal there was a famine. Hence, he had a common meal prepared for all present. One of those preparing the pottage unknowingly put shreds of poisonous gourd into the pot. Elisha had meal added, and the pottage was edible. If he had not done so, all who ate might have become ill and died.

A reporter once asked the late United States senator from New York, Jacob Javitts, who suffered from Lou Gehrig's disease, how he felt about having a terminal disease. He replied, "We are all terminal." How true! The

---

1. *SH* 1762, 1:183.

mortal, physical body is temporal. Yet many spend their lives trying to preserve it and extend the span of life as long as possible.

Unquestionably, "There is death in the pot." What we eat can destroy us. We have come to describe our dietary needs by such words as well-balanced, low-fat, low-sugar, low-sodium, high-fiber, and many more expressions. Much of the population has become more nutrition-conscious and knows the meaning of these words. If we eat improperly, we can expect to suffer the consequences eventually. Numerous fatal diseases are known to be related directly to poor eating habits.

Wesley, of course, is speaking of "death in the pot" at a different level. He moves beyond the contents of the pottage and sees this story as a parable which views our eating as directly related to our relationship to God. When we partake of earthly sustenance without a constant awareness of the Sustainer of life, God, it is fatal. The attempt to sustain life without its Sustainer is futile.

Paul says that whether we eat or drink, it should be to God's glory (1 Corinthians 10:31). How do we eat to God's glory? By thinking and praying seriously about God's gift(s) of life before, during, and after we eat; by eating with the purpose of sustaining the body, the temple of the Spirit; by being a disciplined eater, not eating merely to satisfy our whims and special tastes; by sharing food with others, especially the poor and needy; and by fasting, which increases our awareness of how and for what purpose we eat and live.

We all have eating habits, be they good or bad. Without question there are physical and psychological reasons behind them. If we seek to lead responsible lives before God, we cannot eat thoughtlessly. Our eating habits have a direct bearing on our relationship to God. They communicate to others the quality of that relationship.

Indeed, our mortal bodies are terminal, but the Scriptures and biblical faith affirm that life is eternal. Therefore, we eat to sustain body and soul. Let us eat then for our sustenance and God's glory.

76.

Why pray before eating?
Parent of good, whose plenteous grace[1]

GRACE BEFORE MEAT

Parent of good, whose plenteous grace
    O'er all thy creatures flows,
Humbly we ask thy power to bless
    The food thy love bestows.

Thy love provides the sober feast,
    A second gift impart;
Give us with joy our food to taste,
    And with a single heart.

Let it for thee new life afford,
    For thee our strength repair,
Blest by thine all-sustaining word,
    And sanctified by prayer.

Thee let us taste, nor toil below
    for perishable meat;
the manna of thy Love bestow,
    give us thy flesh to eat.

1. *HSP* 1739, 215–16.

SECTION 7: DAILY LIVING

> Life of the world, our souls to feed,
> Thyself descend from high!
> Grant us of thee, the living Bread
> To eat and never die.

The asking of God's blessing in prayer before a meal, often called a "grace" or "blessing," is common practice in most Christian homes. For some it becomes repetitious and routine. Frequently the same prayer is said before every meal, and the habit can become more meaningful than the words uttered. Although some may pray extemporaneous prayers, many have the tendency to use the same phrases over and over again. Unquestionably there is no perfect approach to table graces. It is the attitude of prayer and the spirit in which we enter it that is of primary importance.

Wesley's grace above reminds us of a number of God's gifts which, when thought of in prayer before meals, will imbue the habit of such prayer with inspiration and meaning. These are God's gifts of power, joy, strength, and love.

The primary attitude with which the Christian comes to the meal table is that what is about to be eaten is "the food thy [God's] love bestows."

Before eating, we implore God's power to bless the food. Hence, mealtime is a time for the imparting of God's power. Frequently, meals become perfunctory. We go through the motions whether eating alone or with others. But meals are times of power or strength—God's strength which embraces us and the food we eat. Furthermore, the entire meal is the time of God's power, not just the grace or blessing beforehand.

Before eating, we ask God to give us joy with which to taste our food. Such joy is God's gift. Eating in despair, when angry or upset, is contrary to the Christian attitude toward mealtime. Such demeanor can be both spiritually and physically negative, for the body's digestive processes are disturbed under such stress. For the Christian, mealtime should be a time of joy.

Before eating, we pray for the renewal of strength that we may live as examples of the new life experienced in Christ. Hence, every mealtime is a time of renewal and resurrection. We become God's instruments of renewed strength and new life even as we break bread.

Before eating, we pray for the gift of God's love. The food we eat is perishable, but God's manna of love is eternal. This is why for the Christian every meal is a feast of love!

WHY PRAY BEFORE EATING?

Wesley makes clear that for Christians each meal is a foreshadowing of Holy Communion, which is the meal of meals. Daily bread is the preparation and sustenance for partaking of the living bread, Jesus Christ, that we may continually sit at his table in this world and the next.

77.

How do we wait on God?
Still for thy loving kindness, Lord[1]

Psalm 46:10: "Be still and know that I am God."

THE MEANS OF GRACE

Still for thy loving kindness, Lord,
    I in thy temple wait:
I look to find thee in thy word,
    Or at thy table meet.

Here, *in thine own, appointed ways,*
    I wait to learn thy will:
Silent I stand before thy face,
    And hear thee say, *"Be still!"*

Be still—and know that I am God!
    'Tis all I live to know,
To feel the virtue of thy blood,
    And spread its praise below.

---

1. *HSP* 1740, 35–39; stanzas 13–16 of a twenty-three-stanza poem.

> I wait my vigor to renew,
> > Thine image to retrieve,
>
> The veil of outward things pass through,
> > And gasp in thee to live.

The Christian vocation of waiting upon God is not a purposeless, idle expenditure of time. It involves careful planning and preparation. From his mother, Wesley learned as a child the value of a method for the living of each day. Hence, time to be still and know that God is God was set apart in the daily schedule. The reason for moments of such stillness and waiting is simple—"I wait my vigor to renew, / Thine image to retrieve." This means becoming more godlike—discovering that God's image in our lives is a reality. It means passing from the outer world to the inner world of who we really are beneath the surface of what others see. When we are still before God, we are given the breath of life that sustains us.

One Christmas during the period when our family lived in Germany, one of our sons returned home from his first semester at an American university. The pastor of the American Protestant Church in Bonn, where we resided, invited him to talk with the youth of the congregation about his university experience. As a counselor of the group, I was privileged to hear his perceptive and wise words on the value of structuring time to wait upon God. He explained that having spent his youth in Germany, he was in somewhat of a culture-shock tailspin during his first semester at a university in the United States. There was only one thing that saved him from emotional shipwreck, he said: routine. "I went to church every Sunday for worship, even when it seemed I could not possibly grasp its meaning. I read the Scriptures and prayed daily, although I often did not comprehend their significance. Finally, I attended classes and did the work prescribed by the professors. These are the only things which held me together and kept me from flipping out," he said. He was grateful for the routine.

We are often waiting upon God in the routine of our daily lives, even though we may not know it. We can easily fall prey to the syndrome: "I don't have time for this or that." Charles Wesley implores us to take time and gives us a prescription for *planned* waiting upon God, which may be routine:

(1) Attend worship.

(2) Study the Scriptures.

(3) Receive the sacrament of Holy Communion.

(4) Practice silence.

(5) Witness—spread abroad God's message of redemption through Christ's sacrifice.

He does not foresee these as optional steps for the growth and nurture of faith. They are requisites for faithful Christian living and communion with God.

The goals we set for ourselves in waiting upon God are crucial to getting the most out of our time. Wesley's poem points out some of the most important ones:

(1) to seek God's lovingkindness,

(2) to learn God's will,

(3) to know that God is God,

(4) to experience personally the meaning of Christ's sacrifice,

(5) to renew one's faith.

When we are scurrying about with too much to do to allow time for God, perhaps we will remember Wesley words. If we follow his prescription for planning our time with God and pursue these goals, Isaiah's promises in Isaiah 40:31 will be fulfilled in us and for us.

> "Those who wait for the Lord shall renew their strength,
>   they shall mount up with wings like eagles,
> they shall run and not be weary,
>   they shall walk and not faint."

78.

How shall we live our lives?
Let him to whom we now belong[1]

Let him to whom we now belong
    His sovereign right assert,
And take up every thankful song,
    And every loving heart.

He justly claims us for his own
    Who bought us with a price:
The Christian lives to Christ alone
    To Christ alone he dies.

Jesus, thine own at least receive,
    Fulfill our heart's desire,
And let us to thy glory live,
    And in thy cause expire.

Our souls and bodies we resign,
    With joy we render thee
Our all, no longer ours, but thine
    Through all Eternity!

This is Hymn 157 published in section 5, "Concerning the Sacrifice of our Persons," in the volume *HLS* 1745 published by John and Charles Wesley.

1. *HLS* 1745, 131.

The hymn has an interesting structure. The opening line of stanza 1 states clearly the theme of the entire hymn: all persons belong to God. Stanzas 1 and 2 affirm the perspective of Holy Scripture that God is the Giver of all life and has claimed all people as his own through the death of his Son Jesus Christ. Stanzas 3 and 4 are a prayer for communicants at Holy Communion that they will give up themselves completely to live for God's glory.

Stanzas 1 and 2 are Charles Wesley's theological prologue to the prayer he prays in stanzas 3 and 4. He understands that coming to the table of the Lord is an offering of ourselves to God. We bring "every thankful song" and "every loving heart" as our own sacrifice of thanksgiving to the God who has claimed us and "to whom we now belong."

While Charles does not specifically say that a "thankful song" is a church hymn, it is interesting to recall that hymn singing in the Church of England was prohibited until 1821. What then does Wesley mean in this hymn for Holy Communion that God should "take up" or receive "every thankful song"? Are we to understand this phrase only poetically and abstractly? Why sing about the offering of a "thankful song" in a eucharistic hymn? Indeed, the soul bursts with joyous song in reflecting on the death and resurrection of Christ and the forgiveness of sin. This is in the spirit of the outbursts of joy one reads in the Psalms:

> "O come, let us sing to the Lord;
> let us make a joyful noise to the rock of our salvation!
> Let us come into his presence with thanksgiving;
> let us make a joyful noise to him with songs of praise!"[2]
>
> "Make a joyful noise to God, all the earth;
> sing the glory of his name;
> give to him glorious praise!"[3]
>
> "Make a joyful noise to the Lord, all the earth;
> break forth into joyous song and sing praises."[4]
>
> "Make a joyful noise to the Lord, all the earth!
> Worship the Lord with gladness."[5]

---

2. Psalm 95:1–2.
3. Psalm 66:1–2.
4. Psalm 98:4.
5. Psalm 100:1–2.

It is interesting that one of John Wesley's liturgical innovations was the introduction of the singing of hymns at the time of communing. This was not an interruption in the liturgy itself and hence was probably not considered a violation, i.e., hymn singing during the liturgy itself. Through such practice, however, the songs of the people became an offering as they came and communed at the Lord's table. We cannot affirm that this is specifically what Charles Wesley had in mind when he wrote the line "And take up every thankful song," but this practice of singing hymns at the time of communing indeed attests the spirit of Wesley words in stanza 1.

In stanza 2 Wesley emphasizes the importance of Christ's atonement for our sin, for Christ "bought us with a price." Hence, in thanksgiving Christians live and die not for themselves but for Christ alone. The apostle Paul also says, "I die every day" with Christ (1 Corinthians 15:31). Certainly, he does not mean that he has to crucify each day every sinful thing he might do, but rather he has taken on a cruciform life. In this style of living one gives oneself each day in service to God and others. One empties oneself, as did Christ, of everything but love. This is the offering worthy of the Christian.

Stanza 3 begins a powerful eight-line eucharistic prayer (stanzas 3 and 4). Wesley prays that God will receive and fulfill the desire of our hearts, which is simply to live to God's glory and to die engaged in God's purpose. It is in this spirit that Paul wrote to the church at Corinth: "do everything for the glory of God" (1 Corinthians 10:31).

Stanza 4 concludes the prayer emphasizing the sacrifice of ourselves. We commit our souls and bodies fully to God. We are no longer our own, but wholly God's throughout eternity.

This is why the people called Methodists continue to pray in their annual Covenant Service:[6]

> Let me be your servant, under your command.
> I will no longer be my own.
> I will give up myself to your will in all things.
> . . .
> Lord, make me what you will.
> I put myself fully into your hands:
>   put me to doing, put me to suffering,
>   let me be employed for you, or laid aside for you,
>   let me be full, let me be empty,
>   let me have all things, let me have nothing.

---

6. "Wesley's Covenant Service" in *The United Methodist Book of Worship*, 291.

SECTION 7: DAILY LIVING

I freely and with a willing heart
 give it all to your pleasure and disposal.

79.

Which is the most important meal?
Author of life divine[1]

> Author of life divine
>   Who hast a table spread,
> Furnished with mystic wine
>   And everlasting bread,
> Preserve the life thyself hast given,
> And feed and train us up for heaven.
>
> Our needy souls sustain
>   With fresh supplies of love,
> Till all thy life we gain,
>   And all thy fullness prove;
> And, strengthened by thy perfect grace,
> Behold, without a veil, thy face.

During his first year at Christ College of Oxford University, Charles Wesley enjoyed himself more than he applied himself to his studies, but of his second year he wrote, "I set myself to study. Diligence led me into serious thinking. I went to the weekly Sacrament, and persuaded two or three young scholars to accompany me, and to observe the method of study prescribed by the Statutes of the University. This gained me the harmless nickname of Methodist."[2] Thus, a small group of friends began to gather

---

1. *HLS* 1745, 30.
2. Baker, *Charles Wesley As Revealed by His Letters*, 14.

with a strong commitment to study, prayer, and social service, such as visits to local prisons, with food for body and spirit of the inmates. These kinds of experiences grew out of the power for loving service received from Holy Communion. "I went to the weekly Sacrament" was the preface to his activity at Oxford and throughout his life.

I remember as a youngster sitting in a church service and counting the rows of communicants and wondering how long it would take for them to be served. I was more concerned about the logistics of Holy Communion than its meaning and power. Reaching adulthood, I realized that various branches of the Christian faith also have preoccupations with the logistics of this sacred meal, though in a different way. Some prefer to receive the elements of bread and wine standing, others kneeling, and yet others seated. These particular postures have become fixed in various traditions with diverse justifications. Standing may symbolize the readiness to go into the world after communing. Kneeling may symbolize the humble reception of God's gifts as the proper prelude to service. Sitting may focus upon the resolute stillness and quiet reception of God's power to rise anew in faithful service. While such postures may communicate important attitudes, which translate into faithful living, it is the power and momentum received from Holy Communion to be God's faithful servants which is of primary importance.

Holy Communion is the most vital meal of our lives, for in and through it God preserves life, a divine gift. Wesley reminds us that we come to the table to be fed. Proper spiritual growth requires regular nourishment by the Spirit, that is, partaking regularly of food at the Lord's table. We also come to the table to be trained in preparation for this life and the life to come. Holy Communion is a training meal of learning and discipline which gives our lives their most meaningful nourishment.

Finally, we come to the table to receive a fresh supply of love. How often Wesley was overcome by the immensity of God's love in the gift of the Incarnation, i.e., Jesus, whose life, teaching, ministry, death, and resurrection were the supreme expression of God's love for all the world.

On May 25, 1738, just two days after he had written his conversion hymn, "Where shall my wondering soul begin," Wesley wrote in his *Journal*: "in the prayer of consecration [during Holy Communion] I saw, by the eye of faith, or rather had a glimpse of Christ's broken, mangled body, as taking[3] down from the cross. Still I could not observe the prayer, but

---

3. Though Charles Wesley wrote "taking," since he was writing in the past tense, he

only repeat with tears, 'O Love, Love!' At the same time I felt great peace and joy."[4]

Strengthened by God's grace and empowered by God's love through Christ as experienced in Holy Communion, Wesley was thrust into the world in search of the poor, needy, outcast, wealthy, and noble, for God's love seeks all people.

---

no doubt intended "taken."

4. *MSJ*, 1:111.

80.

What does one experience at Holy Communion?

Give us this day, all bounteous Lord[1]

Give us this day, all bounteous Lord,
    Our Sacramental Bread,
Who thus his sacrifice record
    That suffered in our stead.

Reveal in every soul thy Son,
    And let us taste the grace
Which brings assured salvation down
    To all who seek thy face.

Who here commemorate his death
    To us his life impart,
The loving filial Spirit breathe
    Into my waiting heart.

My earnest of eternal bliss
    Let my Redeemer be,
And if even now he present is,
    Now let him speak in me.

---

1. *HLS* 1745, 75.

This Hymn was published in section 2, "As it is a Sign and a Means of Grace," in the Wesley brothers' volume *HLS* 1745.

The entire hymn is a prayer for God's presence in the life of the communicants at Holy Communion. The opening words "Give us this day" are reminiscent of the Lord's Prayer (Matthew 6:11): "Give us this day our daily bread." Here clearly, however, Wesley is speaking of spiritual food by which a bounteous God nourishes us. The bread is sacramental. In other words, it is an outward and visible sign of an inward and spiritual divine grace. The word "sacrament" comes from the Latin *sacrare* meaning "to hallow" or "to make holy." Thus, in partaking of the Sacramental Bread in the meal of our Lord, we are made holy. In receiving the bread, we keep alive the faith community's memory of Christ's sacrifice.

The Sacramental Bread is itself a "record," says Charles Wesley, of Christ's suffering for us. It is a visible sign, for as it is placed before us the record of God's salvation history is remembered and relived once more. The bread, the former sign and means of grace, becomes an ever-present sign and means of grace.

This hymn was published relatively early in Charles Wesley's ministry, 1745. His conversion had taken place just seven years previously on May 21 (Pentecost Day), 1738. In the early years of the Wesleys' ministry the practice of administering and receiving Holy Communion was by no means "regular" or weekly for most parishes of the Church of England. Yet the Wesley brothers understood it to be at the very center of the church's life and mission. Hence it is not surprising to find Charles praying, "Reveal in *every* soul thy Son, / And *let us* taste the grace." One of the primary purposes of the sacred meal is that Jesus Christ will be revealed in all who come to the table of the Lord.

Notice Wesley's use of the verb "taste." He intends for communicants to have a sensory perception of grace. One is literally to taste grace in the meal through the bread and wine. The psalmist of ancient Israel similarly admonished all: "O taste and see that the Lord is good" (Psalm 34:8).

For those who may think that Charles Wesley intends for Holy Communion to be thought of simply as a remembrance or as a mere memorial of Jesus' death by the words, "here commemorate his death," one must read very carefully all of stanza 3. In these lines Wesley prays for a life-imparting experience in which a "loving filial Spirit" is breathed into his "waiting heart." The remembrance at every service of Holy Communion is thus a life-transforming and a love-transforming moment in one's life. One comes each time to the table of the Lord with anticipation that a new breath of divine love will fill one's whole being!

Charles often speaks of the "real presence" of Christ at the sacred meal of Holy Communion. This divine presence is a bridge between eternity and the present. Christ, the Redeemer, is the source of eternal happiness, and one of the evidences that he is present is that he speaks in us. Hence the closing line of the hymn pleads, "Now let him speak in me." Though Christ is mystically present in the meal, he is temporally present in us. We become instruments and evidence of the "real presence" of Christ. Therefore we need to ask ourselves with each communion: What do I experience at Holy Communion?

81.

Why do we observe Holy Communion?
Because thou hast said[1]

Luke 22:19: "Then he took a loaf of bread, and when he had given thanks, he broke it and gave it to them, saying, 'This is my body, which is given for you. Do this in remembrance of me.'"

ISAIAH 64:5

Because thou hast said
   "Do this for my sake,"
The mystical bread
   We gladly partake;
We thirst for the Spirit
   That flows from above,
And long to inherit
   The fullness of love.

'Tis here we look up
   And grasp at thy mind,
'Tis here that we hope
   Thine image to find;

---

1. John Wesley, *A Short View of the Difference between Moravian Brethren, Lately in England, and the Reverend Mr John and Charles Wesley* (1745).

SECTION 7: DAILY LIVING

> The means of bestowing
> Thy gifts we embrace;
> But all things are owing
> To Jesus's grace.

This hymn was originally published with the heading *Isaiah 64:5* as one of six hymns by Charles Wesley included at the conclusion of a tract by John Wesley, *A Short View of the Difference between Moravian Brethren, Lately in England, and the Reverend Mr John and Charles Wesley* (1745) and never used in any hymn book until it was published in the British Methodist *Hymns and Psalms* (1983). It is interesting that its original year of publication coincides with that of the volume dedicated solely to the theme *Hymns on the Lord's Supper* (1745), from which most of Charles Wesley's familiar hymns for Holy Communion derive: "Author of life divine," "Come, Holy Ghost, thine influence shed," "God of unexampled grace," "Happy the souls to Jesus joined," "O the depth of love divine," "O what a soul-transporting feast," "Victim divine, thy grace we claim."

The Wesley children learned early the importance of the sacred meal known as the Lord's Supper, Holy Communion, and Holy Eucharist through their devout parents, especially through their father Samuel's exercise of his office as a parish priest of the Church of England at Epworth.

Charles seems almost never to have forgotten that this divine meal provided indispensable sustenance and nurture for his life. Hence it is not surprising that when he recalls his days at Oxford University and the beginnings of the so-called "Holy Club," he records that along with serious secular learning, Bible study, prayer, and visits to prisoners in the Bocardo, he persuaded a few fellow students to accompany him to the weekly sacrament, which was not a popular student practice of the day.

Regular attendance at Holy Communion during his early years became a pattern for Charles's life and ministry. There were times when he records that it had little meaning; yet he did not deny himself the opportunity to receive anew this special means of God's grace. Just like the students of Wesley's Oxford days, there are always those who caution that regular Holy Communion can lead to mere formalism and routine. This hymn, however, reveals that for Charles Wesley the reasons for regular presence at the Lord's table have more profound meaning.

The hymn bears the superscript: Isaiah 64:5, a verse which reads: "Thou meetest him that rejoiceth and worketh righteousness, those that remember thee in thy ways: behold, thou art wroth; for we have sinned: in those is continuance, and we shall be saved" (KJV) . Charles draws upon the inspiration of the prophet Isaiah, who pleads the cause of God's presence among the faithful of Israel, and understands how important it is for the community of faith to *remember* God's ways. In such *remembrance* there is encounter with God and the way of divine redemption. Hence Wesley connects this reality with Christ's mandate in Luke 22:19, "And he took bread, and gave thanks, and brake it, and gave unto them, saying, This is my body which is given for you: this do in remembrance of me" (KJV; see also 1 Corinthians. 11:24).

The first reason Wesley gives for regular participation in the Lord's Supper is paramount: we partake of the bread and wine in remembrance because Jesus said, "this do in remembrance of me."

> Because thou hast said,
> "Do this for my sake,"
> The mystical bread
> We gladly partake.

Charles knew, however, that even in the act of remembrance he could not fully comprehend the mystery of the Sacrament; hence, he speaks of "the mystical bread," of which Jesus said, "This is my body, which is broken for you."

This is a mystery. It is mystical, and we cannot fully grasp its reality. What we can comprehend with Wesley each time we eat "the mystical bread" is that Christ's brokenness entering us becomes the means through which we understand the brokenness of our own lives and the world in which we live. We become with him broken bread for the world, offering all we are and have for others.

Two more reasons for eating this sacred meal are found in stanza one:

> We thirst for the Spirit
> That flows from above,
> And long to inherit
> The fullness of love.

There is a thirst which is quenched only by the waters of the Spirit which God pours upon our parched souls. It is a thirst to which physical thirst can never compare. But oh, how refreshing it is!

There is a longing within us also for love—not incomplete or imperfect love, but love in its fullness. It is the self-emptying love of God in Jesus Christ, which alone makes love complete or full in our lives. Only love which empties itself can be full. What a contradiction: emptiness means fullness! Yet only those who empty themselves in love for others ever know how full of love they can be.

Two final reasons for coming to the Lord's table are stressed in stanza two:

> 'Tis here we look up
>   And grasp at thy mind,
> 'Tis here that we hope
>   Thine image to find.

Paul once adjured the church at Philippi: "Let this mind be in you, which was also in Christ Jesus" (Philippians 2:5, KJV). It is in the act of remembering what God has done for us that we have the possibility of receiving the mind of Christ. That is, our whole mental posture can become so pervaded with a sense of self-giving love that our thoughts will be in harmony with our whole being in personifying love wherever we find ourselves. The Supper of our Lord is the mirror of the soul of God in which we may see the divine image of total and complete love in ourselves. Therefore, with Charles Wesley we lift our voices to affirm:

> The means of bestowing
>   Thy gifts we embrace;
> But all things are owing
>   To Jesus's grace.

When we come to the Lord's table and eat the bread and drink the wine, we embrace the means of grace through which the fullness of love may be a reality in our lives.

82.

What does Holy Communion really mean?

O the depth of love divine[1]

O the depth of love divine,
    The unfathomable grace!
Who shall say how bread and wine
    God into us[2] conveys!
How the bread his flesh imparts,
    How the wine transmits his blood,
Fills his faithful people's hearts
    With all the life of God!

Let the wisest mortal show
    How we the grace receive;
Feeble elements bestow
    A power not theirs to give.
Who explains the wondrous way,
    How through these the virtue came?
These the virtue did convey,
    Yet still remain the same.

---

1. *HLS* 1745, No. 57, 41.
2. Original = man.

SECTION 7: DAILY LIVING

> How can heavenly spirits rise,
>   By earthly matter fed,
> Drink herewith divine supplies
>   And eat immortal bread?
> Ask the Father's wisdom how:
>   Him who did the means ordain;
> Angels round our altars bow
>   To search it out, in vain.
>
> Sure and real is the grace,
>   the manner be unknown;
> only meet us in thy ways
>   and perfect us in one.
> Let us taste the heavenly powers,
>   Lord, we ask for nothing more.
> Thine to bless, 'tis only ours
>   to wonder and adore.

During his first year at Oxford University, Charles Wesley enjoyed himself more than he applied himself, but during his second year, as previously noted, he began attending the weekly sacrament. This became a central activity of a small group of students whom Charles invited to accompany him. In addition, the Wesley brothers developed a strong commitment to study, prayer, and social service, such as visits to prisoners with food for body and spirit. All of these things were intimately related to, and grew out of, the power for loving service received from the Lord's Supper, Holy Communion. "I went to the weekly Sacrament" was the preface to Charles Wesley's activity from his second year at Oxford and throughout his life.

Faithful to his inquiring mind and spirit, Wesley dares to ask honest questions in this hymn about the validity and authenticity of Holy Communion. These are questions with which the church has wrestled for centuries. While punctuated here with exclamation marks in part in this hymn, it was Wesley's practice often to exclaim and question in the same sentence. And sometimes, if you follow the printing of his hymns during his lifetime, there is a fluctuation between the use of question marks and exclamation marks for the same sentences. Such changes may have been made by him, an editor, or printer, but they accentuate the double thrust of declaration and inquiry in the same lines of poetry.

Here he declares and asks:

WHAT DOES HOLY COMMUNION REALLY MEAN?

> Who shall say how bread and wine
> God into us conveys!
> *How* the bread his flesh imparts,
> *How* the wine transmits his blood,
> Fills his faithful people's hearts
> With all the life of God!

The church through the centuries in its many councils and branches has spent much time, created tensions, and often divided itself over precisely the issues raised by Charles in this stanza. Is what transpires during the supper of our Lord *transubstantiation* or *consubstantiation*? Do the bread and wine become the actual body and blood of Jesus? Are the elements of bread and wine God's means of the conveyance of God's nature? Or is God with us at the table simply through a *real presence*? Further, are not the bread and wine merely *symbols* of remembrance and nothing more? And is the meal actually only an ordinance and not a sacrament? Granted, Wesley is not addressing these specific theological questions about the meal of our Lord, but he is laying before the church and followers of Christ in all ages the awesomeness of the divine wisdom which resides in and is imparted by sharing the common table with one another and with Christ. In all humility he faces the question—Who has the audacity to say that one knows the mind of God and the fullness of "the depth of love divine, the unfathomable grace" conveyed at Holy Communion?

Stanzas 2 and 3 take his inquiry further:

> Let the wisest mortal show
> How we the grace receive;
> Feeble elements bestow
> A power not theirs to give.

The sages of the church from the early Church Fathers to present generations of women and men continue to describe what transpires at the table of our Lord. Perhaps many leave the mystery to God, yet the diverse modes of communion indicate that the church wrestles with the most effective way actually or symbolically to receive the grace. *How* shall we commune? Shall we *stand, sit,* or *kneel* to receive the elements? Does it matter? Who shall administer the elements and who shall receive them? How shall we receive the elements? Shall we drink the wine (if wine at all) or grape juice and eat the bread, or dip the bread into the cup? Shall we have a common cup or many small ones? Wesley asks:

> Who explains the wondrous way,
>> How through these the virtue came?

Wesley continues to question himself and others:

> How can heavenly spirits rise,
>> By earthly matter fed,
> Drink herewith divine supplies
>> And eat immortal bread?

How can simple wine and bread, the fruit of the earth and mortal hands, be the link between earth and heaven and mediate divine grace? How can mortal bread become immortal bread? Wesley says we must inquire constantly of God's wisdom regarding *how*. In his conclusion of stanza 3 he affirms that in God's wisdom Christ ordains the means of grace, namely the Sacrament. If mortals think they will explain *how* the elements become "divine" and "immortal," they should beware that "angels round our altars bow / to search it out in vain."

Even if we cannot define or describe the manner of the mediation of God's grace through the Sacrament, the grace and means are real.

> *Sure* and *real* is the grace,
>> The manner be unknown;
> Only meet us in thy ways
>> And perfect us in one.
> Let us taste the heavenly powers,
>> Lord, we ask for nothing more.
> Thine to bless, 'tis only ours
>> To wonder and adore.

Charles Wesley testifies to the surety of the means of God's grace mediated in the Sacrament, while holding in tension the reality that though we "taste the heavenly powers" in this meal, we cannot fully decipher all aspects of the manner in which God's grace is mediated to us through the Lord's Supper. We must be willing to let the mystery be the mystery. "We ask for nothing more" but "to wonder and adore."

Wesley's petition in lines 3 and 4 of stanza 4, "only meet us in thy ways / and perfect us in one," indicates that the church's sign of the means of grace is perfect unity. Unity in the community of faith signals the world that it is a recipient and instrument of God's grace.

83.

How can we know and feel that God and love are one?

O thou who this mysterious bread[1]

Luke 24:13–16, 28–35: "And, behold, two of them went that same day to a village called Emmaus, which was from Jerusalem about threescore furlongs. And they talked together of all these things which had happened. And it came to pass, that, while they communed together and reasoned, Jesus himself drew near, and went with them. But their eyes were holden that they should not know him. . . . And they drew nigh unto the village, whither they went: and he made as though he would have gone further. But they constrained him, saying, Abide with us: for it is toward evening, and the day is far spent. And he went in to tarry with them. And it came to pass, as he sat at meat with them, he took bread, and blessed it, and brake, and gave to them. And their eyes were opened, and they knew him; and he vanished out of their sight. And they said one to another, Did not our heart burn within us, while he talked with us by the way, and while he opened to us the scriptures? And they rose up the same hour, and returned to Jerusalem, and found the eleven gathered together, and them that were with them, Saying, The Lord is risen indeed, and hath appeared to Simon. And they told what things were done in the way, and how he was known of them in breaking of bread." (KJV)

---

1. *HLS* 1745, No. 29, 22–3.

SECTION 7: DAILY LIVING

> O Thou who this mysterious bread
>   Didst in Emmaus break,
> Return, herewith our souls to feed,
>   And to thy followers speak.
>
> Unseal the volume of thy grace,
>   Apply the Gospel-word;
> Open our eyes to see thy face,
>   Our hearts to know the Lord.
>
> Of thee we commune still, and mourn
>   Till thou the veil remove;
> Talk with us, and our hearts shall burn
>   With flames of fervent love.
>
> Enkindle now the heavenly zeal,
>   And make thy mercy known,
> And give our pardoned souls to feel
>   That God and love are one.

Not only was this hymn inspired by the passage from the Gospel of Luke, but also from a statement in Daniel Brevint's *Christian Sacrament and Sacrifice* (1673): "Let my Heart burn to follow thee now, when this Bread is broken at this Table, as the Hearts of thy Disciples did when thou didst break it in Emmaus."[2] An abridged form of Brevint's work appeared at the beginning of *HLS* 1745, probably John Wesley's main contribution to the volume.

Why did Wesley refer to the bread that Jesus broke with the disciples as "mysterious"? It is not the bread of a Passover meal like that broken by Jesus when he celebrated his Last Supper and charged the disciples to remember him in the practice of this meal. The disciples who walked with the resurrected Christ to Emmaus did not recognize him during their walk or their conversation with him. When they gathered with him that evening for a meal, however, "he was known of them in breaking of bread." This was indeed a "mysterious" occurrence and revelation. Shared bread became the means of *knowing* their *unrecognized companion* along the road, namely, Jesus.

Though this account of the appearance of the resurrected Christ to the disciples and their final recognition of him in the course of breaking bread

---

2. *HLS*, 8.

HOW CAN WE KNOW AND FEEL THAT GOD AND LOVE ARE ONE?

was not a reenactment of the Lord's Supper, Wesley appropriates the experience to coming to the table of our Savior in Holy Communion. Wesley yearned, as did Brevint, for the experience of the disciples on that evening in Emmaus to be our experience as we partake of the Lord's meal.

He prays that Jesus will "return" and "speak" with those who follow him:

> Return with him our souls to feed,
> And to thy followers speak.

The Emmaus story reminds us that there is always a grave danger that we will be instructed by the gospel-word, as were the disciples as they walked the road with Jesus that day, and still not recognize the One who speaks it *until the breaking of bread*. This is one reason why faithfulness to the sacrament was a lifelong commitment of the Wesleys and should be for all followers of Christ. Therefore, Wesley prays,

> Open our eyes to *see* thy face,
> Our hearts to *know* the Lord.

He wants to recognize Jesus; he wants to know him, but understands that only God can remove the veil of the Divine Unknown, and this is precisely what happens at Holy Communion. It is at Christ's table that we may hear his words which enflame our hearts with "fervent love."

It is clearly the urgency of the burning hearts of the disciples as they encountered Jesus on the way to Emmaus that Wesley seeks to recover and sustain. Hearts that burn with "fervent love" are closest to God, for "God and love are one."

Stanza 4 emphasizes that the Wesleys understood that Holy Communion is an evangelical meal. It can "enkindle now the heavenly zeal" and make God's mercy known. At this holy table pardoned sinners may *feel*, experience, that "God and love are one."

Two key words of the Wesleys, *know* and *feel*, employed so often by them to express the encounter with God in Jesus Christ, are used here by Charles. They are integral to this prayer-hymn for Holy Communion. As we approach the sacred table, he bids us always to pray "that our hearts may *know* the Lord" and that we may "*feel* that God and love are one."

In breaking bread with Jesus we may *know* him and *feel* (or sense) what love really is, and, hence, who God is, namely, love.

84.

Whom will we invite to supper?
Come, sinners, to the gospel feast[1]

Luke 14:16–24: "Then he said unto him, A certain man made a great supper, and bade many: and sent his servant at supper time to say to them that were bidden, Come; for all things are ready. And they all with one consent began to make excuse. The first said unto him, I have bought a piece of ground, and I must needs go and see it: I pray thee have me excused. And another said, I have bought five yoke of oxen, and I go to prove them: I pray thee have me excused. And another said, I have married a wife, and therefore I cannot come. So that servant came, and shewed his lord these things. Then the master of the house being angry said to his servant, Go out quickly into the streets and lanes of the city, and bring in hither the poor, and the maimed, and the halt, and the blind. And the servant said, Lord, it is done as thou hast commanded, and yet there is room. And the lord said unto the servant, Go out into the highways and hedges, and compel them to come in, that my house may be filled. For I say unto you, That none of those men which were bidden shall taste of my supper." (KJV)

---

1. *RH* 1747, No. 50, 63–66; stanzas 1, 2, 4, 12, 20, 22, 23, 24 from the original twenty-four-stanza hymn.

THE GREAT SUPPER

Come, sinners, to the gospel feast;
Let every soul be Jesus' guest.
Ye need not one be left behind,
For God hath bid all humankind.[2]

Sent by my Lord, on you I call;
The invitation is to all.
Come, all the world! Come, sinner, thou!
All things in Christ are ready now.

Do not begin to make excuse;
Ah! Do not you his grace refuse;
Your worldly cares and pleasures leave,
And take what Jesus hath to give.

Come, then ye souls, by sin opprest,
Ye restless wanderers after rest;
Ye poor, and maimed, and halt, and blind,
In Christ a hearty welcome find.

My message as from God receive
Ye all may come to Christ, and live:
O let his love your hearts constrain,
Nor suffer him to die in vain.

See him set forth before your eyes,
Behold the bleeding sacrifice!
His offered love make haste t' embrace,
And freely now be saved by grace.

Ye who believe his record true,
Shall sup with him, and he with you:
Come to the feast; be saved from sin,
For Jesus waits to take you in.

This is the time, no more delay,
This is the acceptable day,
Come in, this moment, at his call,
And live for him who died for all.

---

2. Original: For God hath bidden all mankind.

SECTION 7: DAILY LIVING

This hymn originally had twenty-four stanzas, from which different stanzas have been combined by editors of hymnbooks to form a variety of hymns across the years. They often begin with the opening line, "Come, sinners, to the gospel feast." Wesley published the text in 1747 with the title "The Great Supper," based upon the parable told by Jesus in Luke 14. The Wesleys did not take lightly the mandate of Jesus: "call the poor, the maimed, the lame, the blind" to your banquet, "and you will be blessed, because they cannot repay you" (14:13 KJV, 14 NRSV). Perhaps this is one of the reasons why they understood the service of Holy Communion as an evangelical meal:

> His offered love make haste to embrace,
> And freely now be saved by grace.

It is a meal to which all are invited; all may partake of the bread of life offered to all. The thirsty may come and drink from the life-giving stream. No one is to be left behind, for God has invited all to come and eat at the table of salvation.

It is not surprising that Charles Wesley appropriated Jesus' parable of "The Great Supper" of our Lord. He had experienced the exclusivity sometimes practiced by clergy of the Church of England at this meal, as an entry in his *Journal* on July 20, 1740, makes clear.

> Our poor colliers being repelled from the Lord's table by most of the Bristol ministers, I exhorted them, notwithstanding, to continue daily with one accord in the Temple, where the wickedest administrator can neither spoil the prayers nor poison the Sacrament. *These* poor sinners *have* ears to hear.[3]

A week later, on July 27, he experienced exclusion from the sacrament himself.

> Heard a miserable sermon at Temple church, recommending religion as the most likely way to raise a fortune. After it, proclamation was made "that all should depart who were not of the parish." While the shepherd was driving away the lambs, I stayed, suspecting nothing, till the Clerk came to me and said, "Mr Beacher[4] bids you go away, for he will not give you the Sacrament." I went to the vestry door and mildly desired Mr Beacher to admit me. He asked, "Are you of this parish?" I answered, "Sir, you *see* I am a clergyman." Dropping his first pretence, he charged me with rebellion

---

3. *MSJ*, 1:274.
4. The rector of Temple Church.

in expounding the Scriptures without authority, and said in express words, "I repel you from the Sacrament." I replied, "I cite you to answer this before Jesus Christ at the day of judgment." This enraged him above measure. He called out, *"Here, take away this man!"* The constables were ordered to attend (I suppose, lest the furious colliers should take the Sacrament by force), but I saved them the trouble of taking away this man, and quietly retired.[5]

Charles Wesley understood personally that the Church of England had excluded from the Lord's table those whom he had invited. Furthermore, he understood what it meant to be turned away from the Lord's table precisely because of his ministry to the poor and outcasts of eighteenth-century England's masses. The local law enforcement officers were going to be enlisted to remove him from the church at the time of Holy Communion, and for fear that the coal miners to whom he had been ministering would come and take the Sacrament by force, he removed himself.

The Wesleys knew, however, that you could not read the gospels and aver that there are *persona non grata* not welcome at the Lord's table. This is a category created by human beings and often propagated by the church.

Charles Wesley expressed Jesus' concern for the poor, for example, in a hymn which had not appeared in any hymn book until 1993 and was left unpublished at his death. It summarizes the concern which cannot permit the exclusion of the poor from the life of the body of Christ, the church, especially from its most important meal.

> The poor as Jesus' bosom-friends,[6]
>   The poor he makes his latest care,
> To all his successors commends,
>   And wills us on our hands to bear:
> The poor our dearest care we make,
> And love them for our Savior's sake.

The invitation to salvation and to "The Great Supper" made to all are one and the same according to Wesley:

> Come to the feast, be saved from sin,
> For Jesus waits to take you in.

The fact that all are welcome at this feast underscores that it is a feast of love.

---

5. *MSJ*, 1:275.
6. *UP*, 2:404. This author first published the text in *A Song for the Poor*, 1993.

SECTION 7: DAILY LIVING

> O let his love your hearts constrain
> Nor suffer him to die in vain.
>
> . . .
>
> His offered love make haste to embrace,
> And freely now be saved by grace.

The concluding four lines of Charles's original twenty-four-stanza hymn express the urgency of responding to Christ's invitation: to God's saving love and the feast of that love—the Lord's Supper or Holy Communion.

> This is the time, no more delay!
> This is the Lord's accepted day.
> Come thou, this moment, at his call,
> And live for him who died for all.

Conclusion

While Charles Wesley's poetry was born in the eighteenth century, it is in many ways still up-to-date. To be sure, at times it employs metaphors, similes, figures of speech, modes of expression, and syntax which are somewhat foreign to us today. Yet he speaks to us in the twenty-first century with an authentic message which addresses us where we are and addresses questions we face personally and corporately in daily life and in the life of the global church. Why are his responses to these questions still pertinent today?—Because he speaks from the depths of human need: conflict and despair, tensions created by injustices in society through the misuse of wealth and power, and the necessity of personal and social redemption.

Many of the questions Charles Wesley asked about the trinitarian God (Father, Son, and Holy Spirit), faith, others, the world, and self are questions people are still asking today. Indeed, contemporary contexts are often very different, but we live as did Charles Wesley amid the tension of the known and the unknown, the revealed and the unrevealed. His inward cry has become our own:

> Come, O thou Traveler unknown,
>   Whom still I hold, but cannot see,
>   . . .
>   Wilt thou not yet to me reveal
>   Thy new, unutterable name?

These brief lines from his poem, "Wrestling Jacob," remind us that we too wrestle with the angel. We long to know the God we cannot see! We yearn for revelation that will make the Unknown known. If we endure, Charles Wesley's affirmation from that same poem will become ours:

> 'Tis Love, 'tis Love! Thou diedst for me,
>   I hear thy whisper in my heart.

CONCLUSION

> The morning breaks, the shadows flee:
> Pure Universal Love thou art.

The Universal Love becomes known in Christ Jesus.

Wesley's poetical journey of faith remains fresh and relevant for us because he does not lose sight of the wonder of creation, the Creator, and the created. He is unendingly awestruck by the possibility of God, the Incarnation, God's love in Christ, and living the reality of that love on earth, and the transformation of human lives through such love. Charles Wesley is unceasingly "lost in wonder, love, and praise." In this way he exemplifies an indispensable pattern for the search for God, the pilgrimage of faith, and the living of faith. Live with a sense of wonder, be continually awestruck by the Creator, creation, and the created. Live the love of Christ by being totally filled with that love, which spills over into the lives of all whom we encounter and which goes in search of others.

Finally, live in constant praise of God even when God seems distantly and painfully unknown. Endure! Be "lost in wonder, love, and praise." Such a life can face fear, hate, conflict, suffering, despair, and violence with confidence and victory, for "perfect love casts out fear" (1 John 4:18).

Charles Wesley's call to be an evangel for Christ speaks to human need as vitally today as in his own time. In every age, and certainly in ours, there is a need for human transformation. Hardly a poem of Wesley's slipped from his pen without somehow addressing this issue. He spent his life committed to Christ, who can transform lives, turn evil to good, hate to love, brokenness to wholeness, and alienation to reconciliation. Wesley saw people constantly transformed by God's love in Christ. Salvation, redemption, reclaiming of life was and is a reality! His poetry calls us anew to be evangels in a shattered and fragmented world where fear, war, and hatred still wreck lives. We are to personify what God's love through Christ does: heals, renews, creates anew, builds bridges, makes friends of enemies, gives wholeness to broken individuals and a broken world. We are not called merely to be bearers of the good news of the transforming power of Christ's love, that is, to be *only evangelists*. Wesley bids us, as does the gospel, to be *evangels,* persons who embody God's love in all that they are in thought, word, and deed. Evangels live, tell, *and* personify the good news of Christ. They do not fear asking the hardest questions that human beings face, particularly if there is the possibility they may discover and personify universal love, the essence of God's nature.

Appendix A

Charles Wesley Time Line

1707	Dec. 18	born at Epworth
1709	Feb. 9	rescued from Epworth Rectory fire
1716		enters Westminster School
1726		enters Christ Church College, Oxford
1730		receives B.A. degree, becomes Oxford tutor
1733		receives M.A. degree
1735	Apr. 25	father Samuel dies
	Sept. 21	ordained deacon of the Church of England by Dr. John Potter, Bishop of Oxford
	Sept. 24	appointed secretary for Indian Affairs, American colony of Georgia
	Sept. 29	ordained priest of the Church of England by Dr. Edmund Gibson, Bishop of London
	Oct. 14	Charles and John embark at Gravesend on the ship *Simmonds* for Georgia; during the voyage they encounter on board the Moravians' deep faith and singing
1736	Feb. 5	lands in Georgia

APPENDIX A

	March	proceeds to Fort Frederica where he takes up his ministry
	March 9	begins his manuscript journal
	July 26	leaves Georgia overland for Charleston where he will embark for England; becomes severely ill before departure and on board;
	Sept. 24	ship docks near Boston for repairs
	Oct. 26–27	departs for England
	Dec. 3	lands in Deal, England, and proceeds to London
1737		meets Moravian leader, Count Zinzendorf, in London
1738		meets Moravian Peter Böhler whom he begins teaching English
	Apr. 3	resigns his Georgia secretaryship
	May 21	Charles Wesley experiences "conversion"
	May 24	John Wesley experiences his "heart strangely warmed"
1739		with John begins major publications of hymns/poems: *Hymns and Sacred Poems*; first Methodist house of worship is established: "New Room" in Bristol
	May 29	preaches in fields for the first time
	Nov. 6	eldest brother Samuel dies
1742		preaches in the north of England with brother John for the first time; they establish their first orphanage and Sunday School
	July 23	mother Susanna dies
1744		first Methodist Conference held at the Foundery; Methodist districts are established throughout England
1747	Sept. 9–	visits Ireland for the first time
	March 20, 1748	
1748	Aug. 13–	visits Ireland for the second time

CHARLES WESLEY TIME LINE

	Oct. 8	
1749		publishes *Hymns and Sacred Poems*, 2 vols.
	Apr. 8	marries Sarah Gwynne; officiant is brother John
	Sept. 1	acquires house in Charles Street, Bristol
1752	Aug.	son John Wesley is born (Note: Charles and Sarah had eight children but only three—Charles, Jr., Sarah, and Samuel—survived infancy and childhood.)
1755		Conference at which separation of Methodist societies from the Church of England is intensely debated; Charles strongly urges unity
1756		ends itinerant ministry and settles in Bristol; Conference reaffirms unity of the societies and the Church of England
1757	Dec. 11	son Charles is born
1759	Apr. 1	daughter Sarah is born
1762		publishes *Short Hymns on Select Passages of the Holy Scriptures*, 2 vols.
1766	Feb 24	son Samuel is born
1771		begins preaching regularly in London and moves to Chesterfield Street, Maryleborne, London
1778		City Road Chapel, London, is opened
1788	Mar. 29	Charles Wesley dies
	Apr. 5	Charles Wesley is buried in Maryleborne churchyard
1822	Dec. 22	Mrs. Charles Wesley dies

Selected Bibliography

Baker, Frank. *Charles Wesley As Revealed by His Letters.* London: Epworth, 1948.
Bonhoeffer, Dietrich. *Gesammelte Schriften.* 3 volumes. Edited by Eberhard Bethge. Munich, 1960.
Burtt, Perxy E. "Comparison of Charles Wesley and Isaac Watts," *Pittsburgh Christian Advocate* 77 (1910) 21.
Capey, A. C. "Charles Wesley and his literary relations," Retford: Brynmill Press, 1983, off-printed from the *Gadfly,* 6:1, 17–26.
Dale, James. "Charles Wesley and the Line of Piety: Antecedents of the Hymns in English Devotional Verse," *PCWS* 8 (2002) 55–64.
———. "Charles Wesley, the Odyssey, and Clement of Alexandria," *Methodist History* 30 (1992) 100–10.
———. "Holy Larceny? Elizabeth Rowe's Poetry in Charles Wesley's Hymns," *PCWS* 3 (1996) 519.
———. "The Theological and Literary Qualities of the Poetry of Charles Wesley in Relation to the Standards of his Age," PhD dissertation. University of Cambridge, 1960.
Gill, Thomas H. "Watts and Charles Wesley Compared," *Congregationalist* 7 (1878) 129–44.
Hodgson, E. M. "Poetry in the Hymns of John and Charles Wesley," *Proceedings of the Wesley Historical Society,* 38 (1972) 131–35, 161–65.
Jackson, Thomas. Editor. *The Journal of Charles Wesley.* 2 vols. Grand Rapids, MI: Baker Book House, 1980, 2:285–86.
Kellett, E. E. "The Poetic Character of Charles Wesley's Hymns," *Methodist Recorder,* 18 (August 1910), 10–11.
Kimbrough, S T, Jr. *Sweet Singer. A Musical Drama about Charles Wesley,* © by the author (1985).
Kimbrough, S T, Jr., and Kenneth G. C. Newport. Editors.*The Manuscript Journal of the Reverend Charles Wesley.* 2 vols. Nashville: Kingswood Books, 2008.
Roth, Herbert John. "A Literary Study of the Calvinistic and Deistic Implications in the Hymns of Isaac Watts, Charles Wesley and William Cowper," PhD dissertation. Texas Christian University, 1978.
Routley, Erik. Editor. *Rejoice in the Lord.* Grand Rapids: W. B. Eerdmans, 1985.
Telford, John. *Charles Wesley.* London: Epworth, 1927.
The Coloured American. (New York and Philadelphia), Saturday, August 25, 1838.
The Hymnal 1982. New York: The Church Hymnal Corporation, 1982.

SELECTED BIBLIOGRAPHY

The United Methodist Book of Worship. Nashville: United Methodist Publishing House, 1992.

Tyson, John R. "Charles Wesley and Edward Young: Eighteenth-Century poetical apologists," *Methodist History*, 27:2 (1989) 110–19.

Watson, J. Richard. "Charles Wesley and the Thirty-Nine Articles of the Church of England," *Proceedings of The Charles Wesley Society* 9 (2003–2004) 27–38.

———. "Hymns on the Lord's Supper, 1745, and Some Literary and Liturgical Sources," *Proceedings of The Charles Wesley Society* 2 (1995) 17–33.

Watts, Isaac. *Hymns and Spiritual Songs.* 2nd Edition. Book 3. London: John Lawrence, 1709.

Wesley, John. *A Short View of the Difference between Moravian Brethren, Lately in England, and the Reverend Mr John and Charles Wesley.* London: Strahan, 1745.

Wesley, John and Charles. *Minutes of Several Conversations Between The Reverend Mr. John and Charles Wesley, and Others From the Year 1744, to the Year 1780.* London: J. Paramore, n.d. (Fifth edition of the Large Minutes).

Whitefield, George. *A Collection of Hymns for Social Worship.* London: Strahan, 1753.

Zinzendorf, Nikolaus Ludwig von. *Das Gesang-Buch der Gemeine in Herrn-Huth.* [Herrnhut]: Wäysenhause, 1735.

Index of First Lines

A charge to keep I have	81
All praise to our redeeming Lord	144
And are we yet alive	155
And can it be that I should gain	32
And live I yet by power divine?	188
At evening to myself I say	236
Author of every work divine	126
Author of life divine	251
Because thou hast said	257
Blest be the dear uniting love	148
Blow ye the trumpet, blow!	151
Can we in unbelievers find	134
Christ from whom all blessings flow	159
Christ the Lord is risen today	91
Christ, whose glory fills the skies	84
Come, divine Interpreter	68
Come, and let us sweetly join	163
Come, Holy Ghost, our hearts inspire	65
Come, let us anew / Our journey pursue	207
Come, let us use the grace divine	141
Come, O thou Traveler unknown	3
Come sinners, to the gospel feast	269
Come, thou long-expected Jesus	36
Death in the pot! 'Tis always there	239
Depth of mercy! Can there be	110
Father in whom we live	18
Father, instruct my docile heart	225
Forgive my foes? It cannot be	197
Forgive my partial selfishness	191
Forth in thy name, O Lord, I go	114
Gentle Jesus, meek and mild	182
Give me the faith which can remove	77
Give us this day, all bounteous Lord	254
Hail the day that sees him rise	48
Hark! the herald-angels sing	128
How can we sinners know	117
How oft have I, like Pharaoh, proved	200
I want a principle within	217
If death my friend and me divide	167
Jesu, lover of my soul	95
Jesus, Lord, we look to thee	51
Jesus, plant thy Spirit in me	63
Jesus! the name high over all	38
Jesus, thine all-victorious love	42
Jesus, united by thy grace	170
Let him to whom we now belong	247
Let us plead for faith alone	102
Like him in piety's decay	203
Lo, he comes with clouds descending	27
Love divine, all loves excelling	131
No, they cry, it cannot be	139
O come and dwell in me	71
O for a heart to praise my God	213
O for a thousand tongues to sing	136
O Love divine, what hast thou done	10
O may I never take the praise	205
O might the gracious words divine	229
O the depth of love divine	261
O thou who camest from above	16
O thou who this mysterious bread	266
Oft as I lay me down to rest	232
Our earth we now lament to see	173
Parent of good, whose plenteous grace	241

INDEX OF FIRST LINES

Rising to sing my Savior's praise	234
Rejoice, the Lord is King	185
Savior of all, what hast thou done?	25
See how great a flame aspires	195
Sinners, turn: why will you die?	105
Spirit of faith, come down	57
Spirit of faith, come down on me	61
Still for thy loving kindness, Lord	244
The table of my heart prepare	223
Their earthly task who fail to do	89
Thou hidden Source of calm repose	13
Thou God of harmony and love	209
Though all the precious promises	193
Thy will, O Lord, whate'er I do	8
'Tis finished! The Messiah dies	45
When he did our flesh assume	30
When quiet in my house I sit	227
Where shall my wondering soul begin?	99
Ye different sects who all declare	87
Ye servants of God, your Master proclaim	179
Your duty let the apostle show	123

Index of Scripture Passages

GENESIS
2:7	127
20:11	191
32	3

EXODUS
8:15	200
9:12	200

LEVITICUS
6:13	16
8:33	82
8:35	81, 83
11:44	165
25:9–10	151

DEUTERONOMY
6:4–5	223, 228, 229
6:6	223
6:4–7	235
6:7	225, 227, 229, 232, 234
6:9	224
26:5–10	49–50

JUDGES
15:14	61

1 SAMUEL
16:23	211

1 KINGS
19:10	203

2 KINGS
4:40	239

2 CHRONICLES
6:11	145

PSALMS
19	19
24:8	186
34:8	255
34:14	146
46:10	244
47	19
51:1	214
51:3	214
51:10	213, 214
66:1–2	248
68	70
95:1–2	248
98	19
98:4	248
100:1–2	248
104:24–30	125
105:8	145
107	70
107:2	50
111:6, 9	49

PSALMS *(continued)*

111:10	218
122:6	145
150	19

ISAIAH

35	199
40:31	246
64:5	257–8

JEREMIAH

31:22	30
31:33	215
32:39	139
50:4–5	141

EZEKIEL

18:31–2	105
36:26	201

JOB

9:20	193

RUTH

2:19	236

MALACHI

4:2	85

MATTHEW

6:11	255
17:20	79
28:20	204

MARK

15:38	46

LUKE

1:78–79	85
6:37	197
8:56	205
14:16–24	268
22:19	257
23:45	46
24:13–16	265
24:28–35	265

JOHN

1:9	85
1:14	30
1:29	41
7:9–10	20
13:34–5	215
14:13	270
14:16–24	268
14:18	204
17:3	93
17:20–1	159, 160
17:22–3	161
19:29–30	45
20:20	110
20:21–2	165
24:13–16	28–35, 265

ACTS

4:11–12	40
17:11–12	134
17:28	19
20:33–4	124
20:35	123

ROMANS

12:11	89

1 CORINTHIANS

1:10	146
1:12	192
2:2	148
5:31	26
10:31	240, 249
11:24	259
15:31	26, 249
15:53	47

15:55	92

2 CORINTHIANS

3:17	71–2
5:17	71–2
5:19	235
12:15	79
13:11	146

GALATIANS

1:11–12	226
1:3–4	46
1:6–7	70
2:20	70
5:22–3	63

EPHESIANS

2:8–10	102
2:14	146
3:16–19	202
4:4–5	144–5
4:7	146
5:19	164

PHILIPPIANS

2:5	172, 260
2:5–8	119–20
2:9–11	38
3:8–9	155

HEBREWS

11:5	72
12:1	204

1 THESSALONIANS

4:13	167
4:14	168

1 JOHN

1:5	85
4:2	85
4:8	31, 215
4:12	216
5:20	93

1 PETER

2:5	212

2 PETER

1:19	85

REVELATION

1:7	27
1:3	68
11:15	186

Index of Subjects

Subjects are followed by the first line of the appropriate hymns/poems and page number.

Advent
  Come, thou long-expected Jesus, 36
  Lo, he comes with clouds descending, 27
  O thou who camest from above, 16
  When he did our flesh assume, 30
Attitudes
  Rejoice, the Lord is King!, 185

Bigotry
  Forgive my partial selfishness, 191

Christ
  Savior of all, what hast thou done?, 25
Christian experience
  O thou who camest from above, 16
Christmas
  Hark! The herald-angels sing, 128
Commitment
  Jesu, Lover of my soul, 95
Conversion
  Where shall my wondering soul begin?, 99

Easter
  Christ the Lord is risen today, 91
Eating
  Death in the pot! 'Tis always there, 239
Education and learning
  Father, instruct my docile heart, 225

Eternal life
  Christ the Lord is risen today, 91
Faith
  Their earthly task who fail to do, 89
  Ye different sects who all declare, 87
Forgiveness
  Forgive my foes? It cannot be, 197
Freedom
  Come, thou long-expected Jesus, 36
  Spirit of faith, come down, 57

God
  Come, O thou Traveler unknown, 3
God's will
  Thy will, O Lord, whate'er I do, 8
God's Word (Holy Scripture)
  Come, Holy Ghost, our hearts inspire, 65
  O might the gracious words divine, 229
Hard-heartedness
  How oft have I, like Pharaoh, proved, 200
  There needed, Lord, no act of thine, 200
Holy Communion
  Author of Life divine, 251
  Give us this day, all bounteous Lord, 254
  Let him to whom we now belong, 247

INDEX OF SUBJECTS

Holy Spirit
  Come, Holy Ghost, our hearts inspire, 65
  Jesus, plant thy Spirit in me, 63
  Spirit of faith, come down, 57
  Spirit of faith, come down on me, 61

Labor (work)
  Your duty let the Apostle show, 123

Loneliness
  Like him in piety's decay, 203

Love
  And can it be that I should gain, 32
  Come, Holy Ghost, our hearts inspire, 65
  Love divine, all loves excelling, 131
  See how great a flame aspires, 195
  The table of my heart prepare, 223

Ministry
  O may I never take the praise, 205

Music
  Thou God of harmony and love, 209

Mystery
  And can it be that I should gain, 32
  Thou hidden Source of calm repose, 13
  When he did our flesh assume, 30

New Year
  Come, let us anew / Our journey pursue, 207

Open-mindedness
  Can we in unbelievers find, 134

Peace
  Hark! the Herald-angels sing, 128

Prayer before meals
  Parent of good, whose plenteous grace, 241

Resting
  Oft as I lay me down to rest, 232

Rising
  Rising to sing my Savior's praise, 234

Sainthood
  Though all the precious promises, 193

Second Coming of Christ
  Lo, he comes with clouds descending, 27

Sickness and Suffering
  And live I yet by power divine, 188

Talents
  Thou God of harmony and love, 209

Unity
  No, they cry, it cannot be!, 139
  Ye different sects who all declare, 87

Waiting on God
  Still for thy loving kindness, Lord, 2

www.ingramcontent.com/pod-product-compliance
Lightning Source LLC
Chambersburg PA
CBHW050337230426
43663CB00010B/1888